Return to Ukraine

TEXAS A&M UNIVERSITY PRESS
College Station

Return to Ukraine

ANIA SAVAGE

*For a complete list
of books in print in this series,
see the back of the book.*

Library of Congress Cataloging-in-Publication Data

Savage, Ania.
    Return to Ukraine / Ania Savage.
       p. cm. — (Eastern European studies ;
    no. 12)
    Includes bibliographical references and index.
    ISBN 0-89096-916-7 (cloth : alk. paper)
      1. Ukraine—Description and travel—1981–
    2. Savage, Ania. I. Title. II. Series : Eastern
European studies (College Station, Tex.) ; no. 12.
DK508.2.S28   2000
914.7704'86—dc21   99-36803
                                      CIP

Contents

Illustrations

Series Editor's Statement

Ania Savage is doing many important things in this book. Following Csaba Teglas—who has published his reminiscences of living behind the Iron Curtain in Hungary, also in this series—she is giving voice to the neglected survivors of Communism, in general, and in Ukraine in particular. One can find many reminiscences of living and dying under Nazism, but relatively few of life under Communism. Although many men have written about Communism as well as Nazism, many fewer women have given their points of view, the most notable being Slavenka Drakulic, who wrote about how she and others survived Yugoslav Communism. Here, Savage contributes one more woman's voice. Finally, because Ania Savage is a professional writer, she writes an engrossing, finely crafted book that gives these neglected voices an eloquence and clarity that is rare.

Future sociologists and anthropologists will have little to go on as they try to piece together the intimate secrets of how and why Communism ruled the former Soviet Union and Eastern Europe. The former gulags are *not* being turned into museums: there is no Communism equivalent of the Nazi concentration camps. Instead, the gulags and prisons of the Communists are either being razed or, worse yet, sometimes still used. The former prisoners and other survivors of Communist oppression are generally *not* getting their reminiscences published in either the West or formerly Communist nations. Their compatriots are too poor to buy books and the West seems uninterested. Western art museums still feature "their own" artists from Germany, France, the United States, Great Britain, and the Netherlands, but rarely if ever venture into exhibiting the works of artists who worked under or escaped from Communism. Is it ethnocentrism that prevents the West from being curious about Eastern Europe and the former Soviet Union? After all, Nazism fascinates the West because it is an affront to its high image of itself as civilized, and, for that reason, had to be dissected and examined. Germany was and is considered a part of the West. But Western scholars have exhibited an arrogant disdain for Russia, Poland, Croatia, Ukraine, and other lands to the East. For example, the famous social theorist, Max Weber, literally dismissed the lands of the Orthodox religions from his grand scheme of Protestant-based capitalism and rationalism. Weber thought Russia was and would always remain barbaric.

Or is the neglect due to the prevalence of many Marxists in academia who just cannot bring themselves to criticize an aspect of their ideology that turned sour? Indeed, many Marxists deny any linkage between Communism and their academic Marxism. Yet it cannot be denied that Communists tried to create a purely Marxist mathematics, sociology, economics, medicine, and every other endeavor known to humankind. A notable exception to this state of denial by Marxists is Zygmunt Bauman, a former Communist and Marxist from Poland who is now a sociologist in Great Britain. In his book, *Intimations of Postmodernity,* and other books, Bauman argues that Communism and Marxism were modernist phenomena whose fall in the East signaled the coming postmodern collapse of modernity. It is an intriguing and provocative theory, yet it is still abstract, still subtly and ironically Marxist in its grand vision of history.

What Savage does is to give the reader the concrete, intimate details of living under Communism, of fleeing Communism, of living with relatives who remembered the fear that drove them away, and of seeing so little change in post-Communism. This is the stuff of real life. Communism was more than abstract modernity: it was a cruel and oppressive system that tried, but never succeeded, to stamp out the cultures, the habits of the heart, of the peoples it ruled. In this regard, Savage's book brought back so many memories for me. Growing up as a boy in Communist Yugoslavia, I remember hearing the knocks on the door in the middle of the night, and that the person taken away was never seen again. I remember the fear and whispers in saying *anything* about Tito and the government. Above all, I remember the mystery of my father's death, labelled a "suicide" by the Communists, but most likely it was murder, the ultimate payback for his noncompliance. Now that Communism is gone in many but not all parts of the world (let us not forget North Korea, China, Serbia, and Cuba); now that Communism in some form may be attempting a comeback in impoverished areas of the former Soviet Union; now is the time to bear witness to what Communism was and how it oppressed the human spirit. It was more than modernity gone amuck.

Whatever postmodernism is—and its exact definition need not concern us here—one of its alleged characteristics is to allow "voices" from the margins of society to be heard. Women, minorities, and all those who had been oppressed, repressed, and kept out of mainstream debates are supposed to have a better chance of expressing themselves nowadays. But again, there is an ethnocentric irony here even regarding this welcome, feminist development. For example, relatively little attention or concern was paid by Western women, or men, to the rape of Bosnian women in the most recent Balkan War, in contrast to the enormous amount of attention paid in the West to issues from Nannygate to Monica Lewinsky. An ironic provincialism exists in the West such that Western women and minorities are given more of a chance to express themselves, but non-Western women and minorities are not. This is another reason why Ania Savage's book is important. As someone who identifies herself as an American and also as someone with cultural roots in Ukraine, she comes across as a stranger in both lands, and thereby as someone who can act as a cultural bridge between the two worlds. What was the role of all the millions of babushkas in formerly Communist lands as their fathers, husbands, and sons went forth to create this monstrous system? How did the women eke out a living in a system that promised so much wealth but basically could not feed its own people adequately? What values did the women impart to their children in a system that tried to destroy the family along with the nation and minority cultural identity? (After all, one was supposed to be a Soviet, not a Ukrainian; a Yugoslav, not a Bosnian.) The reader gets glimpses into these important questions from Savage's intimate portrait of her family and the people that she met in Ukraine.

Finally, Ania Savage is clearly a gifted writer. She is able to draw the reader into her family life, into the frightening aspects of Ukraine, and into the nostalgic charm and dreams of a by-gone Ukraine. Because she draws on the reader's empathetic understanding, the author is able to bear witness to the horrors of her family's past, but also, more importantly, to build bridges to the oppressed histories of many others. A universalism emerges out of all the particularism, all the concrete details, in this story. I believe that Kurds, Bosnians, Albanians, Palestinians, and many other oppressed peoples will find themselves in this book. Perhaps it will inspire them to bear witness to their own suffering, and help open the West's eyes to the rest of the world.

—Stjepan G. Meštrović
Series Editor

Return to Ukraine

Chapter 1

MASS GRAVE IN SLAVSKE

We are looking, you and I, at a ridge of mountains that resemble the Blue Ridge in Virginia and the Adirondacks in upstate New York. These ridges are rounded at the pinnacles, their flanks shaggy with conifers that tint the landscape a bluish hue and sweeten the air. Yet, we are not on the East Coast of North America. In fact, we are not in North America, but half a world away, in mountain terrain about the same age as the Appalachians, the Carpathian Mountains of Eastern Europe. It is early September, a clear, bright day. The sky is without a cloud but its color is not the blazing, heart-tugging blue I am used to from living in the Colorado Rockies. The blue is gentler, softer, not unlike the rounded peaks on the horizon. The color reminds me of the soft blue flannel of a pair of L. L. Bean pajamas one of my sons wears in fall and winter. I think of him, safe and asleep on the other side of the globe. The time in which I'm living is eight hours ahead of his, but I might as well be in a different era.

In the clear, flannel-blue sky, the late morning sun gives off little warmth. There's a bite in the air that hints of a coming frost. Being a mountain climber, I know about treacherous weather. An hour ago I pulled out my Gortex parka, which has protected me on the summits of two dozen of Colorado's highest peaks. I think it is appropriate apparel for a day in the mountains, but I fail to recognize its fatal flaw. It's bright red, a color that is considered—as I will learn in the months ahead—unsuitable in this time frame, and in this society, for a woman my age.

But neither the illusory good weather nor my warm parka gives me

Although Russian and Ukrainian both use the Cyrillic alphabet, they are transliterated differently. Rather than standardize one language to the other, I have transliterated proper names in each language according to its own system.

comfort. I am working my lower lip in consternation. Or is it fear? A boy—a boy no older than my sleeping son—is holding out for my inspection a discolored and crushed human skull.

We are, you and I, in a country of contradictions and labyrinthine history, a country that is two weeks old on this day, but one that marked the millennium of its civilization three years ago. This country has not been independent for a hundred years in the last five centuries, yet it has a unique language, literature, and culture. This country is Ukraine, and it won't impress its name on the American public for another three years, until a fifteen-year-old figure skater named Oksana Baiul will edge out America's and Disney's darling Nancy Kerrigan for the gold medal in skating at the Winter Olympics in Lillehammer, Norway. It is then that Americans will see a yellow and blue flag alongside the stars and stripes. Television viewers will wonder impatiently about the long wait for the medal ceremony. Later, we will learn that a missing tape—the tape of the national anthem of this unknown country—caused the delay. The tape will be found, the blue and gold flag will be hoisted above the stars and stripes, and the anthem will be played, although Oksana Baiul will tell Oprah Winfrey that she's Russian. Oh, well. What can you expect if you're an unknown country?

On this September day, these events are still in the future, and hardly anyone in the West is thinking of Ukraine. The myth of Ukraine's mighty "big brother"—the Soviet Union—will not be shattered for another four months.

This is my fourth day in Ukraine, and I have sought out the gravediggers on purpose. Although I came alone to the gravesite, I am not alone in Ukraine. In a pseudo-Tyrolean chalet up the scarred hill behind me are my two traveling companions, my mother and my aunt. My mother, Anna Bojcun, is seventy-five; her sister, Katia Kovshevych, seventy-seven or so. I'm not quite sure how old Katia is, but neither do I ask, now nor later. (All three of us have fiddled with our ages sometime in our lives, but that's another story.) It is obvious that my mother and Katia are sisters, but I don't resemble my mother. I am blond-haired and pale-eyed, while she and Katia have honey-colored skin and dark eyes under black, winglike eyebrows. My mother's black hair turned white overnight when my father was killed, but Katia's is still salt and pepper, perhaps because she was able to anticipate her impending widow-hood since her husband died after a lingering illness.

"You even have your father's long nose," my mother said in an aggrieved voice at the beginning of our trip as I stood in front of the mirror in the bathroom we were sharing.

"She has your hairline and the high forehead," Katia said diplomatically to her sister from the bathroom doorway, but by then my mother's thoughts had fled somewhere else.

I said nothing. Even when I was a child, people seldom realized that I belonged to my mother. They assumed that Katia's older daughter, Christine, dark-haired and dark-eyed, was my mother's child. Perhaps that is why my mother, when addressing my father, would refer to me as "*your* daughter."

Besides age manipulation and kindred genes, my mother, Katia, and I share one more peculiarity. Each of us was born in Ukraine, and for half a century each of us was afraid to go back to our birthplace. But now, in the last decade of the twentieth century, we are back, although each for a different reason. Three months earlier, my mother was diagnosed with Alzheimer's disease, which has already devastated her short-term memory, although her long-term memory remains, for the most part, intact. I read in her chocolate-brown eyes that she knows this is her only chance to see her homeland one more time. Katia's agenda is quite different. She came to keep us company, but she is also thinking of initiating legal proceedings in the hope of regaining property that was confiscated from her husband's estate fifty years ago. I'm on a pilgrimage, coming back to forge a link with a country a birth certificate says is mine, but which I neither know nor remember.

On this robust September morning, we are in Slavske, a town that does not rate a dot on most maps. I did not know Slavske existed until two days ago when a man sidled up to me in the lobby of a hotel in Lviv, the capital of Western Ukraine and our first stop, and whispered into my ear. He said that, being a journalist, I had to go into the Carpathian Mountains to a town called Slavske to see—and then to write about—the mass grave of NKVD (the precursor of the KGB) victims.

I knew immediately why the man was whispering. The lobby of Hotel Dnister had been bugged for years. I was warned about the surveillance before I left home. "If you want to discuss private matters, go for a walk in the Jesuit Garden across the street," a veteran of trips to Ukraine advised. "You never know . . . " She left the sentence unfinished, but I understood her warning. My parents were political refugees who had fled Soviet Ukraine at the end of World War II, after being warned that they would be arrested and deported to Siberia if they did not leave. Although this is the 1990s, old fears spin around me like Indian summer cobwebs.

The boy is holding a human skull for me to inspect, but I don't know what to do. What is the etiquette on handling human remains? In

Ukraine? Anywhere? Mother and Katia, my guides to this land, to the past, to a time I know only from stories that made me sad, are up on the hill, sunning themselves on the brick patio of a chalet for the proletariat, a contradiction in terms and images. They are the ones who told me that Slavske was simply a ski resort, a pleasant alpine village. I equated "ski resort" with "Vail, Colorado," which also has pseudo-Tyrolean chalets. Slavske, my mother and Katia said, was famous because it was the first ski resort to be built in the Carpathian Mountains, its ski trails dating back to the 1930s. Katia said that her husband Bohdan had skied Slavske as a university student. Mother, after looking from Katia to me, then concentrating on a memory that was working its way to the surface, added that Slavske was near the Stryi River, and therefore would also be near her birthplace, a tiny village called Krushelnytsia. Thus, lulled by images of another Vail and hoping to mine the lode of family history, I arranged the day before for us to visit Slavske. My curiosity is tickled not so much by the rumor of a mass grave but by seeing a second Vail and Krushelnytsia.

This impromptu side trip has not been going well. A recently acquired acquaintance was driving her daughter to spend a week with a grandmother in the mountains and agreed to drop us off in Slavske. We started out late, were caught in a downpour, and reached our destination hours behind schedule, after the town, the restaurants, and the chalets had closed for the night. After much cajoling, accompanied by "a little extra" for the night clerk, we found lodgings in the chalet, which turned out to be a rest home that a trade collective built during the flush years of Brezhnev's rule. During the night I dreamed that a man with a carbine slung over his shoulder had crept into my room through the partially open window and was staring down at me. Frightened, the image of the intruder as vivid as if I had actually glimpsed someone, I woke up, but it took me a moment to screw up my courage to look around. The night was graying into dawn and I could see without turning on the light that I was alone. As I drifted off to sleep again, I realized I knew who the intruder had been.

A moment later, someone was calling my name. Someone was knocking on the door. I sat up. The air was crisp; the morning had turned sunny. Mother and Katia were urging me to hurry because breakfast was being served. They had been up for hours.

Breakfast turned out to be another bad omen. We followed other guests to a bare, utilitarian room. Narrow wooden tables crowded either side of a center aisle. Hard, straight-backed chairs flanked the tables. A stern matron in a gray uniform refused to give us a table until all the other guests were seated. When I saw where she was going to assign us, my heart sank. The couple already at the table set for six was from central casting for "From Russia with Love," a James Bond movie filled with Russian villains. His black hair was glossy with pomade. Dark, hostile eyes examined us from beneath bushy eyebrows as he bit into a piece of bread. Bulldog jowls trembled as he chewed. He looked mean enough to be a stand-in for a member of the Politburo. His wife was a female clone, big, dark, and belligerent. Imagine the female commissar who kicks Bond in the shins with her orthopedic shoes, the tips of which suddenly grow knife blades. And then, as we watched, the woman stabbed at the communal butter plate with *her* knife.

Yes, we did smile and said good morning in Ukrainian. Neither he nor she returned our greeting. Soon the waitress rolled her trolley to our table and began dishing out breakfast. To our consternation, it turned out to be thin, pale green fish soup. We made faces at each other, but said nothing, afraid the Politburo couple would overhear our carping. Fish soup, for breakfast? How odd! I stole a glance at our table companions. As soon as it was placed before them, they dipped into the soup plate with gusto.

"How can you benefit from the cure if you refuse to follow the regimen?" demanded a patrolling matron, who noticed that we were not eating. She stalked over to complain loudly to the head matron in the gray uniform, who, after seating us, had returned to guarding the dining room entrance. People at the other tables turned to stare at us. The Politburo couple bent their heads over their soup bowls and slurped on resolutely, pretending we did not exist.

That was breakfast.

But the weather was glorious, as if the deluge of the preceding night had never happened. The flannel-blue sky hung above us like an umbrella. A strand of mist, a scarf of gossamer silk, had draped itself against a distant, blue peak.

"Look," my mother said, pointing to a mountain on the horizon. "Isn't that Hoverlia?"

I knew that was the name of the tallest mountain in this part of the Carpathians and that my mother had climbed it as a young woman. Katia was not sure. "I think you have to go farther into the mountains to see Hoverlia," she said.

"How about going into town?" I asked. Katia and my mother exchanged glances, consulted their watches, and said they would rather wait until later in the day.

I had decided during breakfast that I would not contribute to our developing reputation as troublemakers by asking the clerk in the lobby about the mass grave. I waited until I descended into the town, then stopped a passerby. I had rehearsed the question in Ukrainian (I could have asked the question in Russian, which I had studied in college and, more recently, with a Russian émigré in Denver, but decided on Ukrainian both because I am fluent in it and because this *was* Ukraine). I asked, "Could you direct me to the digging?" consciously refraining from using the word *grave*. Either the question or the language frightened the woman. She did not say a word, only gestured to a road and scurried away, her face tense with disapproval.

I set out thinking it would be a long walk. I imagined a dense fir forest, perhaps a meadow set amid heavy underbrush, trees that blotted out the sky. But when the road crested, I saw the diggers, out in the open. They were on the left side of the road, at the base of an escarpment bare of any vegetation. All around them were piles of black dirt. What soil had been left undug glistened like black ice, but its skin was deceptive. This seemingly hard surface was in fact shiny, wet mud. I discovered this as I stepped off the road and my new white Reeboks sank into the mire. I retreated.

The skull had not been discovered yet. The two diggers paused momentarily to acknowledge my presence with nods, then continued digging. I looked around. Ahead, the road sloped down to a pasture. It, too, was dotted with piles of excavated mud. Directly across the road from me was a run-down country store—not unlike a rural vegetable stand—but there were no other buildings. The sun grew warmer; a bird twittered in a nearby tree, a jay perhaps. Behind me, in town, a church bell tolled, its bass tones echoing dolefully against the walls of the narrow valley.

Probably because he had been conditioned by years of denials and fearful silences, the boy closest to me did not shout his find when his shovel crunched against bone. He motioned to the other boy to shield him as he dropped to his knees. With a gesture that was like a caress, he sank his fingers into the shiny mud. I saw the change of expression on his face and held my breath. But I was not the only one who realized something was happening. Across the road, two stocky men suddenly appeared in the doorway of the country store. Four pairs of eyes bored into the boy as he slowly stood up. In his cupped hands he cradled a brown object, a chalice of bone.

Suddenly, I feel very cold. I fancy I'm smelling something raw, something rotten and forbidden. One of the watchers at the country store swears loudly, grinds out his cigarette in the dust of the road, and hurries back toward town.

"Secret Police," the boy says, his voice matter of fact. His gaze—intent and brittle with hate—follows the departing figure. "He's going to the post office to call in a report," he continues. "They watch us day and night, have since the beginning."

"Who?" I say.

"KGB."

"Oh."

"Look," the boy insists, extending toward me his supplicant, cupped hands. I gaze into the valley they form, at a collapsed human skull. The bone is dark brown, discolored by the viscous black mud.

"You can tell he was shot in the head. See the missing bone in the forehead?" the boy says, pointing.

I look, but have no idea how to interpret what I'm seeing. The skull's forehead is cracked and has a jagged, rectangular hole where the left temple should be. What I want to know is why the bullet did not leave a neat, round hole, but how can I ask such a callous question?

"The NKVD brought them here from all over," the boy says. He wipes mud from the skull with the sleeve of his shirt. "From the bunkers in the mountains. From jails in other towns. They lined them up along the ditch—there used to be a deep gully here—then shot them. Some who were buried were not dead. Old women say the topsoil trembled for days after an execution."

The image horrifies me, but not the speaker. He has become used to it. He adds, "We think there may be fifteen hundred to two thousand bodies buried here."

My gaze shifts to my mud-caked sneakers. Am I standing on top of a thousand, or perhaps two thousand, skulls like the one I am being shown? A cemetery with no crosses? A cemetery of people buried alive?

But I ask no questions about who the "them" were. I know. The armed man in my dream was one of them. The "them" were the UPA, a name forbidden for fifty years. The UPA was the Ukrainian Insurgent Army that fought the Red Army in the Carpathian Mountains for nearly a decade following World War II. UPA guerrillas fought to separate

Ukraine from the Soviet Union as Chechen guerrillas would fight to separate Chechnya from Russia a half century later. Moscow considered both conflicts civil wars and retaliated harshly.

I know something about the cruelty of Bolsheviks, the NKVD, and the KGB. I grew up hearing stories about it and how it was applied to family members—a grandfather, a grandmother, two uncles. I also know something about the UPA. My first encounter with partisans came when I was about six years old. One day, after lessons in a makeshift classroom in the refugee camp where we were living, I saw a group of men chain-smoking in the yard. Since my father was a smoker, I approached the huddle of men thinking I would find him there. At the last possible moment, a woman snatched me back. "Those men carry weapons," she hissed into my ear. She told on me and I was spanked by my mother.

Over the years, I picked up details by eavesdropping on adult conversations, then by reading about the UPA in Ukrainian-language books. In the 1970s, an émigré publishing house in Canada began issuing eyewitness accounts of soldiers and medics who had participated in the UPA war and who had either escaped to the West—as had the group of chain-smoking men I came across as a child—or had had their memoirs and documents smuggled out. I devoured these accounts, as, later, I devoured CNN clips of the Chechen war.

Even today I find it impossible to define or comprehend the depth of evil during the UPA era, to measure the suffering, or to assess the loss of lives. Cornered UPA partisans were burned alive when the houses in which they were hiding were set on fire by grenades or mortars, just as in 1996 Grad missiles were deployed in Chechnya to firebomb rebel villages into oblivion. Women and girls suspected of serving as UPA couriers were raped, then gored with bayonets. Partisan bunkers were dynamited with the guerrillas trapped inside. The UPA retaliated, as the Chechens would a half century later. Communist organizers sent into the villages were shot. Their families were driven out. Hostages were taken and exchanged for safe passage, or freedom for captured comrades. In the late 1940s and early 1950s, both sides insisted that they had to destroy in order to create a society to their liking, not unlike the arguments offered by both sides in the Chechen war of the 1990s. Of course, in the West, no one cared about the guerrilla war behind the Iron Curtain during the deep freeze of the Cold War. Even if it had been publicized, would the Western Allies have intervened? The Soviets characterized the UPA guerrillas as fascists, crazed remnants of Hitler's war. Besides, certain real estate on the globe was off limits then, as it remains today.

Did the United Nations interfere in the Chechen war as it did in Bosnia or in Kosovo? Yet all three were civil wars.

Here is an excerpt from a 1997 Amnesty International report on Russian Army behavior in Chechnya: "According to witnesses, Hasan Khamidov, from the village of Terskoe, was subjected to torture while he was detained at the 'filtration camp' in Mozdok in January 1995; the Russian guards, reportedly, cut his feet with a blade and burned him with cigarettes."

I never touched the skull. Looking back, I think I held my breath, afraid of inhaling the bad odor I had smelled or had fancied. What was I afraid of? A whiff of something foul, of that odor of death or rottenness Anne Rice evokes so well in her novels? I continue to wonder whether unearthed bones reek. And I cannot say if the skull in Slavske had an odor or not.

In Slavske, I am so frazzled that I fail to notice other things that are happening around me. Only when the boy holding the skull says: "Vitya is getting protection" do I notice the absence of the other digger.

Vitya returns with a woman and two men, who don't fit my idea of revolutionaries. Irena Sen is extremely thin and nervous and chain-smokes. She wears her dark hair clipped close to her skull, and this, combined with the dark hairs on her upper lip, give her an uncannily masculine appearance. She looks toward the man loitering outside the country store, then motions to me to follow her up the muddy slope. Sliding and stumbling, we climb a dozen or so feet above the road. She sits down, and I follow her example. Her two companions catch up and sit down also. Zenoviy Dosiak, broad shouldered, stocky, and openly curious, does most of the talking. Vasyl Shybystyi, a small man with a small smile, smiles. Dosiak says the three of them constitute the committee in charge of the digging, then shuts his mouth with a snap.

Irena says: "We don't know you." But as we talk and they learn something about me, she and the two men drop their reserve. I think they eventually tell me almost everything they know about Slavske's mass grave.

We learn from each other's stories. Sitting with Irena, watching emotions sweep across her face, I begin to recognize the mass grave in Slavske—where I came as an afterthought—as the axis of her life. Sitting on that slope, I grasp the reasons why Irena and the others are digging. She and they must make some sense of the killings, even if it is only to compile a list of the dead. As she speaks, Irena pulls me back into a childhood where the stories were about the dead, the dying, and the suffering, not stories of princes, princesses, and pumpkins that turned into gilded chariots.

"Whispers about what happened here never died out," Irena Sen says. "Old women would shake their heads and weep when we began to ask questions. With time and patience we learned that three cottages and a communal outhouse stood here." She points up the hill.

Sometime in 1946, she says, about the time when the Soviet regime outlawed the Ukrainian Catholic Church, two priests and a cantor were executed and their corpses were hurled into the outhouse. "This is when we think the cottages were razed and the gully at the bottom of the hill became a garbage dump and an execution site," she says, her dark eyes glinting with wetness. "There, where the boys are digging."

She falls silent. She passes the back of her hand over her pinched face and sighs. Now Dosiak explains: "People were herded here and forced to witness the executions. The idea was to frighten the population into not helping the partisans." He says Slavske became the killing field for twenty-seven neighboring villages. Irena adds that five Jewish doctors, captured when a UPA hospital where they worked was discovered, were also brought to Slavske and shot. Some time later, the execution site was bulldozed over, leveled with the road, and abandoned.

"Did you come here to collect information on the grave?" Vasyl Shybystyi finally speaks up.

I shake my head, although I wish it were otherwise, but I'm not going to lie to these people. Irena places a forgiving hand on my arm. She says that if I meet with them that evening, she will show me a list of those who died in Slavske's ditch.

"We will provide you with a bodyguard who will escort you back," Dosiak promises.

I stare at him. I do not consider myself easy to spook, but I'm spooked.

"We'll show you our drawing for a memorial here," he adds. "It will cost forty-seven thousand dollars. Perhaps you can help us."

We scramble down to the road and Irena and the two men leave. I linger because I want to talk with the boys. I also want to photograph the skull. The boy who found it poses.

I ask him, "What will you do with it?"

"We have a place where we store the bones and then assemble the skeletons," he says. "We have put together nineteen thus far."

He is fidgeting. I know he has something on his mind. The other boy comes up. He's acting very casual, offhand. I look into their faces, but cannot read them. They are still more boys than men. A light fuzz cov-

Workers assemble skeletons dug up in Slavske from the mass grave. Photograph courtesy Slavske Mass Grave Committee.

ers their cheeks. Their skin has yet to feel the scrape of a razor. They have long arms and legs and possess that certain awkwardness that accompanies sudden growth. Only their eyes are foreign land. Their eyes are pale, hard and flat, revealing nothing.

"Did they search your bags when you arrived?" one asks.

"No, I don't think they search foreigners any more. We just fill out a customs slip."

The boy moves closer to me. He reaches into his pocket and pulls something out. He opens his palm. A small black pistol lies on it. "We need more of these," he says. "People like you can bring them in for us."

"What do you need them for?" I demand, while my mind says, *Oh, my God.*

"To protect ourselves from people like them," he says and gestures with his head across the road.

I glance over my shoulder. The second man is gone, although I did not notice him leave either. "I—we Americans—don't smuggle in weapons," I blurt.

The boy's face crumples in disappointment. He puts the pistol away. "How about miniature cameras, the kind your CIA uses?" he asks hopefully.

"What would you use them for?" I say, incredulous at the conversation. I feel I am watching a bad movie in which someone who looks and speaks like me is acting out an overwrought melodrama.

The boy explains: "We need to photograph the documents we find before they're confiscated by them," and he gestures again toward where the two watchers stood.

"You would be better off taking them to a place that has a copying machine and making a dozen copies and distributing them among people you trust," I counter, speaking briskly, thinking I'm giving good advice. "I know there are copy machines in Lviv."

The boys regard me with pity—or is it disdain?—in their hard, pale eyes. "We don't trust people with copy machines," one says.

I am a disappointment. A coward. They shrug and return to digging. I try to find something to say, but the chasms of age, of outlook, of culture are too great. As I form one explanation after another, the words flounder and sink as my Reeboks have in the deceptive mud. I think: Little boys play at war to snatch a moment of make-believe glory for themselves. My sons still do so when they play a game called Risk. The point of the game is to deploy the armies at your command until you have conquered the world. Sometimes even big boys do not realize that glory's companions are injury or death. The boys in Slavske are standing at the threshold between childhood and adulthood, mesmerized by visions of glory, yet too inexperienced to see glory's flip side. I shudder. These two boys seeking glory are no older than my sleeping son, the boy who delights in playing Risk. *Oh, my God.*

I climb the hill scarred by ski runs back to the pseudo chalet. I feel as if the dream I had during the night has returned at midmorning and I am somnambulant. It is one thing to read—or even have a nightmare—about atrocities, but it is something entirely different to witness a skull being unearthed from a roadside ditch, or to see a revolver that is ready for use, or to be told that you need protection if you dare visit someone in the evening. I cannot forget the hatred in Irena's and the boys' eyes. How she and the boys must have begun to hate—and fear—early in their lives! I see her pinched, masculine face and wonder whether she would ever be able to forgive.

A building with a tiled sloping roof and dark wood trim looms above me. It is a pretty building, like a barmaid in "The Student Prince." Curvaceous red tiles give way to creamy walls framed by black, heavy beams like coils of braids. I doubt that Irena or the boys have ever been up here. The formidable couple at breakfast, or even the local woman who gave me directions an hour earlier, have little, if anything, in common with Irena or the grave diggers. More likely than not, the Politburo couple and the local woman resent having someone disturbing their peace of mind by probing a past best left forgotten. How will Irena, the boys, and the rest-home guests ever find common ground to keep together this newborn country?

In the lobby, the Tyrolean charm disappears. The interior is Soviet utilitarianism at its starkest. A rubber plant is dying in a bleak corner from lack of care. A sign someone forgot to take down, or perhaps intentionally kept, proclaims that rest-home sojourns are rewards "for the deserving proletariat." Next to the sign hangs a meticulously copied timetable of train departures from Slavske's station, the same station through which fifty years ago prisoners were dragged to the execution site at the roadside ditch.

The conundrums of what this country—my birthplace and my birthright—is, are multiplying.

As I pass through the unadorned, gray-painted lobby, the time warp disappears. Mother and Katia are still sitting on the patio, exactly as I left them. For a moment they do not see me and I study them covertly. They are a handsome pair. Age has not robbed Katia, the acknowledged beauty of the family, of the finely chiseled features and striking eyebrows above dark, flashing eyes. My mother, suntanned from life in the Florida sun and significantly slimmer from the ordeal of MRIs and psychiatric tests that diagnosed her illness, looks uncommonly young and healthy. Her white hair contrasts well with the bronze cast of her skin and her brown eyes are as animated as Katia's.

When Baudelaire said that women did not possess "a taste for the abyss"—by which, I think, he meant "the unknown"—the kind of women common in my family must have been outside his circle of acquaintances. Before she became ill, my mother circumnavigated the globe by herself. Katia still drives a four-wheel-drive vehicle, a "Jimmy," and I climb mountains. My curiosity brought us to Slavske, will take us to Krushelnytsia and, eventually, even farther into the Carpathians. Mother and Katia thrive on adventure and newness, but how will they react to the past I have glimpsed?

I sit down with them, yet say nothing as I try to read their faces. My mother is smiling and happy. The wariness and fear that veiled her eyes following the diagnosis of Alzheimer's is gone. She has been transported back to a joyous time that she has no difficulty recreating. I listen to them talk about a different life, another way of living, a homeland light-years away from the mass grave and the fear in the valley below.

Anna and Katia, 1991. Photograph by Ania Savage.

Life is choices. A long time ago, when I was still an adolescent and many years before the advent of her disease, I realized that my mother lived in the past. She chose the past over the present, over her future. The past was worth remembering; the present was best forgotten, or ignored. Perhaps her disease derives from this self-imposed breach. She chose the safe world before the war, not the frightening world of the immigrant. "Before" was a magical time. "After" was horror. When war swept over her and she became an immigrant, she reached back for the "before," suspending it in a magic bubble. For years, she kept that magic bubble sealed inside herself, uncontaminated by the new life. I can re-create and understand her reasoning: Nothing recommended her new life. The sweatshop where she was paid a nickel for each pair of men's pants she sewed, as well as her daughter's school where the other mothers talked about cooking and shopping, were alien worlds. Her study of English faltered; she chose not to master it (although she spoke Ukrainian, Polish, Russian, and German well), and in the last few years, English increasingly abandoned her.

Sitting and watching her in Slavske, I begin to wonder about the wisdom of bringing her back to where her past had taken place. What will happen to her mind, her equilibrium, when the resplendent past collides with, is challenged by, and becomes contaminated with the inferior present? Will she continue to remember the Carpathians solely as a magical place, will she accept the fact that horrible things happened here, or will she go mad?

Yet, perhaps because I am a journalist, I cannot keep quiet: "I met some people," I say. "They're excavating a mass grave from the UPA war. If you want, I'll introduce you to these people."

The glow and the happiness disappear from their faces. Suddenly they are old, sad women. Neither meets my gaze.

"They . . . " I begin, but it is Katia, not my mother, who interrupts.

"We've seen enough horrors," she says, hugging her sister to her breast.

It is the afternoon of the same day. We take the road into town. Whatever lingering ideas about Vail I might have harbored evaporate. The shops are few; their shelves are dusty and empty. The potholed main street is deserted also. We pass the hostel where I am to meet with Irena Sen and the two men, and I memorize its location. I feel better because the inn looks like one of the old Vail condos, wood-clad, Tyrolean, familiar. We return to the rest home in late afternoon. After dinner, which begins with the same fish soup we encountered at breakfast, I return to town, leaving my mother and Katia to watch a film being screened in the auditorium.

"I'm going for a walk," I lie.

Inside, the inn reveals a different self. It is unkempt; the air is sour. A game club on the first floor is not yet open. The air reeks from a leaking toilet that has emptied a brown rivulet onto the linoleum. In the silence, I hear a baby wailing behind a distant door. I climb the staircase and start knocking on doors. Finally, one opens. A distracted woman with the wailing baby on her hip asks what I want. I ask where I can find two men and a woman.

"Oh, them? The ones involved with the crazy diggers? They're next door. They play cards and argue politics," the woman says.

"Everyone's gone out to eat," she adds. She shifts the baby to her other hip and gives me directions to a restaurant. I go there, but it is closed. I return to the inn, but no one answers my knocks. I wait; no one comes. The baby is no longer crying. Night is falling. There are no lights in the hallway. The building is silent, empty, and scary. I retrace my steps up the scarred hill. As I think about the bodyguard Dosiak promised, the thought crosses my mind that I may be an accomplice to the circumstances I have encountered in Slavske. I ask myself whether my fascination with the UPA is somehow skewing my Slavske experience. How intense is my imagination as it filters events? How contagious is the past?

Surreptitiously, I glance over my shoulder, but I see no one. I am a solitary figure on the road—a lone shadow illuminated by the blue light of the full moon. Did UPA couriers climb this hill fifty years ago to deliver messages to bunkers deep among the conifers? Did the women, afraid of being stopped and searched by Soviet patrols, coil the messages into thin flexible tubes, which they hid inside the spiral of thick braids they wore like coronets? As I climb the hill, I breathe deeply and taste the cool night air. Soon the pines swallow my shadow and the forest closes around me, until I think that the slender pines are bending to hide my passage. I stop and shake my head and reprimand myself for the double barrel of imagination.

Four days later I will come to regret that I did not take Dosiak's warning more seriously.

Chapter 2

THE COWARDLY BROTHER

When my mother became ill, her face changed. Particularly her eyes. They used to be sparkling and dueling. Mostly they dart about or stare unblinking. Often, they burn with hurt and rage as if she were seeing something terrible. I think she is saying to me, "If only you would listen and understand."

Mother and I were never close, but now I can hardly comprehend her, except for the palpable fear and rage. Although I realize that she does not know how to speak of that fear because she cannot grasp it, I cannot come to terms with its presence. I hear it in her words, read it in the half-grin on her face that makes the corners of her mouth go down instead of up. When she speaks, the words are painful and hard. They are like pebbles a child throws at a rival in consternation, not realizing that the pebbles will hurt before falling to the ground. At such moments I make a valiant effort to understand, not judge and condemn. I ask myself: What do I know of her fear? What do I know of waking up in the middle of the night and not knowing where you are? Can I possibly imagine what terror surges through her when she looks in the mirror and does not quite know her past?

I think of my father. He died in an automobile accident. One moment he was there; the next he was a statistic a state trooper left at our door. My father seldom reminisced about his youth. When something went wrong he would say, "This is America . . . " He would accompany this phrase with a shake of his head, as if to say that the trek across Europe and the transatlantic journey might not have been worth it. Yet he never complained about his life as an immigrant. He died instantly when his truck struck a tree, the state trooper said.

It took time for me to understand the futility of my parents' lives, frittered away by war. To leave her homeland became a death sentence for my mother. A part of her was amputated and she never felt whole again. Perhaps my decision to take her back to her homeland was an attempt at reversing the maiming.

I grew up into an adult who equated the Soviet Union with a penal colony. I had no desire to go back, to step outside the charmed safety of the United States. Then in 1991 came an offer I could not refuse. I was invited by the Ukraina Society, an arm of the then still Communist government of Ukraine, to be a guest editor at the society's English-language newspaper, *News from Ukraine,* and to teach a course on Western media at Kyiv State University in the capital of Ukraine. (Following independence, Ukraine changed the transliteration of the name of the capital from the Russian Kiev to the Ukrainian Kyiv.)

I sent a fax accepting the invitation and began planning a three-stage trip that included my mother. We would stop in Poland to visit her older brother Oleksander Vlasenko, who had had a successful career as a lawyer and was now retired. Then we would travel through Western Ukraine to the village where I was born and to the villages and cities where my mother had spent her girlhood and young adulthood. Finally, we would arrive in Kyiv, where I would stay while my mother returned to the United States. Since she could not travel alone and since her doctors strongly recommended that two adults accompany her, I invited Katia to take the trip with us.

In the weeks preceding our departure, I was either excited or mortally afraid. What if *they* decided to arrest me once I got there? After reading the UPA memoirs, I had translated smuggled *samizdat* from political dissidents in Ukraine. The translation had been published in the émigré press. What if *they* ignored my American citizenship? What if . . . ?

But how could I pass up such an opportunity for both my mother and myself? How could I not heed her desire to visit the places where she grew up? How could I not go, see for myself, understand the heritage she had bestowed on me? The urgency to get at the facts, I would realize later, had two sources. The first source was obvious: It came from my training as a journalist to poke into things, to ask questions, to find out what I did not know, and to understand what I did not understand. The second source, I would discover, derived from a longing that went beyond a desire to know the facts to a desire to understand who I was. The melting pot theory had not worked for my parents and was only partially successful in my case. I had thought in high school that if my name was Anglicized I would be "more American." In college, I discovered the values of individuality, but in my first job for a Gannett newspaper I found myself returning to my high school theory as news sources and editors struggled with my unpronounceable surname. Marriage gave me the gloss of an American middle-class identity and took me to the suburbs, but, to my surprise, the Anglo-Saxon surname, a house, a car, and children failed to close the gap. What interested the women I carpooled with to Montessori, for the most part, did not interest me. Over time I became resigned to the fact that I would always be someone looking in. If I went back to Ukraine, would I feel at home?

Our trip was nearly aborted. Two days before our departure, the August, 1991, coup in Moscow began to unfold. Ukraine declared its independence of Moscow. Other Soviet republics did likewise. We boarded the plane for Europe unsure whether we would be permitted entry and whether those who had championed "the cultural exchange" in which I was to participate were still in their jobs. In Germany, we bought tickets for a train going east. We had hoped to get off in Lodz, a city in western Poland where Oleksander lives, but a message reached us that we should continue to Warsaw, where he would meet us. Was he altering our plans because of the changing map of an imploding empire?

We met Oleksander at the Forum Hotel in Warsaw. It was a disastrous afternoon. Mother wept while Katia and Oleksander quarreled.

"So, you were a Communist?" Katia said.

Oleksander winced. "Everyone was."

"President of the bar association, my, my," Katia said.

"It was a job," he said.

A little later, soft-spoken, good-natured Katia went into a frontal attack.

"I looked at the map," Katia said sweetly. "You know, Warsaw is not all that far from Ukraine. Day's train ride."

"I settled in Lodz early on," Oleksander said, suspecting what was coming next.

"You could have gone back, seen our parents when the war ended," Katia said. "You had all the right connections."

"I wrote," Oleksander said.

"But never went back," she insisted.

"Not until the eighties, no."

My mother swung her round face from one to the other as they parried. She didn't take sides. I don't know whether she understood what was at stake. Her face was placid. Now and again, she squeezed Oleksander's hand affectionately.

"You didn't care if mother starved to death," Katia cried and began weeping.

Oleksander shifted on the black leather sofa. "You don't understand how life was here," he said.

"Our father was beaten to death!" Katia cried.

I had never seen this side of Katia before, and would not see it again. She is a cheerful, mild person, smoothing over the wrinkles of life, always yielding to my mother, the more excitable and aggressive one. But at the Forum Hotel Katia was like a lioness avenging the death of a cub, although the wrong she was redressing had been committed a half-century ago: Oleksander had not only been too cowardly to help his parents but had denied his parentage to save himself. He had let his parents die alone, abandoned, because he had been afraid to return to Ukraine and admit that he was Ukrainian, not Polish. The two sisters knew what he had done; over the decades and across thousands of miles the facts had piled up slowly, but inexorably. Was it surprising then that at their reunion after so many years Katia dwelt on the past? But, even in her anger, Katia could not bring herself to disavow Oleksander. I would have. Families are riddles to outsiders. At the Forum Hotel, I was an outsider.

For a few moments, Oleksander sat silent and hunched over in the corner of the black leather sofa. Then suddenly he burst out with: "What do you know about life here? You've been living in luxury in America, while my pension barely puts food on the table. Look at my sweater and look at your suits. My wife was never able to afford such fine clothes."

Katia found a new place to draw blood. "We were wondering why your wife did not come with you. Are you ashamed of your 'foreign' sisters?"

Oleksander rolled his eyes.

"I guess that's why you didn't invite us to your home in Lodz."

"It's a tiny place. I thought you would be more comfortable if we met here," he said and began getting up.

I interrupted for the first time to say that we had a reservation in the hotel's restaurant for dinner.

"I guess it's time for me to leave," Oleksander said.

"But I thought we would eat together," I protested.

"I don't think so," he said. "The train ride to Lodz is long."

"Sianiu!" my mother suddenly cried, using the diminutive of his name. "Don't go." She grabbed his hand and hung herself on his arm, then bawled. On the sofa, Katia sobbed. Oleksander was a coward, a weakling, and an opportunist, but he was also their brother. Katia let my

Oleksander Vlasenko with his sisters Anna (standing) and Katia during their meeting in Warsaw, 1991. Photograph by Ania Savage.

mother coax Oleksander into going into the restaurant and sitting down at a table. But he wouldn't look at the menu. Katia and my mother also refused to order. They said they could not possibly eat anything, although they had missed lunch in the excitement of waiting for and greeting Oleksander. A waiter came to the table to glare at us as we sat in embarrassed silence, staring down at the white tablecloth.

Suddenly my mother was standing up. She was taking charge as she used to do in the past. She swept past Katia, who had reverted to her usual more passive behavior. We watched as my mother rushed to Oleksander and kissed him.

"You look exactly the way I remember," she said. "My handsome, Sianio."

Oleksander raised the white linen napkin to his eyes and dabbed.

"Katia," my mother commanded and beckoned to her sister.

Katia wiped her eyes with the hanky she had crumpled in her hand, then blew her nose and joined her brother and sister.

As they hugged, I took out my camera and snapped a photo. Oleksander was probably eighty then but looked sixty, with an unwrinkled brow, pale blond hair hardly touched by gray, clear blue eyes, and a healthy pink complexion. He was so different from his two dark-eyed and olive-skinned sisters that I could find no family resemblance between the sisters and the brother, but I could easily have been his daughter with my blond hair and pale eyes.

The cease-fire was followed by a truce that would not be broken again that day. The three siblings tried to outdo one another in tactfulness and kindness. Oleksander agreed to order dinner, even letting slip the morsel that he had never dined at the Forum and had been looking forward to the treat. His sisters beamed.

When dinner arrived, we ate and talked about our families. By the time dessert was served, Oleksander had charmed his way back into Katia's good graces and she was smiling. By the time late afternoon shadows fell across the dining room, sisters and brother were reconciled. At the train station, Katia stuffed dollars into Oleksander's trouser pocket as we waited with him for an evening train to Lodz. But the rapprochement was only on the surface, and we knew it. None spoke of a second meeting, although we planned to spend three more days in Poland.

The next morning, I went to buy train tickets for Ukraine while my mother and Katia planned our sightseeing, since both had visited Warsaw as young women. I had not bought tickets for Ukraine at the start of the train journey because I had not known how long we would stay with Oleksander.

"Get your tickets in Krakow," the woman behind the wooden cage at Orbis, the government travel and ticket office, barked at me. Before I could ask another question, she slammed down the grating because it was lunchtime, although it was barely eleven o'clock in the morning. I watched her unwrap a sandwich, made from thick bread and a pink slice of ham, and begin eating. The other cages were also shut.

I mulled the idea over as I made my way past newly minted capitalists selling everything from nylon stockings to Barbie dolls to canned hams on the teeming, sunwashed sidewalks of Aleje Jerosolimskie, one of the major streets in Warsaw. The sidewalks were crowded with improvised stands. Usually rickety folding tables displayed the jumble of merchandise, although occasionally the hood of a car, or an open trunk, served the same purpose. Advertising was accomplished by grabbing passersby by the arm or outshouting a rival at the adjoining table. Less than two years before, this kind of activity would have resulted in a charge of "speculation" and a jail term. When I reached the hotel, I told my mother and Katia about the difficulty with the tickets, but they did not seem to be concerned. They liked the idea of going to Krakow. Both had visited it when a cousin had attended the university there in the 1930s.

A friendly travel agent at the hotel arranged both train tickets and accommodations, although she could not get tickets for the train across the frontier into Ukraine, but she assured me I would have no trouble getting them in Krakow. I was foolish enough to believe her.

Lulled by the ease with which our plans could be changed, we went sightseeing. At the base of Aleje Jerosolimskie, we stopped at the outdoor Armed Forces Museum because the day was warm and lovely. We wandered amid the trucks, tanks, and heavy artillery used in World War II. I stopped in front of a T-34 tank that the Red Army had used not only to rout German panzers but later to destroy entire Carpathian villages that aided the UPA.

I looked back at my mother and Katia. Katia was looking bored and was fiddling with her scarf, while my mother was sitting on a bench and was gazing peacefully toward the Vistula River. I left them alone. They did not want to know what I was thinking. And then, beyond the tanks, I saw a flimsy metal rack mounted on the back of a flatbed truck and caught my breath involuntarily. I had seen this equipment before, I was certain of that. I walked up to it and read that it was a Katyusha, which was an antiaircraft rocket launcher Russians used against the Nazis. In my mind I saw a Katyusha firing a salvo into the nighttime sky. My heart began beating fast. I was back in my childhood.

I was a toddler when we began our journey by train, by truck, by wagon pulled by an ox, and finally on foot, across Europe. A road, a set of rails, a path stretching far to the horizon are what I remember. Along this trek there are stops, my memories. I remember my father shielding my mother and me with his body as he backed away from a group of partisans—or perhaps they were German Army deserters because they wore uniforms—upon whom we stumbled in a forest somewhere in the mountains. But were those mountains the Carpathians or the Alps? I also hold a memory of waking up one night in the back of a truck and watching flares exploding in the black sky, while shells from antiaircraft guns streaked across the horizon like so many giant fireflies.

And here before me, on a sunny afternoon in Warsaw, that memory was coming alive as I stared at a Katyusha. Ignoring my earlier resolve, I hurried back to my mother.

"How close were we to the front?" I asked.

Her face registered no comprehension.

"During the war, were we ever near a battle?" I persisted.

She looked at me, her placid face blank. "What war?" she asked.

Two days later, at the Orbis tourist office in Krakow, I tried to buy train tickets again and made the mistake of speaking broken Polish with a Ukrainian accent, instead of English. The blond-haired clerk looked down her nose at me, then turned away, saying, "No tickets." At the train station I heard the "No tickets" refrain again.

Later, after studying the map of Poland I had brought with me, I asked Katia what she thought about us going farther east to the frontier town of Przemysl (or Peremyshl, as it was known when it was part of Ukraine before World War II). Katia beamed and my mother sat up, unusually vivacious. Hadn't the Basilian Sisters operated a boarding school for girls in Przemysl before the war, she asked, and hadn't one of Katia's best friends gone to school there? She would love to go to Przemysl.

Thus, we crept farther east on a rickety local train. We arrived in Przemysl late at night and hired a taxi. The driver was a dark-haired, nice-looking man in his thirties named Yan. When he heard me address my mother and Katia, he switched to Ukrainian. His father was a Pole born in Lviv, but his mother was Ukrainian.

Katia liked Yan. She suggested that we hire him to give us a tour of the city the next morning. Yan appeared at our hotel punctually and had an itinerary ready. The Basilian Sisters school, which Katia had mentioned to him the night before, was a boarded up, neglected building that, during the Cold War, had been used as army barracks. The Ukrainian Catholic Church was negotiating with the Polish government for return of the property, Yan said. We stopped at the Ukrainian Catholic parish. An old woman opened the door a crack and said the priest was in Lviv, where he was to meet with the recently arrived Ukrainian cardinal. Katia opened her purse and took out her wallet. She pushed a ten-dollar bill through the crack and asked that the priest, upon his return, say a mass for our family. My mother was looking around with interest, but seemed unaffected by the poor state of the buildings or the apprehension in the old woman's face.

"What you need is a good view of Ukraine," Yan said. "Your first?" he added, turning to me. I nodded. We drove to the town's highest hill, which was surmounted by the ruins of a castle. Seven centuries earlier, this castle had guarded the Sian River valley from Genghis Khan and the Mongols. The morning was misty and we could barely make out the east bank of the Sian River. "There, your first glimpse," Yan said.

As I looked into the haze, I felt both awe and terror. All the fears I had been fighting surfaced. *At last,* I thought. *Finally.* And then: *What will they do to me?* Katia, standing beside me, took out a handkerchief and wiped her eyes. Mother looked into the distance placidly, unmoved. Did she know she was almost home?

The train station was hot and crowded. The airless waiting room reeked of garlic, whiskey, and the sweat of many bodies. The clerk selling tickets laughed in my face. It was impossible to buy train tickets to Ukraine. "Come back in a week," he said.

I turned to Yan, who had come with me, and pointed to the crowds inside the waiting room and outside on the train platform. The platform teemed with people. Solidly built women sat on large, lumpy bags. Children dashed in and around the clumps formed by extended families. Young women in flower-patterned summer dresses carried babies on their hips. Old women wore black dresses despite the heat and had tied heavy black kerchiefs under their chins. Men stood in small groups, smoking. It seemed that a large segment of the population was on the move, along with all of its possessions.

"What's going on?" I asked, dismayed and puzzled.

"People are 'handling,'" Yan explained, using the term that encompasses the capitalistic activities of buying, selling, and trading. The turmoil in Moscow, he said, was making people brave. Enterprising farmers from Ukraine were crossing into Poland to sell produce, while Poles were crossing into Ukraine to sell their Western wares.

I peered into the faces of the crowd. I saw no scowls or impatience. No worry, agitation, or exasperation. No one seemed to mind the inconvenience of waiting. Eventually I would come to realize that delays and hardships were regarded as vital signs of life in this part of the world. How else would you spend your free time if not in a line, gossiping, waiting for a train, or trying to buy a scarce ticket or consumer item?

"I'll take you to Lviv," Yan volunteered suddenly. "For dollars."

I pretended to consider the offer, but, of course, I was delighted. Yan's unabashed desire for dollars demonstrated the high regard accorded Western currency in Eastern Europe, and I would both remember and turn to this lesson in the future.

Yan had a roomy old Mercedes taxi. It was white on the outside and had dark brown leather seats. In the back, the leather had cracked to expose strips of white muslin. The trunk was big enough for our five suitcases. While we packed, Yan went to fill the car with gas. He also had time to wash it; it gleamed when he returned.

A few miles outside Przemysl we ran into a snaking line of lorries, trucks, vans, and cars. The customs ramp at Shegini, the border crossing, was miles ahead of us. Engine exhaust shrouded the road in a gray pall. Families were picnicking on the shoulder of the road. Scores of vehicles had overheated and drivers were bent double under the hoods working on engines. No one was going anywhere fast. I was about to ask Yan to turn around and return to town when he suddenly swerved out of the right-hand lane, pressing the palm of his hand on the horn, and the taxi shot forward into the oncoming lane of traffic. Luckily, the lane was empty. We breezed past the trucks, the vans, the cars, and the gaping people. The occasional car or truck that barreled down upon us would honk testily and swerve around us.

Yan drove us right up to the customs ramp, where a uniformed Ukrainian customs inspector had left his booth to watch our approach. I noticed that he was a young man, not much older than the sons I had left behind in America, and that he had a bad case of acne. I jumped out of the car, ready to beg indulgence. My American passport was in my hand.

He wasn't angry. If anything, he was amused after he glanced at our passports, as if he were thinking, "That's exactly what an American in a hurry would do, take a taxi." But when we addressed him in Ukrainian, he was astounded. He wanted to know how and when we left Ukraine. I told him that my father had bribed his way onto a westbound train in the waning days of World War II. "I tried, but couldn't do the same coming back," I added.

Chapter 3

COSSACK ANCESTRY

The chalets rise at my back, creating a false picture of Old World charm. I'm on my way down the hill in search of transportation to Krushelnytsia. Unlike the train station in Przemysl, Slavske's train station is deserted and locked. The autumn sun hangs heavily in the sky and for a moment I'm dazzled by the glare and do not see the man who jumps out of the building's shadows. He proves to be a pleasant old man and my fright subsides. He suggests I come back around five that afternoon when a train will be passing through Slavske and there might be someone at the window. He says there is no taxi stand in town. "There's nowhere to go."

I turn back toward the rest home dejected, dreading to report bad news to two women who have assured me of their complete faith that I will "come up with something." Mother and Katia want to visit Krushelnytsia, but they also said at breakfast that they want to leave Slavske. They gave several reasons—the bad food and cramped room among them—although what was bothering them most was that they were being treated like foreigners. Word of our presence had spread. People stared at us and whispered in the dining room. The formidable couple had demanded that we be moved to a different table, and we had eaten dinner and the second morning's breakfast in isolation. No one had talked to my mother or Katia when they sat on the patio or when they went to see a film playing in the auditorium. In retrospect, I know what the problem was: people did not know what to make of us. We were in a rest home operated by a trade collective for its members, but it was readily apparent that we had no connection with a trade collective. Although we spoke Ukrainian, it was obvious we were foreigners. There had been a coup attempt in Moscow; it was a time of uncertainty, and a time when it was prudent to pretend that people like us did not exist.

The second breakfast had been a replay of the first, and again we bolted outside as soon as it was over. We went to the edge of the patio and looked down. From our perch we could see white cottages amid lush greenery about halfway between us and the commercial district at the bottom of the valley. The distant crowing of roosters and the occasional mooing of milk cows audibly corroborated the existence of Slavske's old village. Charmed and waylaid by a promise of a rustic wonderland, we located a flight of old wooden stairs and descended on them, instead of using the modern gravel road that ran along the periphery and into the center of the town. At the bottom of the staircase, it seemed that, indeed, we had stumbled upon a different world. Trim cottages lined the unpaved streets. Some of the houses were of wood, but many had been stuccoed and whitewashed. Each was fenced in and had a garden and an orchard. The orchards were glutted with ripe apples. Fat geese and plump chickens foraged in the muddy ditches paralleling the street. Buxom women in slippers were hanging out wash, scratching with a spade for potatoes, or shooing off pesky geese.

This was the Ukraine of my mother's stories—charming, prosperous, peaceful. She was looking around with absolute familiarity and it seemed, at that moment, that this scrap of land had been left untouched by a half-century of trouble and deprivation. Mother and Katia said they would rather wander through the village than go with me to the train station. We agreed to meet on the brick patio before lunch. Nothing could go wrong, I said to myself, and we parted.

As I hunt for a taxi, I look in at the post office where a row of telephones lines a wall. I recall what the gravediggers said about their watchers using these telephones to file their reports. No one is telephoning today. The post office fronts on a pedestrian promenade where flowerbeds have been overwhelmed by weeds. I cannot find a taxi stand. In fact, it seems there are many more trucks than automobiles in Slavske. A mountain stream with high, steep banks separates the promenade, the post office, and the train station from the rest of the town. A flimsy metal bridge that throbs and shakes whenever a vehicle crosses it spans the tumbling water. On the opposite bank, a street runs along the stream. A block or so to the right stands the two-story sports club where I tried the night before to meet with the committee of three. I go inside. The committee of three has moved out, the woman with the baby tells me. "They caught the early train," she says. I follow the road to the mass grave. The diggers are gone. The two watchers no longer loiter in front of the country store. Could I have frightened them all away? Were it not for the piles of excavated mud, I could have been convinced that I had imagined my encounter with the gravedigging boys, the crushed skull, and the conversation with Irena Sen and the two men.

I turn around to look up the slopes of the valley. The twisting ski runs terminate near the rest homes — a separate world in this strange, divided town. I'm unwilling to return to the hilltop existence just yet. Instead, I head for the gleaming cross of a whitewashed church I passed on my way to the gravesite.

A mass is under way. There are no pews in the icon-decorated nave, so I hang back near the door. The congregation consists of about a dozen women, each holding a lit candle. I am wearing a pair of slacks and my red parka because the morning is cool. Several women turn around to stare at me in disapproval. The years of toil make them all look alike. They have sallow, pinched faces and are clad in black, including black headscarves. I feel intimidated, yet hold my ground and stay for the service. It is chanted in Old Church Slavonic, but it differs from any I have ever attended. To this day I don't know whether this was a Greek Catholic mass or an Orthodox mass, or perhaps a hybrid of the two. At this mass, the congregation of women forms an ever-moving phalanx. Throughout mass, they are busy. They borrow tapers from each other to light their candles. They blow the candles out after the Gospel and stow them away. They cross themselves in unison and bow toward the altar. They kneel, stand up, and rekindle the candles for the procession of the bread and wine. They are like a flock of milling crows, intent on a sparkling object in their midst — the priest, clad in vestments embroidered with gold thread. I keep back, although I know I would like to link with these women. Now and then, one of them glances over her shoulder to see if I am still standing by the door, but none beckons to me to join them.

During Communion, I follow the women forward to receive the host. The priest looks me over, pauses, decides, then turns away and climbs back to the altar without offering me the host. I am a stranger, a foreigner, and an alien. I creep back to my place by the door, my face scarlet.

The humiliations of this morning are not yet over. A few minutes later, I find my mother and Katia in tears. They have been the butt of a scam. They relate that as they were wandering among the houses, they heard a woman scream. "She flew out of her house crying," Katia says. "She asked us for help. She said her son was beating her and she had nowhere to go."

"We said we would walk her to the militia," my mother injects.

"She said she didn't want to go to the militia," Katia resumes the story. "She said we could help her in a different way by giving her money. I pulled out some local money . . . " Katia begins to cry.

"She got very angry," Mother says, her lower lip also quivering. "She wanted dollars."

How had the woman known they were from the West? I have no idea, but people could tell instantly, not only in Slavske, but everywhere we went. It may have been the clothing, well made and pressed. Without good detergent and dry cleaners, most of the population looked slightly seedy. Perhaps it was the way we walked; I would later hear a discourse on how Americans walked. Or perhaps our Western leather shoes and handbags gave us away. Yet, we spoke Ukrainian, considered ourselves Ukrainian—especially my mother and Katia, two little old ladies walking arm in arm down the village street. But there was something about them that was different. Something marked them foreign.

The hell with Slavske, I say to myself. Aloud I suggest that we hire a private car to take us to Krushelnytsia. Both Katia and my mother brighten at the prospect. The clerk in the lobby finds us a driver, Stefko, within the hour. The only stipulation Stefko insists upon is that I pay the fare in dollars.

I had heard about Krushelnytsia all my life. My maternal grandfather Mykhailo Vlasenko, a priest in the Uniate Catholic rite, which allows seminarians to marry at the time of ordination, was the parish priest in Krushelnytsia for a number of years. Mother, who was born there and spent her early childhood in the mountains, would remember Krushelnytsia as paradise. Her stories about her life there would begin thus: "Long ago, Krushelnytsia was rich and well known. It lay in the heart of a mining region, hence its name, which means, 'place where they crush.' People living there used huge sledgehammers to crush rock to extract gold." If there ever had been a mine or a surface quarry to exploit a mother lode, or if the lazy, sprawling Stryi with its shoals and shifting islands of pebbles and river rock had been dredged for placer gold, evidence of such activity had disappeared long ago. Small-lot farming is the mainstay of present-day life.

We have been traveling for an hour by the time we approach Krushelnytsia, first leaving Slavske's valley, then picking up the main road that hugs the bank of the Stryi River, which over millennia has carved a broad fertile valley through the Carpathians, not unlike the valley of the Blue River in the Rocky Mountains. The river is lined with birches and aspens, their leaves fluttering and gleaming in the afternoon sun. The river meanders, spilling now again into a wide channel before narrowing into braided streams separated by elongated islands covered with willow brush. As we near the village, Mother points to a particularly wide stretch of the river and says to Katia: "Do you remember how one summer father went swimming and almost drowned?"

She proceeds to relate how he became caught in the current and was heroically rescued by a local man. Katia listens for a moment, then shakes her head.

"Annuytka," she says gently, using the affectionate diminutive of Anna, "it happened to the other way around. Father rescued a man caught in the current."

Mother begins to argue, then her eyes mist over and she bites her lower lip. She has become very sensitive about memories and when one of us gives a different version of a recollection, she tends to sulk and refuses to speak to us. Sometimes this self-imposed silence becomes depression, from which it is difficult to draw her out. "I'm not crazy," she repeats over and over again.

I will speak first about the ancestry of my maternal grandfather Mykhailo Vlasenko because his family came from Eastern Ukraine and I know little about them. Mykhailo's grandfather or great grandfather fled from Imperial Russia following the unsuccessful Decembrist Revolt in 1825. This ancestor was a member of one of the secret political organizations that evolved into the Decembrist movement, the aim of which was to abolish serfdom and overthrow autocracy. His escape into Western Ukraine and into Austro-Hungarian jurisdiction—in the nineteenth century and up to World War I, Western Ukraine was part of the Austro-Hungarian Empire—saved him from a severe sentence to Siberia or death. I don't know whether my grandfather had any siblings, where he grew up, or when the family (or he) converted from Orthodoxy to Catholicism. I do know that he was a seminarian in Lviv and was a contemporary and friend of Metropolitan Andriy Sheptytsky, the Uniate patriarch who attempted to forge closer links between the Ukrainian Catholic Church and the Vatican. My grandfather married my grandmother before he was ordained a priest. And I know that my grandmother's family and not my grandfather's dominated my mother's childhood.

Elena, my maternal grandmother, came from a well-to-do Western Ukrainian family and was one of eleven children—eight girls and three boys. The children were healthy and long-lived. Only one son died as a child, when he was thrown from a horse. Elena and Mykhailo had five children: Roma, Myroslav, Oleksander, Katia, and Anna. All reached adulthood, although Roma and Myroslav were mentally ill.

Elena's ancestors were old Cossack gentry, who had lived in Western

Ukraine for many generations and were pillars of the petite bourgeoi-
sie. Her maiden name was Chubaty. The word means "man with big
hair" and was probably an alias for a runaway sixteenth-century serf who
joined the horsemen of the steppes. His name, according to family lore,
was Hryc Chuba (big hair). He was in the army of Bohdan Khmelnytsky
when the Dnipro Cossack hetman stormed Lviv (held by the Poles) in
1649. Instead of returning with Khmelnytsky to central Ukraine, Hryc
settled and prospered near Lviv. Among the Cossacks, men were identified by a physical characteristic or by the prowess they showed in battle.
A legend from that era recounts the exploits of a Cossack leader whose
name was Ivan Pidkova. Pidkova means "horseshoe." This Cossack was
famous for his unusual physical strength: he could bend a new and unused horseshoe as if it were a willow branch.

Hryc must have had a most striking head of hair. As I think of this,
I glance at Katia and realize that this physical characteristic has come
down to the present. Even in her late years, Katia has abundant hair,
and I recall a photo of her as a young woman. In the photo, she wears a
simple white dress, perhaps the better to show off an awesomely thick
braid of blackest hair that coils over her shoulder and falls heavily to her
waist. I think of Katia's daughter, Irene, and her abundant bronze hair.
Unfortunately, my mother did not inherit those Chubaty genes and
neither did I. But one of my sons has. His hair is blond, but it is so thick
that barbers used to thin it when I took him to get a haircut.

There is a romantic story about my Chubaty great grandfather, who
was an officer in the Austrian Army. He fell in love with the beautiful
daughter of a Polish aristocrat. Marriage was out of the question, since
the suitor possessed neither the desired wealth nor the right nationality.
The lovers eloped and the young bride lived with her mother-in-law until
her husband finished his army service and had acquired a position that
could support a wife and a family. If children are a measure of happiness, then this union that produced eleven was an exceptionally happy
one. Of the eight girls, three never married, possibly because of a rule
that their father forced them to obey: Each girl would have a coming
out party and have a gown imported from Paris, but a younger sister
could not be affianced or marry until her older sister or sisters had. Eventually the rule was relaxed, but by then the marriageable age for three of
the older sisters had passed. My grandmother was one of the younger
daughters who did marry, and my mother told stories of spending holidays with the maiden aunts.

The Chubatys were a large clan. They were part of the Catholic intel-

The three Vlasenko sisters. Left to right: Katia, Roma, and Anna, about 1930.

ligentsia and clergy and their children attended universities in Prague and Krakow. Some became priests, while others were doctors and lawyers and lived privileged lives. One of my mother's fondest stories recounted a trip she took with an uncle who had imported a Model T Ford in which to explore the Carpathians in the 1920s. Her job was to turn the crank while he revved up the engine. Another Chubaty became a painter of icons.

Like my mother, my father, Ivan Bojcun, also came from a family of five children, but he was the eldest of the siblings, three boys and two girls. The Bojcuns were townspeople and my paternal grandfather was a postman. My paternal grandmother died during the 1920s, from cholera, which also almost took my father. My father, who was not a storyteller, did tell me a story once. I was a little girl then and was delighted when he could pick me up high from the floor as I held onto his forearm, which was muscled and hard. I once asked him why he was so strong and he told me about the cholera epidemic. "The doctor came and looked at me. I was unconscious and close to death. He turned to my father and said, 'If he pulls through, he will be a very strong man.'"

He did pull through, and he was not only physically strong but also the emotional bulwark of the family. He used money he received from my maternal grandfather and bricks of butter from the dairy cooperative where he was the director to obtain train berths for us, for Katia's and Roma's families, and for his two sisters and younger brother and their families to leave Ukraine. World War II and emigration scattered my mother's and father's families all over the world. Some immigrated to the United States, others to Canada, England, and Australia.

Perhaps I would not be here telling this story if it were not for a sympathetic Russian commissar who befriended (and perhaps was in love with) my mother. She once told me the story thus: "When the Russians arrived in September, 1939, following Germany's invasion of Poland and the signing of a nonaggression pact by Hitler and Stalin, I was teaching in a one-room schoolhouse in Zariche [a village southwest of Lviv where my grandfather was the parish priest]. The commissar assigned to our district often came to school to make certain that I had hung up Lenin's and Stalin's photographs and was teaching the curriculum I had been given. I met this man when I was still single and we got along well. I sometimes flirted with him to get supplies for the schoolchildren. In any event, we became friends."

This friendship must have continued after my mother married, or perhaps the commissar did not know she was no longer single. In June, 1941, he came to see my mother for the last time. "The Russians were retreating east and the front was moving toward us. We could hear the distant boom of cannons," my mother recalled. "Then one day, he came back. He was on a horse that was foaming with exhaustion. He rode into the schoolyard and came inside to say good-bye. He said, 'I've been able to protect you and your family from Siberia. When we return— and return we will—someone else will come in my place and you and your family will be in great danger. Your family is too well off, your father's a priest who refuses to accept Orthodoxy. You will be killed or exiled to Siberia.'"

The commissar's predictions came true. In 1944, the Red Army returned. As the front neared again, my mother, now with a baby in her arms, convinced my father and her two sisters that we had to emigrate. My grandparents, however, could not be convinced and refused to leave. Both perished tragically within two years of the Communists' return.

In the 1990s, there is no one in Western Ukraine who is close kin. Oleksander is in Lodz. Myroslav, the other brother, disappeared many years ago into Lviv's Loncki prison and we do not know to this day how or when he died. I grew up in the shadow of this family disaster. We know there are no Chubatys in Krushelnytsia or elsewhere, but we hope to see the house where my mother was born and the church where my grandfather was a pastor.

Our driver spots the wooden sign pointing to Krushelnytsia and turns left, off the main road. Immediately we find ourselves in a narrow lane shaded by fruit trees, their canopies escaping untidy stockades protecting run-down houses on either side of the lane. Our car bumps along on the unpaved lane until it narrows into a path. Stefko finds a place where he turns the car around while we get out. Ahead of us lies a village green dominated by a beautiful wooden church. Three cupolas rise majestically in tiered pyramidal roofs. The roofs are shingled, as are the walls. They blend together into a unified whole, a soft brown-gray color. An incongruous yellow-painted door marks the entrance to the church. It is padlocked. We knock but no one answers. We circle the church but find no other entrance. A woman, wearing a shapeless dress and with her head wrapped in a flowered kerchief, comes toward us and asks our business. We say we would like to see the priest and the interior of the church. She studies us carefully for a moment, then says that there has not been a priest for a long time and the church is permanently closed.

"Where's the house you lived in?" I ask my mother and Katia when the woman leaves.

They silently point past the church to a large field that lies fallow and empty. Weeping, they turn back to the narrow lane where the car and Stefko wait.

It is still only midafternoon and none of us wants to go back to Slavske. We ask Stefko to drive deeper into the mountains. As we climb out of the Stryi valley, the scenery becomes one of vivid contrasts. White-and-brown cows dot emerald green meadows. Whitewashed houses crowd along silvery streams. Smoky-blue hills rise to a clear blue sky. To my delight and astonishment—since I take inordinate pleasure in identifying the peaks in the Rockies whenever I hike or drive in them—Katia and my mother, forgetting Krushelnytsia, start calling out the names of the distant mountains. Stefko, who has said little, nods and volunteers that once the road crests we will see Slovakia. We drive to the top and I am about to urge him to continue when a squall sweeps down from nowhere. The mountains disappear and sleet pelts the car as we careen down the slope back into the valley.

Chapter 4

COUNTER-MONUMENTS
IN THE CARPATHIANS

If we are putting ourselves at risk, we aren't overly worried. Katia and my mother sit with their knees under their chins on the narrow back seat of the temperamental Lada. Up front, I accidentally nudge a metal plate on the floor below the front passenger seat and my right foot momentarily falls through the hole I uncover. I feel the lumpy gravel of the road through the sole of my sandal before I hastily pull my foot back into the car. Next to me, Stefko, the driver who took us to Krushelnytsia, is fiddling with the starter and cursing the Lada under his breath. In the back, our luggage, precariously fastened down with rope, hangs out of the tiny trunk.

The car's cramped and aging interior is incidental. We are savoring the promise of the unfolding day. We leave Slavske with the general objective of going farther into the Carpathian Mountains and the specific one of visiting Kolomyia, the historic center of the Hutsuls, an ancient highland people famous for their melancholy music, their intricate wooden churches, and their flat woven geometric rugs that Ukrainians call *kilim*s. For the third day, the weather is benign, sunny and warm. The morning sky is cloudless and, again, the color of blue flannel. On the horizon, the mountains shimmer as if they were being viewed through a pane of uneven glass. I speculate about subtle distortion of the horizon and decide that the anomaly is due to the moisture in the air. As we sit patiently in the sunlight waiting for the Lada to start, it suddenly does so with a splutter and a heave of the chassis. The engine jerks the car forward, splutters again, then roars into life. We are off.

The little red car does not let us down again. It chugs all morning past black-blue forests that creep up the flanks of the mountains. We drive through bright green valleys nourished by streams that glisten in the sunlight. The few villages we see are tight, small communities that, from a distance, look like colonies of gray-white mushrooms. Around midday, a breeze sweeps in clouds that drift in cotton wisps above the peaks. By midafternoon, the clouds swell into a mist that blots out the mountains. Yet my mother and Katia, who hiked these mountains as young women, have no trouble recognizing the landscape. Story after story pours out as a panorama of memories opens before them. My mother becomes animated and the lurking fear in her eyes fades. Katia chatters and laughs. Remembering softens the wrinkles on their faces and infuses their cheeks with color, and I realize I am seeing them as they must have looked a half-century earlier.

The road leads us into a village, where I look for the traditional thatched straw roofs that I remember from sepia photographs my mother kept in her journal. None of the cottages has one. I question Stefko, who says all thatched roofs have been replaced because they leak and are a fire hazard. The new roofs are ugly. They are fashioned from corrugated squares, not tin but some kind of mastic, about three feet by four feet. This roofing material comes in a variety of gray shades that the roofers did not bother to match. As a result, most of the roofs look like skewered chessboards of gray rectangles. I'm still mentally disapproving of the roofs when we approach a granite monument of overscaled human figures. The chests of the helmeted warriors are thrust forward, while their arms are raised in defiance. I recall a similar monument we had seen from a distance. As we pass the monument, I see that the concrete from which the monument was poured has been left jagged at the base by the sculptor to imitate rock—a miniature Mount Rushmore. The Lada slows down because the monument is at an intersection, and I have time to read the bronze dedication. It commemorates a Red Army victory in a battle I have never heard of. A few hundred feet past the monument, we see a new, Cossack-style burial mound that is topped by a white birch cross. A large blue plaque, emblazoned with a golden trident, sways in the breeze from the crossbeams of the cross. I remember a burial mound we saw yesterday, to which I had paid scant attention. It also had been decorated with a trident, which had been cleverly executed in a precise planting of marigolds. I know that the trident is the historic symbol of Ukraine, as the bald eagle is of the United States. I also know that the trident was used by the UPA and was banned for fifty years by the Soviet regime.

I turn to Stefko. He isn't forthcoming, but my repeated questions finally elicit some information. He says that burial mounds began appearing in the late 1980s and early 1990s, as *glasnost* swept across the Soviet Union. The mounds honor the UPA guerrillas who died in the same battles celebrated by the concrete Soviet monuments. I marvel at how alien and galling the Soviet monuments must have been for people to begin erecting "counter-monuments" as soon as such actions would not be subject to punishment. I am astounded. I make Stefko stop. I examine the burial mound and, yes, it is as he had said: it commemorates the same battle as the concrete monument at the crossroads. As I stand there in the bright sunlight, I wonder: Which version of history is the right one? I grapple at an answer: It depends on who you are—a Ukrainian or a Russian. Soviet propaganda had tried to erase the differences among the many peoples whose homelands were gobbled up by Moscow. The propaganda worked so well that even a pragmatist like Mikhail Gorbachev came to believe it. He insisted that the Soviet Empire had created a Soviet man. Would Gorbachev have persisted in this belief if he had come this way and seen the cross-topped counter-monuments?

We reach Kolomyia at dusk and the pleasant day fractures. Even today, I wonder whether our faces betrayed our disappointment. Kolomyia turns out to be a dusty grid of narrow streets lined with run-down, buff-colored buildings—poured concrete sticks in my mind—not the picturesque town I have been looking forward to seeing. We pass through a section of stucco and brick homes, the architecture of which harks back to the turn of the twentieth century, but they all look as though they have not been repaired in years. The Lada enters a forlorn park that funnels us onto an untidy boulevard. Both testify to the town's better days. What is most striking, however, is that the cracked sidewalks are nearly empty of pedestrians. Having done my reading, I know that before World War II, Kolomyia was a regional commercial and literary center; thirty newspapers and journals thrived in the city, along with a flourishing nightlife of concerts, lectures, and theater. I look for the cafés, but there are none.

Stefko halts the Lada in front of what he says is the town's best hotel, a plain, buff-colored building. I go inside and ask for accommodations. The clerk behind the desk stares at me as if I were mad. "You're not with a tour?" she asks incredulously.

"No."

"You have no reservations?"

"No."

She says all rooms are booked. I cajole, plead. She scowls and shakes her head. Would any other place in town have rooms? I ask. She walks away without answering. On the way back to the car I wonder where we will sleep the night. In the Lada?

"Did they ask you for documents?" Stefko asks.

"Yes."

"Did you put some dollars inside your passport?"

"No," I say.

He shrugs knowingly as I chastise myself for being naïve and for making uninformed assumptions that I will find lodging in a forgotten mountain town simply because once, long ago, it was a center of progressive thought.

"There used to be a fancy place around here that belonged to the provincial governor before the war," Stefko says as he directs the car into a residential section shaded by oaks and lindens. After several wrong turns, we pull up in front of a Victorian house that may once have enjoyed the pretensions of a mansion. It huddles behind a rusted wrought-iron fence and a tangle of shrubs. I hesitate, but then any accommodations will be better than a night in the Lada. The doorbell is not working, so I push the heavy oak door open and enter the front hall. On my left, a fine mirror hangs above an elaborately carved Victorian hatrack. The heavy front door, the curving staircase, and the scuffed parquet floor all testify to yesterday's elegance, and I become hopeful. I call out hello and eventually a woman bustles in. She wipes her hands on her large, white apron and her smile is quick and engaging. Immediately I know she will help. But I shore up my intuition. When I hand her my passport, inside lies what Stefko had called "the essential supplement," a ten-dollar bill.

I say: "We are three women who need a haven for the night."

I will never know whether the fact we were women seeking shelter, or the moment of trust between us, or the money, or all three, made the difference. The matron's eyes widen at the sight of my passport and its contents, but the engaging smile does not leave her face. There is a room, she replies, but dinner is over and she cannot serve us anything but tea and crackers.

She introduces herself as Anna Ostapova. Although during the Hapsburg rule Western Ukrainians had adopted the use of a first name with a surname and dropped the use of the patronymic in polite conversation, the Soviet regime had reintroduced the patronymic as the polite form of address between both strangers and acquaintances. I introduce myself and she leads me to the room I have just rented, which once was the front parlor. It is a square, well-proportioned room with a high ceiling and an elaborately carved overmantel above a nonfunctioning fireplace that is partially hidden by a large bed with a brass frame. A crystal chandelier hangs precisely above the foot of the brass bed and looks out of place. Two smaller beds stand against opposite walls.

"This is where the generals sleep," the woman explains.

It takes me a moment to understand what she is saying. And when I do, I giggle. I apologize to the puzzled housekeeper, but how can I explain to her my amusement and the irony of the situation? I have booked a room in a rest home for veterans of the Red Army, the same army from which my parents fled during World War II. Half a century later, we are going to sleep in the same beds in which the generals of this Red Army sleep during their annual vacations. What a find.

As we unload our belongings from Stefko's Lada, he assures us he will have no difficulty locating a place to sleep and will meet us the next morning. An hour later, Anna Ostapova brings us dinner, modest but adequate. Hot tea comes with biscuits that are followed by a bowl of new boiled potatoes and a tomato salad liberally sprinkled with dill. We sit by the bay window in the generals' quarters, at a round table spread with a fresh tablecloth, carefully darned. After dinner, we choose beds. Mother says she wants to sleep in the generals' brass-fitted bed. Katia and I settle on the two modest and smaller beds against the walls.

When Katia and my mother retire, I go to the kitchen to thank Anna Ostapova. Word has spread that *Amerikantsi* are staying the night. Old men gather around me. They wear shiny, threadbare jackets with rows of medals pinned across their chests. A bottle of vodka appears on the wooden kitchen table, then black bread and *salo*. A party is being organized.

Anna Ostapova clicks her tongue critically as she surveys the plate of tidbits. A moment later she produces dill pickles, which she arranges next to the slivers of salo. Next, she pulls out a sharp knife and begins slicing a tomato while holding it in the palm of her large, reddened hand. I hold by breath, thinking that at any moment she will cut herself. But, of course, she does not. Balancing the slices on the flat side of the knife blade, she transfers them to the plate. Then she steps back and surveys the *zakuski* with approval.

The tastiness of salo is hard to describe, since there is nothing comparable to it in the West. It is cured pork backfat that, when done well, can be sliced into paper-thin wafers, melts in the mouth, and tastes as good as butter. As we are about to begin, one of the veterans tsk-tsks and disappears. He returns moments later with a head of garlic. He shows me what to do with the garlic. After peeling a clove, he rubs a slice of bread. Next, he places a slice of salo on the bread. He says the garlic clove can be placed on top of the salo and the trilevel combination is eaten like a canapé. But it is okay, he says, not to eat the garlic, which suits me fine.

More veterans trickle in, more tomatoes are added to the platter by Anna Ostapova. The veterans shake my hand and sit down at the table, or lean against the wall. They ask how it happened that an American speaks Ukrainian, and I relate my family history. Others ask why three women are traveling alone. "The older men in the family, the men who would have come with us, are dead," I say. They nod wisely and their rheumy eyes are kind, as are Anna Ostapova's. The man who had fussed with the salo edges toward me. He wears what looks like an undershirt under his shiny jacket, his face is etched by many years, and his sunken cheeks are glazed with gray stubble. He asks: "Where in America do you come from?"

"Colorado," I say in all innocence, "a state in the mountains."

His brow furrows and his smile disappears. "You gave us the Colorado beetle," he says severely.

Oh, dear. Now what? I have no idea what he is talking about. I tell him I am not familiar with the Colorado beetle. Conversations around us have died away.

"Do you have potatoes?" the veteran asks in the silence.

"Of course," I answer. *Oh, dear; oh, dear,* I think.

"If you have potatoes, you have the Colorado beetle," he says triumphantly, while the others nod, including Anna Ostapova.

It takes some time and a bit of diplomacy, but eventually I learn that the Colorado beetle was first introduced into the Soviet Union in the shipments of American wheat that Nikita Khrushchev purchased in the 1960s. The beetle had no natural predators and proliferated. It eats the buds of potato plants. The normal way to kill it is to pick the beetle off the plant and squash it between the thumb and forefinger. A riskier method is to douse the plant with gasoline, but that might kill the plant, and gasoline is expensive.

"What about pesticides?" I ask.

"We don't have pesticides," the old veteran says. He grins slyly at me. "Your CIA is very clever. It was your CIA that put the beetle in with the wheat. It wanted to make life harder for us."

The weather holds the next morning. The mist drifts off, revealing another day of bright, if lukewarm, sunshine. A light breeze propels tat-

ters of clouds across the sky, which has darkened to indigo. Our first
sightseeing stop is the Museum of Hutsul Folk Art, a handsome stone
building with a cupola surmounting a corner tower, and therefore easily found. As we walk toward it on a narrow cobbled street, a man comes
from behind and starts talking to us. He knows we are foreigners and
asks for dollars. He follows us into the museum. Katia and my mother
cower as he demands money. The ticket seller calls a guard and the man
is ejected, waving his fists at us. Mother's and Katia's faces are ashen and
they are trembling. I hurry them into the exhibition hall. It takes some
time, but eventually the richly patterned kilims, intricate carvings, lav-
ishly embroidered clothing, and ornate decorations on ordinary household items capture our attention. By the time we leave the museum, the
unpleasant incident has been forgotten. We make our way to the main
square, but cannot find Hutsul kilims and have to settle on woolen socks
with Hutsul motifs knitted into the cuffs.

Despite the incident at the museum, we have enjoyed Kolomyia. As
we pack, we exchange remorseful comments about the wonders we will
miss if we drive directly to Lviv. I ask Stefko what city is on the way and
he says: "Ivano-Frankivske." Both my mother and Katia perk up. Yes.
Let's go to Ivano-Frankivske, they urge me. I have my doubts since
I have read that Ivano-Frankivske, the capital of the Carpathian *oblast*
(province) and a former UPA stronghold, remains closed to foreigners.
(I later hear that the reason it is closed is because there's a factory in the
city that manufactures ICBM parts.) Stefko says he doesn't think we will
encounter a roadblock. He is proven right; no one challenges us as we
drive into the center of town.

Mother and Katia want to see Ivano-Frankivske because it is another
of the cities that figured prominently in their youth. Both describe it
as a cultural center, with many gracious old buildings evoking its illus-
trious past. Stanislav Potocki, a Polish magnate whose family members were kingmakers in Poland for many centuries, founded it in the
sixteenth century and named it Stanislaviv. In 1962, Khrushchev renamed the city after Ivan Franko, a Ukrainian peasant from the turn of
the century who became a prominent writer, ethnographer, and early
socialist. Ivano-Frankivske turns out to be another example of a half-
century of civic neglect. It is dusty, run-down, and in the throes of a
water shortage.

Our appearance on the pedestrian mall in the city center attracts attention. Once again, we look foreign. Mother is wearing a khaki trench

coat and a hat with a feather curving across its narrow brim. Katia has on a fine tweed suit and heels. I am in my red parka. A middle-aged, portly, and balding man comes up to us and asks: "You're from *Amerika?*"

Over the years, I have noticed that, in Colorado, ranchers begin a conversation with reflections about their livestock, while farmers comment on the prairie's unpredictable weather. In the lands of the former Soviet Empire, the first step in establishing contact between strangers is to determine the other's nationality. This will decide your conduct.

"Yes," we respond in unison.

"Ah! *Amerika!*" America must be okay. He clicks his heels, and instead of shaking our extended hands, he plants a fleeting kiss on each in turn. We will discover that kissing a woman's hand is one of the gallantries from Austro-Hungarian times that never died. Perhaps it was a small protest one indulged in to negate the rough comradeship of Communism. In any event, this man earns both Katia's and my mother's approbation. They beam at him.

"Where in America do you live?" he continues his gentle interrogation.

"In New Jersey," Katia says.

"In Florida," my mother says.

"I have relatives in Chicago," he says, mentioning a surname. "Do you know them?"

He is disappointed that we do not, since he has a message he would have liked us to pass on. He bows again and disappears.

"Charming man," my mother and Katia say in unison. A little farther down the mall we see a restaurant and decide to have lunch early.

"We're closed," the waiter says. "No water."

We leave the mall and rejoin Stefko, who is reading a newspaper. "There's no water in the city," he informs us.

As we leave town, we see a café and a large sign: "Fresh coffee." Stefko stops and I head for the open door. The café is dim and deserted. "Can we get some coffee?" I ask.

The waitress says, "No water and we're out of coffee beans."

"But your sign," I protest.

"That's from yesterday," she says.

Maybe I am being overparticular or, perhaps, childish. As we drive to Lviv, I realize I am expecting my mother's embroidered tales of a spectacularly beautiful landscape to turn out to be fact. Since our trip to

Slavske had been shrouded in rain and fog, we had not had a chance to examine the countryside of the plateau east of the Carpathian Mountains. I swing my head from right to left and back again, intent on missing nothing, but what I see is quite ordinary. Land falls away on either side of the road in untidy fields. Stout women hunch over furrows or whack at the clumped soil with battered hoes. Soon I begin to notice the absences: no grain combines or clanking harvesters although it is September, no silos for storage, not even stacks of hay or rectangles of harvested alfalfa. Rickety wagons or solitary cows on tethers replace the rusted pickup trucks or cars we saw in the fields in Poland and Czechoslovakia. Each cow is tended by an old man in a well-worn jacket, a man whose eyes are as lusterless as the war medals pinned to his jacket lapels.

Even the road itself is a disappointment. It is potholed and narrow, a far cry from the megahighway portrayed on the map. We see few passenger cars. Instead, huge lorries and battered trucks rumble by, enveloping us in clouds of diesel smoke. We pass people waiting for a bus under primitive cement overhangs that serve as bus stops. There are no light poles or benches at these stops, no newspaper dispensers or other amenities. The shoulders of the road are strewn with litter. We come to and go through villages. Small, neglected cottages peer from behind uneven fences. Children and dogs play in the ditches on either side of the road. Even in the center of one village, where a flock of geese momentarily blocks our passage, there are no sidewalks. We see more people here, sauntering along the road, eating ice cream, than in the miles of fields we have passed. Yet this is harvest season; it is early afternoon and the day is sunny and cool. Where is the "land of bread and honey" I have heard about? Is this untended landscape the breadbasket of Europe? Is this the agricultural jewel of the mighty Soviet Union?

I become aware for the first time that the farther we have traveled east across Europe, the more desolate and unkempt the land has become, and the more dispirited the people. In Germany, every scrap of land was under cultivation. Towns and villages teemed with activity. People swept, cleaned, worked. In Czechoslovakia, we admired the fields planted with hops and the dogged diligence of farmers who had erected hundreds upon hundreds of high poles around which the vines wound luxuriantly. Even in Poland, the fields were dotted with people harvesting potatoes and cabbages, assiduously gathering the spent vegetation, which they burned in huge bonfires. Yet here in fertile Ukraine, fields lie fallow. In the villages, fenced yards are filled with rusting machinery. Except for a few old women, no one is working. The *kolkhoz* of collective ownership has drained the countryside of pride and hope and, therefore, initiative.

Negley Farson was a bold foreign correspondent who covered the Soviet regime during the 1920s and who returned to Russia during World War II. He predicted in 1956 that if Communism were to fail, it would be "because of just one thing those bloody and bloodless doctrinaires in the Kremlin left out of their calculations: the soul of man—in this case, the Russian peasant's love for the land. . . . You can't go on murdering the men who feed you." Stalin collectivized farmland in Eastern Ukraine by creating the artificial famine of 1932–33. Seven million Ukrainians perished when soldiers confiscated the harvest of 1932 and did not leave enough grain for the planting in 1933. Similarly, the famine of 1946–47 in Western Ukraine was used to force peasants into village collectives. A million people died in this famine. Subsequent Kremlin policies further destroyed the breadbasket.

"Oh, dear." The dismay in Katia's voice is palpable. "Everything's broken down. No one's working," she says, echoing my thoughts.

Stefko laughs. "Even if you work, you get nothing," he says.

I look at Mother. Her face is pale and her eyes are very sad.

As we drive on, I muse that we have passed through two Europes into a third. In Germany we were in Western Europe, confident and rich. In Czechoslovakia and Poland we saw a Central and Eastern Europe that was doing better, was pulling itself toward prosperity. But in Ukraine, we have entered a land poor and desperate, a Third World that masqueraded as a superpower. Why didn't the foreign correspondents of the 1970s and 1980s tell us the wretched truth?

Perhaps my expectations of a bucolic countryside were naïve, yet I was unprepared for the poverty of the land and the fear lurking among the people. Had fifty years of Soviet rule broken the Ukrainian peasants as Farson had foreseen happening to their Russian counterparts? Then, on the outskirts of Lviv, we see something that declares that the spirit may have been bridled, but it is not vanquished. Someone has been systematically changing the road signs from Russian to Ukrainian. The signs have white lettering on a dark blue background. Someone has removed the Russian vowels in the place names and replaced them with vowels from the Ukrainian alphabet. (Ukrainian and Russian alphabets have similar consonants, although vowels differ, as does pronunciation.) The new letters are on a pale blue background and every alteration is starkly visible. The lighter blue creates gaps, like the toothy smile of a jack-o-lantern.

"Good for them," Katia says, grinning.

"Yes," my mother says. "It's nice to read Ukrainian instead of Russian."

"Stop," I command Stefko.

He pulls the car onto the shoulder of the road. We pile out to examine one of these altered signs close up. Stefko sits in the Lada with a dumbfounded expression on his face. He is even more surprised when I return to the car to take out my camera and ask him to take a photo of the three of us standing in front of a road sign and grinning foolishly.

Chapter 5

LVIV, RESILIENT CAPITAL
OF WESTERN UKRAINE

Cities have a personality and, often, a gender. New York is male, while Miami is female, as is New Orleans. The latter two are cities of charm and seduction. Lviv is like a once pretty woman who must contend with bad times and the accumulation of years. I think of Lviv in the feminine, even though its name means "lion."

Mother once told me that before World War II, Lviv residents called their city "Little Paris." But its suburbs are grim and make you think of industry, like in Detroit. Perhaps this is because Lviv manufactures buses. Lviv is the capital of Western Ukraine and has close to a million residents. When he founded it in the thirteenth century, Prince Danylo Romanovych named the fortified town after his son Lev. For centuries, Lviv was called Leopolis in chronicles. The prince probably did not realize he was locating his citadel on the continental divide of water flowing to the Baltic and the Black seas. Perhaps this quirk of nature has molded the city's consciousness. It has consistently tried to reconcile the influences of East and West. In this trait, Lviv also shows its feminine, pliable nature.

The Austro-Hungarian Empire called the city Lemberg and fashioned its center on the European model—narrow, cobbled streets opening into unexpected piazzas, red-tile roofs above the beige façades of buildings, municipal parks embellished with classical statuary. When Western Ukraine was annexed to Poland in the early 1920s, the city became known as Lwow. A generation later, the Poles were rounded up and exiled to Siberia by the Red Army and the Jews perished in the Janowska concentration camp. The camp was situated north of the main train station, which was called Vienna Station. Under Soviet rule, Lviv was called Lvov.

The heart of Lviv is Rynok Square, the central piazza of the city. It is lined by an engaging assortment of medieval, Renaissance, and Baroque buildings. We had eaten lunch in a café on Rynok Square on the second day of our stay and we returned to the square repeatedly since it was Katia's favorite spot. She would point out Neptune brandishing his trident atop a fountain at one end of the square and Diana frolicking in a field of flowers at the fountain at the other end and compare the fountains to the finest we had seen in Prague, Warsaw, and Krakow.

We see the outskirts of Lviv twice—once those in the west as we drive in from Poland and once those in the south as we return from Slavske. These suburbs don't share in the charm of Rynok Square. They are clusters of vertical, unadorned concrete buildings with untidy grass areas and cracked sidewalks, a few scraggly trees, and some wilted shrubbery. When we pass through a warehouse and industrial district, we see a sprawling manufacturing plant that I learn later builds buses for export. At an intersection, a shadow falls across the car and we crane our necks to look up at a towering statue of Lenin. It is on the roof of the main trolley and bus depot. The statue has glowing yellow eyes. Perhaps they are lightbulbs that someone forgot to dim during daylight.

I detect in myself a growing disappointment at the prosaic urban landscape. With the exception of the startling statue of Lenin, the new Lviv tends toward reduction rather than ornamentation. It lacks even such typical urban embellishments as a park or a well-equipped playground, let alone a fountain with classical statuary. As I try to suppress my disappointment, I simultaneously upbraid myself. What did I expect? I know. I expected a charming "Little Paris" and I don't see it. When Katia married in the 1930s, Lviv became her home, and she has been talking about it as if she had visited it a week ago. All my life I had heard my mother describe Lviv as a cultural and social center. Her years at Lviv University were a highlight of her youth. Wherever I go, I look and cannot find the charm both of them had cataloged. Even in the city center, our 1960s modern hotel has a façade of poured concrete slabs and stingily crowded windows. It is not charming, nor is the dark utilitarian lobby, nor our minimally furnished room.

Not until days later do I make a discovery. As I stand at the window contemplating the bald gilded domes of the Byzantine churches, the green copper spires of the Roman Catholic cathedrals, and the Italianate expanse of red-tile roofs, I am rewarded with a glimpse of the Lviv of my mother's and Katia's memories. It is late afternoon and the pale façades of the buildings have turned pink in the rays of the setting sun. Below, in the dark, twisting streets, the cobbles ring with the footsteps of hurrying pedestrians. As I watch, a hand pulls a lacy curtain across a window in the building opposite and the breeze carries what may be the scent of rosewater. I remember that moment because it communicated the existence of an old, European gentility, threadbare, perhaps, but nonetheless still there.

To my surprise and dismay, Mother refuses to leave the Dnister Hotel. After breakfast one day, she returns to our room and climbs into bed. She is adamant in her refusal to go sightseeing. She has been so happy and so ebullient that I have forgotten her illness. I am annoyed, then beset by guilt. Her doctors warned me that she might find it difficult to cope with the barrage of stimuli she would experience. She was irritable all through breakfast, ate little, which was unusual, and tottered on the verge of tears as we left the dining room. I know one reason for her distress: Katia has left us. She has accepted an invitation to stay with Mirka Petrashek, her friend from university days. I wonder whether the joy in Katia's face has made my mother jealous.

Katia brings Mirka to the hotel the following day, and I am taken by her regal elegance. Ten years in Siberia turned a swath of her hair snow-white while the rest has remained black. She combs the silvery swath into a circlet at the crown of her head and wears it like a diadem. Because she was a university student and her husband was an attorney, the Soviets declared them bourgeois and exiled them to the north in the late 1940s. They worked essentially as slave laborers on a collective farm until Khrushchev's amnesty following Stalin's death. They had left behind a small daughter who was hidden by Mirka's mother, otherwise the child would have been placed in an orphanage and most likely lost. Yet, Mirka is not a bitter woman. She has an impish sense of humor and chatters with Katia a mile a minute, as if nothing happened in the intervening forty-five years.

I see in Mirka one of those fated Europeans who live where borders of nations meet. When she was born in the early 1900s, she was a subject of the Austro-Hungarian Empire. During her university days, she was a Polish citizen. In her middle years she was a Soviet subject, and now in her old age she is a Ukrainian. And throughout her life, she has called the same house, the same street, and the same city home.

With Katia gone and my mother depressed, I begin to organize items I will need for solitary sightseeing. My attention is riveted on the overnight bag I had taken to Slavske. The rolls of exposed film are missing. I ask my mother if she put the film away in her suitcase, but she shakes her head. The only record left of our trip to Slavske is my notepad, which

I carried in my purse. Inside the notepad are two photos of skeletons Irena Sen gave me. Had it been Stefko, who had appeared so conveniently and with whom we left our belongings during the occasional stops we made? Did someone follow us from Slavske? Had some unseen hand orchestrated our overnight stay at the Red Army rest home? The paranoia I fought when debating the safety of returning returns. I look around the room, expecting to see a camera and a microphone on the wall. I am being pushed back into a time warp I have no desire to revisit. I am scared again.

"Leave," my mother orders from the bed. "I want to take a nap."

I want to leave. I am thinking of walls that eavesdrop and two-way mirrors that spy. It is safer on the street, mingling with the crowd, disappearing in the shadows of the old buildings. I go out into the hall to arrange with the woman on duty to keep an eye on my mother while I am gone, but I do not mention where I am going. Perhaps I am being silly, and perhaps the rolls of film were lost because of my carelessness. But I do not believe for one minute that simple explanation. Even today, I cannot imagine how I could have lost a plastic bag filled with film canisters.

If anyone is interested in my movements, he or she will be disappointed. I am on my way to St. George's Cathedral, the world seat of the Ukrainian Catholic Church, known also as the Uniate Church. Western Ukraine reverted to Catholicism with the Union of Berestia in 1596, when several bishops with flocks in what would become Western Ukraine abandoned Orthodoxy and recognized the Roman pope. In return for rejoining Rome, the Eastern Church could keep its customs, including the use of Old Church Slavonic (instead of Latin) in its liturgy, and its priests could marry.

If Lviv is the center of Ukrainian nationalistic fervor, then St. George's is the soul. A year before our visit, the cathedral reverted to Ukrainian Catholics, who were persecuted by Soviet authorities as members of a "political religion." St. George's is the church to which a returning immigrant must make a pilgrimage. We did so on the afternoon of our arrival from Poland. We did so again upon our return from Slavske. This is when we met Father Zenon, the quiet and kindly pastor of St. George's. During our conversation, my mother mentioned that as a university student in the late 1930s she had met Archbishop Volodymyr Sterniuk, who was then a young missionary priest. Father Zenon said the archbishop was in residence at St. George's and that he would arrange an audience. I tell myself I'm going to St. George's to inquire about the audience, but that is only part of the truth. The Dnister Hotel is near St. George's and I don't feel guilty about sightseeing by myself since I'm only a few blocks away from Mother.

Designed in the 1740s by the Italian architect Bernard Merettini, the cathedral, which took twenty-five years to complete, stands on the site of a medieval church of the same name. The metropolitan's palace across the cobbled courtyard from the cathedral took only two years to build. The beige façades of both are fine examples of Ukrainian rococo architecture. A statue of St. George the Dragon Slayer looks down on the cobbled square from the pinnacle of the cathedral's tallest cupola.

Religion and people watching are the two occupations in St. George's square. From early morning into late afternoon, the square swarms with laymen and with black-robed clerics. Inside the cathedral, services begin early and continue through the day. Young couples come to see Father Zenon to legalize in the eyes of the church their common law or civil marriages. Many have never been baptized because there were no priests to administer the sacraments during Soviet rule. Before he will permit a church marriage, Father Zenon requires couples to take basic religious instruction, learn the "Our Father," the "Hail Mary," and the "Apostles' Creed," and be baptized. Twenty-five marriages are performed each Saturday and Sunday, and there is a year-long waiting list.

Across the courtyard, on the steps leading to the palace and the chancery, young men with intense faces seek a different kind of fulfillment. Vocations blossomed during glasnost. Traditionally, priesthood bestowed a special status and was considered an exalted calling. A vocation could also be a passport to the West.

I meet a seminarian whose name is Ostap. Tall, blond, handsome, and vulnerable in his flowing black cassock, he attracted attention as he stood leaning against the graceful rococo balustrades of the staircase rising to the cathedral's main entrance. I ask him if he knows the whereabouts of Father Zenon. He points to the sacristy and then accompanies me.

Father Zenon says that I can see Archbishop Sterniuk in about an hour. Ostap offers to wait with me. He says he was in the seminary for a year and has many stories to tell about studying for the priesthood. The intense expression in his blue eyes promises an enormous disclosure, the revelation of the dark secret, to which only those initiated into the resurgent priesthood are privy. I am intrigued.

We settle on a cool stone bench on the right side of the chancery. To my disappointment, Ostap speaks in generalities of the kind one hears from the pulpit when the priest has not prepared his Sunday sermon.

I become more intrigued with the late morning light playing on the scales of the dragon writhing at the feet of the heroic St. George than with the drone in my ear. I know then that this would-be priest does not possess the charm to seduce with words.

When he asks for a hundred dollars, I am more or less prepared. "Why?" I ask.

"So I can buy a ticket to Rome to the seminary."

"Doesn't the ticket cost more than that?" I ask.

"Yes, but I have some money. I only need the final hundred. Then I can do God's work in the West."

A scam is a scam anywhere. I tell him a hundred dollars is a lot of money, and if I had that much to spare, I would rather give it to the church for its work in Ukraine.

"So for a measly one hundred dollars, which means nothing to you, you are going to keep a man like me, a man who wants to do God's work in the West, from going?" he demands.

"Yes," I say.

Ostap walks off in a huff. I see him talking with another tourist as Father Zenon comes to fetch me for my audience with Archbishop Sterniuk. The archbishop has snow-white hair and a flowing white beard. The years of imprisonment have left their mark on his body. His hands are knobby from severe arthritis. He walks with a cane and moves cautiously, as if he has a body that aches most of the time. But his words are gentle and an enormous goodness radiates from his face. I think, "This is a holy man," and bend down to kiss the bishop's ring on his finger.

He is eighty-four years old and has been a priest for sixty-four years. After his return from Siberia in 1952, he could not be a priest or get a good job. Instead he worked as a watchman, an orderly, and a medical assistant. He practiced his faith covertly. Father Zenon told me the archbishop had been his mentor and the one who had secretly ordained him while the church was outlawed.

I hear a cock crow before dawn. Strange at first to hear a rooster's cry in a city, but it seems less so when I remember the empty stores in Rynok Square and a woman in a line saying, "Any day now, I'll dig my potatoes." Whether office workers or retirees, people till whatever scraps of earth they can find, and Katia tells me that Mirka was complaining about seed prices quadrupling in three months. People seem to sense the turmoil and the hard times ahead.

Again, my mother is not feeling well. Father Zenon told me about

Archbishop Sterniuk.
Photograph by
Ania Savage.

the plans to bring the body of Josyf Cardinal Slipyj from Rome for in-
terment in the St. George's crypt. I relay the information to her but she
is not interested, which worries me since she has been very proud of her
association with the cardinal. In the late 1960s and in the 1970s, my
mother spent several years in Western Europe, where she worked on her
doctorate in Slavic languages. During this time, Cardinal Slipyj was released from the Siberian gulag, where he had spent eighteen years, and
was establishing a seminary for Uniate priests in Rome. I don't know
how my mother met the cardinal, but she taught Ukrainian at the seminary for a year or so and lived in a nunnery. When the cardinal came to
the United States, she arranged an audience for me, which resulted in
an article I wrote for the *New York Times.*

"Cardinal Slipyj," she says vaguely. "No, I think I'll stay in bed."

Thus, again, I venture into Lviv alone. In front of our hotel stretches
the Jesuit Garden, a pleasant park that borders on Mickiewicz Avenue,
where Lviv's trolleys trundle by, day and night. I know that I can take a

trolley, then transfer to another, to reach the museum and home of Ivan Franko, my destination. But I choose to walk. I soon discover that Lviv is a city of forgotten squares and streets that twist and turn. I lose my bearings in one of these mazes and ask a passerby for direction. "No more than a ten-minute walk. Less than half a kilometer," she says. A half-hour later, I am still trudging up one of Lviv's innumerable hills.

A young couple and their little girl are walking ahead of me. When I catch up with them they say they will point out the building to me. They are on their way to a woman who keeps a goat in her backyard and sells goat's milk to parents of small children, since cow's milk is scarce. From their matter-of-fact explanation, I see that they do not think it odd that someone is raising a nanny goat in a metropolis with a million residents.

We are in a quiet, tree-lined, residential neighborhood. The buildings are old and mostly of red brick. At one time, many were private residences, but during Soviet times the houses were partitioned into flats, or several families were assigned to a house and had to share the kitchen and the toilet. I went inside one such partitioned house when Katia took me to show off the building her husband's family had owned. This is the inheritance she wants the government to return to her.

Franko's house is at the crest of the hill and has been spared partitioning. I marvel at how a man who was proud of the fact he was Ukrainian found favor with the Soviet regime. The explanation is that Franko was imprisoned several times by the conservative Austrian government for his socialist views and, therefore, could be considered an early socialist martyr. Following the October Revolution, Franko appeared on Moscow's approved list of Ukrainian writers, and a museum featuring photographs and copies of his many literary works was built in the 1950s adjacent to his home. Between the two buildings, an ancient gnarled pear tree is bearing abundant fruit. The brittle branches groan under the weight of giant, golden pears. The courtyard is littered with rotting pulp. The aroma of nectar is sweet, pleasant, and strong. Frenzied bees buzz through the air. But Franko's house appears closed. I ring the bell and eventually am rewarded with a shuffle of feet. A heavy woman with swollen ankles opens the door. She is both the guard and the guide through the house. I ask her for a tour and she nods without much enthusiasm. I prepare myself for a dreary time, but am pleasantly surprised. Once she gets going, she warms to the subject and speaks with feeling and empathy about Franko's declining health, his problems with his eyes, and the arthritis that crippled his hands and made writing extremely painful and difficult. "But he never gave up. Never stopped," she says.

Aggravating Franko's arthritis was a cold, brick house with no central heating, although heating systems were known at the turn of the century when the house was built. Instead, each room has a "stove," a tiled affair which is a cross between the Western potbellied stove and the traditional *pich,* the cooking and heating stove found in Ukrainian village cottages. The stoves were incorrectly designed and threw off little heat but prodigious quantities of smoke, the guide says. She adds that the building remains miserably cold during the winter and is responsible for her swollen ankles. I nod sympathetically since the house is chilly although a heat wave has enveloped Lviv.

After the tour, the guide sits down heavily on the bench beneath the fertile pear tree. I sit down next to her reluctantly, aware of the danger lurking above our heads. Franko planted the pear himself, she says. During World War II, when Lviv was being shelled by Russian artillery, a bomb landed in the tree and exploded. It damaged the roof and the back end of the house, and took half of the tree as well. The house was repaired and the tree survived. After some years, it began bearing fruit again. However, it is deemed too unstable for anyone to dare climb it to pick the fruit or trim the branches. In August and September, the guide says, the tree becomes a menace as overripe pears plummet to the ground at the slightest stirring of a breeze. As she finishes her story, a pear explodes between us, the pulp splattering our clothes and skin with soft shrapnel.

Franko's bronze bust dominates the museum and is an example of the excesses of Soviet heroic art. It is on the scale of a haystack and obstructs passage into the museum, which contains a time-line biography rendered in photographs and documents as well as a library of Franko's works. He was an exceedingly prolific writer and researcher. If he were living today, Ivan Franko (1856–1916) would be lionized as a Renaissance man. From folklore to politics, from drama and prose to poetry, from linguistics to translations, he not only contributed a sizable body of work in each area but also excelled in what he did. The son of a village blacksmith, he would have received the cursory four-grade education had not his intellectual brilliance focused attention on him. He had a photographic memory, easily acquired foreign languages, and wrote his first novel when he was nineteen. He is considered Ukraine's foremost ethnographer and translator, having translated Homer, Dante, Shakespeare, and Goethe as well as Neruda and Ibsen. His translations span an astonishing fourteen languages. I browse through Franko's memorabilia and first editions.

When I return to the hotel, I bump into Bohdan Seniv, who is pacing like a tiger in a zoo cage between the front door and the reception desk. I met Bohdan in Munich, where we stopped on our way to Poland. He was buying a car and we almost drove back with him to Ukraine instead of taking the train. Bohdan is on the verge of erupting. His return to Ukraine in the ten-year-old BMW he purchased did not go well. He refers to "certain irregularities" with the car's ownership papers and tells me the vehicle has been impounded at the frontier. Just as well that nothing came of our plans to make the trip together, I say to myself, our problems in Poland with train tickets notwithstanding. Bohdan is upfront about what he wants from me: *valiuta*—hard currency, to buy his car out of hock. Do we need a guide? He also owns "a perfectly adequate Fiat," which is at our disposal.

Bohdan, a native of Lviv, learned long ago to be resilient. As a sixteen-year-old boy full of patriotic fervor, he enlisted in the all-Ukrainian Division Galizien that was formed in 1943 by Germany. The decision to fight Russia by siding with Hitler was a questionable one and would carry enormous political liability for Ukraine and Ukrainians after the war. The division remains a hotly debated subject to this day. In the summer of 1944, the ten-thousand-member division faced the Russian Army and was decimated. Survivors of the rout fled into Czechoslovakia, then Italy, where they became POWs. Other survivors joined the UPA in the Carpathian Mountains and died or were captured and sentenced to Siberia. A small number of men tried to return to civilian life. Bohdan was one of them. He was immediately arrested, although he was not yet eighteen, and sentenced to prison.

A few days after our meeting, I am sightseeing with Bohdan in his tiny, Polish-built Fiat. As we turn the corner around an imposing building, I ask Bohdan what the building is.

"Loncki prison," he says. "NKVD headquartered here. They used to question people here." He falls silent. His normally pale face looks even more pinched. "Deep in the foundations, the Gestapo had constructed a bomb shelter, which later became filled with sewer water. When the NKVD took over, they threw people in there who refused to confess."

Again Bohdan pauses, as if he has to rally his resources to go on remembering. "Some interrogation rooms faced on the street. They used to play music very loudly so that passersby would not hear the screams of the tortured."

"This is the prison in which my family thinks my uncle Myroslav died," I say.

Bohdan's tapered, sensitive fingers grip the wheel tightly. They are the hands of a craftsman, which he was for most of his life. He made gold crowns for teeth. His business was good until a new alloy—which is yellow like gold and supposedly as strong but also much, much cheaper—was introduced for capping teeth. The alloy destroyed Bohdan's business.

Before he drops me off at the hotel, Bohdan agrees to drive us to Zariche, the village where my life began and where my grandparents died.

Chapter 6

RETURN TO ZARICHE

For years, Zariche tantalized me. Only a few yellowed photographs survived World War II and the five postwar years we spent in refugee camps before we were allowed to come to America. As I was growing up, my mother would tell stories that I suspected were embroidered—about a cherry orchard, an oxbow in the river where fish were so plentiful that they could be caught by hand, chestnut Arabian horses that were the envy of the entire parish.

I harbored two memories of this wonderland, one not so wonderful. I remembered a flock of geese that ruled the yard and terrified me. I'll relate the second memory later. When I was invited to teach in Kyiv, I knew I would go to Zariche.

I wanted to see the rambling three-hundred-year-old house in which I was born. And I was fascinated by the figure of my grandfather. Well-educated, liberal, and a Uniate priest, he had been an outspoken opponent of both Nazism and Bolshevism and had written birth certificates for Jews hiding from the Germans. He died under mysterious circumstances when we were still in a refugee camp. Frightening rumors reached us, never denied or confirmed. Was he really murdered because of his politics, or because he refused to become Orthodox? Was my grandmother really allowed to starve to death afterward? In America, my mother and her sisters whispered about these mysteries and wept.

I was determined to learn the true dates and circumstances of my grandparents' deaths. I also wanted us to visit and mourn at their graves.

The day is cold, foggy and rainy. During the hour-and-a-half drive from Lviv we hardly speak, ignoring Bohdan, who tries to point out the sights. Anticipation mingles with dread. I realize that we are trying to suppress our expectations, but every so often my mother or Katia starts

*Ania Savage in
Zariche, 1944.
Photograph by
Ivan Bojcun.*

to say, "Do you remember . . . ?" and describes a happy event from her girlhood. I conjure up an enchanting old house in a cherry orchard.

We almost miss Zariche.

The road has become a narrow, one-lane country road paved with some sort of aggregate that drums against the underside of the Fiat, while rain pounds the windshield. The fog has thickened into a yellow-gray pall that obscures the countryside. In the distance, on a hillock, we see the outlines of a truck and a group of figures. The people are huddling under black umbrellas, Rorschach blots on a gray sheet.

"Funeral," Bohdan says.

I am still staring at the inkblots when, out of the corner of my eye, I glimpse a familiar name on a small wooden sign on the shoulder of the road. It says: "Zariche."

"This is it," I cry.

"I don't think so," Bohdan says. "It's just a lane to a few houses."

I turn to my mother and Katia. They haven't recognized anything. In another moment, we are on a low bridge, crossing a shallow, untidy river.

"That's our river," Katia and my mother say in unison. "We missed the village."

Bohdan swears under his breath, then finds a place to turn the Fiat around and we head back. At the sign, we turn right. The Fiat, not too big to begin with, barely squeezes through the wrought-iron arch marking the entry. Immediately, a flock of honking, angry geese surrounds us. I am sure we are in the right place.

To the left is a pond filled with assorted fowl—dozens of ducks and geese and an occasional flock of hens supervised by roosters. The unpaved lane is slick with oozing mud. I have never seen such mud before. It is coal black and viscous like glue and, unlike the mud in Slavske, it ripples and flows. I remember the T-34 tank from the military museum in Warsaw and begin to understand why Russians designed their tanks to be lightweight and broad-hipped.

Enormous puddles, reflecting like mirrors, dot the lane. As we drive farther into the village, the Fiat slides and wobbles dreadfully and Bohdan's knuckles turn ghost white as he grips the steering wheel. None of us says anything. We are silent with dismay, struck dumb by blighted hopes. The village is poor and spent. Small cottages on either side of the lane are partially hidden by untidy wooden fences. Some of the houses are no better than shanties with crudely patched roofs and cardboard to replace broken windowpanes.

When we come to the small, gray stucco church, Katia and my mother recognize it. Their voices rise in excitement as they are catapulted into the past. They instruct Bohdan how to get to our house. He turns into a lane, then into another, and we come to a dead end. Bohdan stops the Fiat as my mother and Katia roll down the car windows and peer out into the mist. Katia says we made a wrong turn. My mother points to a hillock and says this is the place. Their confusion is understandable. The house, the barns, the orchard, the pastures, the fenced-in yard are gone. In their place stand two sturdy, one-story brick homes. The orchard has been uprooted to make a field, which lies fallow. The oxbow is hard to make out since it is overgrown with weeds and littered with rusting cans and household garbage.

What has happened to the low-ceilinged house with massive beams supporting the thatched roof? What has happened to the rooms filled with kilims, books, and French furniture? Where are the yard pond and the flock of geese? How could someone destroy a cherry orchard? Min-

utes tick by as we sit in the car saying nothing. Then Katia reaches into
her purse, finds a handkerchief, and blows her nose. My mother sits
quietly, her face bewildered, her eyes fearful and darting as if she is trying to find an escape hatch.

I tell Bohdan to turn the Fiat around and take my mother and Katia
back to the church. I get out of the car and when I think they are out of
sight, make my way to the brick houses. Mud splatters my sneakers and
my jeans. It sucks at my feet and oozes up my ankles. Rivulets of water
run into my eyes, and my hair is plastered to my face by the pelting rain.
I slip and slide on the narrow, uphill path. Desperately trying to resur-
rect a memory, groping for something—anything—that will jog remembrance, as the flock of geese did, I stop and look around. A hazy image
rises at the edge of consciousness, an image so distant that I cannot date
it, or even be certain it is remembrance. I see a large tree, its canopy lush
and rustling. *I'm sitting on someone's lap. In my left hand is a fistful of pebbles
and, as I transfer a pebble from one hand to the other, I'm learning to count.
The day is sunny, a spring day, and I and the man—an old man—are sitting
under this giant tree, in dappled shade.* Rain obscures my vision, or is it
tears? I look toward the oxbow where a solitary tree looms through the
fog. The tree is bare-branched and dead. I step off the path. I slide and
slip and almost fall. Wet weeds coil around my legs. I can hardly move.
I, who have climbed fourteen-thousand-foot peaks, cannot ascend the
hillock of my childhood.

Weeping, I turn around and retreat. Later, Katia tells me that Bohdan
stopped the Fiat and they watched me walk up to the first of the houses,
stand at the door, then turn away. I only remember thinking, *"What can
I say to the people who live here?"*

I see a lane that cuts diagonally behind the houses and surmise that
it's a shortcut back to the church and the center of the village. As I start
out, someone clears his throat nearby. Driving a rickety old horse wagon
is a small man, crinkled by hard work and hard times, his shoulders
hunched against the rain. The wagon is a long contraption with a bottom made from wide boards, while the sides are like ladders attached at
a wide angle to the bottom. The old man sits on a board, the ends of
which are bolted to the two side ladders. What strikes me is that the
wagon rides on automobile tires instead of high, wooden wheels.

"Your family's from around here?" the old man asks. I nod, afraid I
am going to bawl if I open my mouth. I work my lips—they are parched
although rain covers my face—and eventually form two words. I say my
grandfather's name, "Mykhailo Vlasenko."

The man's face lights up. "I knew him," he says.

"What happened to the house?"

"Burned down."

"Who lives here now?"

"Two families."

I have other, more important questions but the old man makes a clicking sound with his lips and snaps the reins and the wagon rolls away.

By the time I reach the village church, word has spread that *Amerikantsi* are visiting and people are coming out of the houses. These are old women, bent over and aching, their square bodies supported by swollen legs that end in lumpy, arthritic ankles. One woman with a florid face comes up and begins to pump my mother's hand. She says her name is Vira and that she was a student in the village school where my mother taught before the war. Vira has full, thick lips and many teeth capped with gray metal, not even the ersatz gold that put Bohdan out of business. Her hands are big, rough, and callused by hard manual labor. The nails are broken and dirty. A few strands of graying yellow hair have escaped the black woolen scarf tied tightly under her chin.

"Oh, yes, Vira," my mother says vaguely.

Vira volunteers to meet us at the cemetery and point out the graves of my grandparents. She walks while we ride in the car and we reach the cemetery before her.

The cemetery is a desolate, forgotten place. Weeds grow knee-high. Crosses lie toppled every which way. Katia, who is wearing open-toe shoes, steps into a puddle and almost falls. She begins to weep quietly. My mother's face has turned white. She clutches at her purse and is whispering to herself. We begin to search.

"This is not the cemetery," my mother says. "We had a beautiful cemetery."

"Of course this is the cemetery," Katia cries. "No one moves cemeteries, not even Communists."

I'm the one who finds the double grave of my grandparents near the center of the cemetery. A rough concrete cross rises above the graves, paid for with money my mother and Katia had sent to the village a few years into Mikhail Gorbachev's glasnost. A metal plaque bearing my grandparents' names hangs from the cross. It does not give the dates of their deaths.

We place the gladioli we have brought with us at the foot of the cross and bend our heads in prayer. Our tears mingle with the raindrops falling on the graves.

Suddenly my mother and Katia are pulling at the weeds on the graves. Katia says she will come back and plant flowers. Mother objects. "Who's going to take care of flowers?" she demands. "Let's plant a bush."

"A bush?" Katia objects. "A bush?"

They begin to argue. Mother insists a bush would look tidier and require less weeding.

"A bush is ugly," Katia says.

They are arguing and crying. I tug vainly at the wooden forms still attached to the crude concrete apron around the graves. This is how Vira finds us, but she does not seem to notice that something's amiss. She takes credit for having the cross erected. She seems to be saying: *You left, but I stayed. I have kept your graves. I did not forget my Christian duty.* I resent her attitude. I don't like her at all. I ask her about the war. She says she was orphaned and was taken in by neighbors like my grandmother after my grandfather's death.

"When did he die?" I ask.

"After the war."

"But when? What month? What year?" I insist.

Vira stares at me. She is stingy with her words. "He had sores all over his body."

"From what? Beatings?"

"I don't know," she says.

But I don't believe her. "What about my grandmother?" I try a new tack, as a journalist would.

"The lady had nothing, nothing. Everything was taken away."

"Even her journal?" I hear my mother ask behind me. I turn around, surprised. I have never heard about a journal. Mother is her old self, alert and keen-witted. "She had a trunk, a leather trunk, where she kept her things."

"She left nothing," Vira says, her voice growing stubborn and sullen.

I have the impression that Vira is telling us what she thinks we ought to hear, rather than what actually happened.

"I was only a child myself," she says.

"But she had a trunk," Mother insists, but her voice has lost the authority it had a moment ago. Vira sighs.

While searching for my grandparents' graves, I noticed a grave that had been weeded; its cross stood erect and a new looking yellow-and-blue plaque hung suspended from the cross arms. The plaque was embossed with a gold trident.

"Who's buried there?" I ask Vira, pointing.

"Two brothers."

"Do you know their names?"

"Volycki."

"I grew up with them," my mother says. "They were a few years younger."

"How did they die?" I ask, but I know already.

"In a fight with the NKVD," Vira says. "They were with the partisans. They were visiting their parents when the NKVD found them. They ran out of ammunition and killed themselves with a grenade. The house burned down with them inside."

She recites the horrific story in a matter-of-fact voice. I turn to my mother to comfort her. But her face has gone blank and she is bending down and weeding. So is Katia.

As we leave the cemetery I see three more graves embellished with the blue-and-gold plaques. Before Vira departs, Katia slips her several bills and asks her to take care of the grave.

When we return to the church, the priest is waiting. A young man nine months out of the seminary, Father Ivan is tall, fair-haired, with blue eyes that shine with enthusiasm. He unlocks the church with a flourish and invites us inside, out of the rain. He says that the church stood locked and unused for forty-three years, after the death of the last priest— my grandfather. Its exterior walls, pockmarked with bullet and mortar holes from World War II and the partisan war that followed, were never repaired. The bronze bell removed by Germans to make ammunition was never replaced. Zariche suffered greatly during the war, Father Ivan says. The German-Russian front halted for two days in the vicinity of Zariche and artillery or fire destroyed half of the village. Later, the NKVD and the UPA clashed several times in the village, and more houses burned. As Father Ivan speaks, I begin to understand why the village is so small and what happened to the old homestead.

The church, though damaged, survived the bombardment and the battles, and in the past two years, Father Ivan tells us, it has undergone repairs. The nave was whitewashed, the wooden filigree gilded, and the icons of the saints restored. He points to several large icons that flash and sparkle with gold leaf. They are draped with linens embroidered in blue and white thread. Father Ivan says that on Saturday, three days hence, the village will celebrate the feast of the village's patron saint and dedicate a new bell that was recently cast. He invites us to return and be the parish's guests.

A new birch cross commemorating a fallen UPA soldier in Zariche cemetery. Photograph by Ania Savage.

We hesitate. Our excuses stumble on our lips. Father Ivan urges us to reconsider.

Returning to Lviv, we discuss what we should do. Mother and Katia weep whenever they—or I—mention what we saw in Zariche. Too many years, too much grief has piled up.

When he leaves us at our hotel, Bohdan says he will keep Saturday open in case we decide to go back.

I vacillate, flounder, change my mind, and then decide to attend the village festival. Mother agrees to accompany me. Katia, crushed by the desolation, declines and remains in Lviv.

Saturday turns out to be sunny and warm. In the sunlight, the mud is no longer so menacing. It's drying out and shrinking, no longer a viscous morass. The village also looks better. The cottages are decorated with greenery and colorful bunting, as are the post office and general store. In

Interior of Zariche church. Photograph by Ania Savage.

church, the congregation is wearing its Sunday best. Little boys are dressed in white linen shirts with tight stand-up collars embroidered in orange or red. The long braids of little girls are caught up in enormous organza bows in the colors of the rainbow. Dozens of candles illuminate the church altar and the sweet smell of incense perfumes the air.

A choir sings responses to Father Ivan's clear tenor. As he prays, I catch the familiar sound of my grandfather's, my grandmother's, my mother's, and Katia's names. He mentions that my grandfather was the last priest in this parish and he, Father Ivan, is the first one after nearly half a century. He says that Mykhailo Vlasenko's daughter and granddaughter have come to celebrate the feast day with the parishioners and people turn around to stare and stare. At the end of the service, Father Ivan joins the choir in singing *Vichnaia Pamiat,* the hymn of remembrance, for our family.

After mass, people surround us. They shake our hands, ply us with questions, and invite us to their homes. A bent old woman hobbles up.

Tears glisten in her eyes. She tells us she worked for my grandparents before the war.

Although he had not known for sure that we would be back, Father Ivan asked two families to join in preparing a welcoming feast. When we enter the three-room cottage, we find the table already set, as is the local custom, with *zakuski,* to whet the appetite for the main event. There are salads of cabbage, carrots, and beets, an aspic of pork studded with garlic cloves, a platter of sliced hard sausage, which resembles salami, and a second platter of sliced yellow cheese. Two bottles of vodka stand high in the center of the table together with a towering bottle of Crimean champagne. We are given seats of honor, on either side of the priest, who sits at the head of the table. Bohdan finds a chair with the other men at the other end. The women, wiping their hands on their starched white aprons, come out of the kitchen. After Father Ivan blesses the food, serious eating begins. Baskets of sliced rye and white bread are passed around. Instead of butter, wafers of *salo* accompany the bread. A welcoming toast is raised, then another one, and a third. Conversation flows.

As a platter empties, another one stacked high with a new *zakuska* takes its place. Pickled beets accompany sliced cold meat. A platter of hard-boiled stuffed eggs is decorated with tomatoes sprinkled with chives and dill.

Then the zakuski disappear. In a moment, hot chicken bouillon called *rosil* makes a fragrant entrance in a huge tureen. Platters of fried chicken, dilled potatoes, and meat-stuffed rolls of cabbage called *holubci* ("little doves") follow the soup. We drink the champagne, which Father Ivan brought, with dessert, which consists of two enormous tortes and a sweet roll layered with dried fruits and jam.

A groaning table is the traditional sign of hospitality, but remembering the empty stores in Lviv and the unappetizing food in Slavske, I am amazed by the bounty of Zariche. There is plenty of meat. There is plenty of everything that the garden, the orchard, the rich, fertile soil—and hard work—can provide. As if reading my thoughts, our host turns to us and says: "The land is not poor. The problem lies with the government."

America fascinates our hosts, as their lives fascinate us. Information is exchanged, questions asked. Do we serve meals such as this? Is vodka available in America? Are we all rich? There is much to tell, to learn, and only an afternoon to do it in.

As the party breaks up, I turn to the grandfather, who was both imprisoned and exiled for his political views. With my voice lowered so that only he can hear, I ask about my grandparents.

He says he does not remember when or how they died. "It's so long ago," he says, and looks away.

I don't believe him.

But he is more forthcoming about the homestead.

"After the house burned, the land lay unused for years," he says. "Then a man returned from Siberia and wanted to settle here. He built one of the houses. Another one like him built the second one. They are good people," he adds, looking me straight in the eye.

It is a long, wise, eloquent look. It says: Let the past rest.

The afternoon is fading into long shadows. It is time for us to leave. Everyone comes out of the house to say good-bye. Neighbors appear also. Hannia, a very old woman who was a neighbor of my grandparents and who had just heard of our visit, hobbles down the street. She pulls at my mother's sleeve until we go to her house for a brief visit. Her table is set for a party. We protest, but to no avail. We are served tea and eat tiny sardine sandwiches.

I ask Hannia about my grandmother. She looks away and says, "Whenever I could, I took milk to her."

"When did she die?" I ask.

Hannia looks away again. "She died a year, or perhaps a little more, after your grandfather. It was a very bad winter," she adds, then turns to speak to my mother about something else.

Bohdan is standing at the door clearing his throat, too polite to urge us to hurry. As we say good-bye, Hannia rushes to a cupboard and pulls out a bottle of homemade vodka, which she presents to my mother. Then she rushes to the cupboard again, to return with beautiful embroidery, which she wraps around the bottle. "It won't do for a woman your age to walk into a fancy hotel with an unwrapped bottle of vodka under your arm," she admonishes.

Dusk has darkened the village by the time we leave. A procession follows our car as Bohdan, trying to bypass the worst of the puddles, weaves the Fiat slowly down the street. I ask him to halt by the hillock and look toward the two brick houses. When I first saw the houses four days ago, I raged. But the rage has evaporated. When? I don't know. Perhaps when Father Ivan was celebrating mass. Perhaps when I saw how hard good people had worked to make us welcome. Perhaps when I watched Hannia drape the embroidery around the bottle of moonshine she had given Mother. Instead of being angry, I find myself feeling grateful. Zariche continues to exist and I have seen it.

Chapter 7

EATING AND DRINKING SLAVIC STYLE

Martha Stasiuk, a relation of a radio journalist I met when we stopped in Munich, invites us to her apartment for dinner. Martha is a city woman, blond, energetic, well dressed and efficient. She and her husband Roman and his parents live in central Lviv, not far from Rynok Square and a few blocks from the Grand Opera. Their building is a nineteenth-century dowager flawed by age, arbitrary partitioning, and lack of care. Neglect obscures the traces of the old elegance.

In silence, my mother and I climb the stone steps behind Martha to the top floor. Martha unlocks a door and we are ushered into a tiny, tasteful, and scrupulously clean room. The room is furnished with a sofa, a small end table, and flat-weave Hutsul kilims of fine geometric design and deep jewel colors, the kind we had looked for in vain in Kolomyia. One hangs on the wall; another is elegantly draped over a sofa. A third kilim lies on the wooden floor. We sit alone in that room for a long time, perhaps thirty minutes, and I begin speculating on the room's function. Once, long ago, it may have been the reception foyer for a large apartment. It serves that function still, as our present circumstances indicate, but the room is probably also a bedroom. I examine the sofa because it "feels" familiar. I decide that the sofa is like a futon, where the back can be lowered into a flat position, thereby creating a bed that is slightly larger than an American twin. This bed is hard and it has a crease in the middle where the back and the seat meet, but it is not uncomfortable as long as you do not tumble into the crease. I had slept on this type of sofa once already, when we were in Prague and stayed with a Ukrainian family.

Eventually, Martha reappears and ushers us into a bigger room where a table is already set with zakuski of herring and sausage. We sit on a banquette that is also draped with kilims. A large, dark sideboard against the far wall is heaped with porcelain and books.

Martha's father-in-law joins us. He has white hair and parchment-like skin that is stretched tightly across his sharp features. Like our Lviv-to-Zariche driver Bohdan Seniv, he exudes nervous energy. He also has classic prewar manners. He bows elegantly over our extended hands, plants a fleeting kiss, clicks his heels, and launches into easy chitchat. I can tell that my mother likes him at once because of the coquettish smile she bestows on him as her brown eyes flash and dance. Mr. Stasiuk explains that his wife is an invalid and will not be joining us.

The conversation centers on America. What happened between 1939 and 1991 seemingly does not exist for Mr. Stasiuk. He pours full-bodied red wine and we all have several glasses, lean back into the banquette, and chat easily. The food on the table is equally wonderful—a tender beef roulade, rich, brown gravy, and mashed potatoes flavored with butter. When I compliment her on the meal, Martha says that one of her relatives owns a meat packing firm. This relative is trying to expand his business under new laws permitting private collectives and is trading meat for assembly-line equipment from Dnipropetrovsk, where the Soviet government used to manufacture rockets. Martha assures me that an assembly line for making sausage is not unlike an assembly line for making ICBMs.

Mr. Stasiuk asks me where we live in America. I tell him that I have lived in a number of states and cities, including in the heart of New York City for several years.

"And where do you keep your Negroes?" he asks.

"Pardon?" I say, not quite sure I've heard him correctly. My head clears. I'm on my guard.

"Your Negroes. Where do you keep them?"

"Keep them?"

Mr. Stasiuk is becoming exasperated with me. "Where are the areas in your cities that you cordon off with barbed wire? That's where your Negroes live."

I am dumbfounded. I say that we don't cordon off cities with barbed wire and that blacks are not restricted to any one neighborhood.

"But I saw it on television," he insists. "I saw barbed wire on television."

"It might have been a temporary barrier during a riot," I suggest, because I think I remember seeing such a barricade during a riot in Miami.

"No, it's the sections you cordon off," he insists.

"We don't cordon off sections of our cities," I insist, in turn.

"They have really brainwashed you in America, haven't they?" he says, shaking his head sadly.

When I recall this conversation, I stop to consider being "brainwashed." If he meant by my being brainwashed that I root for America, then he was right. The last two lines of Emma Lazarus's poem, which is inscribed on the pedestal on which the Statue of Liberty stands, read:

Send these, the homeless, tempest-tossed to me:
I lift my lamp beside the golden door.

America gained my loyalty because it kept its promise by offering a safe haven to my homeless parents. And it also kept the promise of the "golden door" by enabling them—albeit through hard work—to earn a decent livelihood. My parents were not exceptions. Everyone in my extended family—uncles, aunts, and cousins—who immigrated in the late 1940s and early 1950s prospered. Like other immigrants, we came to America with the clothes on our backs and not much more. The extent of my parents' wealth at the moment they sailed past the Statue of Liberty to Ellis Island were two gold twenty-dollar pieces sewn into my clothing. (My maternal grandfather gave them, and more, to my father as he and my mother set out on their trek to the West. My parents gave them to me at the birth of each of my sons. I gave one to each boy on his eighteenth birthday.) Yet, by the mid-1960s, my parents had prospered to the point that my father bought a piece of land and built a house on it, while my mother stopped working on a General Motors assembly line and went back to school for a master's degree and a doctorate. America paid for my education all the way through graduate school. Our modest success was not unique by any means. All my cousins went to college, without exception. Eventually, every family in our extended family had saved enough to buy a house.

I remember those early years in America. We were called the DPs (Displaced Persons). We settled near one another and in the evenings and on Sundays after mass, the families would come together. The adults talked about the war years and the DP camps, while we played nearby and absorbed their stories. The families clung together for companionship, not because of fear. It was okay to talk in a foreign language, sing foreign songs, and cook foreign foods. You could do all these things in America without fear of reprisal. I think we children were imbued with the gratitude the adults felt.

The ancestral table tells much about our families and our history. In my family, language, religion, and culture were intimately linked with food. Our great family feasts were religious holy days, celebrated first at church, then at the dining room table. During the week and for most of the year we ate very modestly. Mother would usually stretch a cut of meat into three meals, while on the remaining days the meals were meatless, often simply boiled eggs in a sauce over noodles or potatoes. But on the great feast days! There was no holding back my mother or my aunts. In their wisdom, gleaned in the years of hardships, they knew that hard work could leave time for enjoyment. Celebration and good food softened hardships; the feast left an afterglow that made it a little easier the next morning to face the foreign country lurking outside the front door.

My mother had a cookbook, its pages yellowed and the edges brown and crumbling, which had belonged to my grandmother and which was pulled out with ritualistic pomp on these rarified occasions. This cookbook had notes written in the margins by my grandmother in an elegant, elongated script made with a real fountain pen that, upon occasion, spat droplets of ink. As I paged through the cookbook, I could imagine my grandmother bending over the earthen stove, stirring a savory goulash, then rushing to the wooden kitchen table to note in the margins of the cookbook how long it took for the sauce to bubble, or how many hours passed before the meat was tender to the fork. The meat dishes from this cookbook were elaborate sauced creations, thick and rich, probably overcooked. But it wasn't the hams or the beef ragouts that I looked forward to. I dreamed about the tortes. These cakes rose to monumental heights as marzipan or butter fillings flavored with almonds, vanilla, citron, and chocolate were stacked one upon the other with only thin wafers separating the different flavors. After consuming these rich stews and even richer cakes, we sat for many hours at the table, drinking tea or coffee, leaning our elbows on the embroidered tablecloth (manners were relaxed after dinner), and listening to stories of my mother's and my aunts' golden youth or my father's exploits on a motorcycle.

These feasts, and the Eastern European dishes served on these occasions, are an intrinsic part of the immigrant life I remember. Thus, was it a wonder that when we returned to Ukraine, I found myself thinking about the Old World cuisine I grew up on? I soon recognized that I was harboring expectations of a culinary string of feasts, of savory dishes, of delectable desserts that I associated with my grandmother's cookbook. I don't think these expectations were out of line. During my earlier travels — to France, Great Britain, Portugal, Spain, and Australia — dining was a large part of the discovery and pleasure of the experience of travel. Although I did not speak to them about food, I realized that my mother and Katia were nurturing similar expectations. Since I had been told that my grandmother's cookbook had been at the elbow of every good cook in Western Ukraine, I assumed that this culinary magic was still being practiced. Perhaps that is why we were so appalled and disheartened by the lackluster food we were served in Slavske and later in the hotel in Lviv. Breakfasts invariably consisted of sliced sausage, cheese, and a weak herbal tea. No coffee. Ever. "Not available," the waiter or waitress would say. Lunch often was a repetition of breakfast, except that a salad of pickled beets or sauerkraut accompanied the sausage meat. The bread was thick, heavy, and indifferent. It came sliced, and if the slicing had been performed a few hours earlier, the bread was stale. At dinner, "beefsteak" appeared, although it might as well have been called "mystery meat." It looked sometimes like skirt steak, but overcooked into stringiness and hidden under a sauce made from onions. "Mystery meat" was accompanied by potatoes and often by dilled tomatoes, the best items on the plate.

The longer I stayed, the more I fantasized about dumplings, a signature dish of the Ukrainian table. Dumplings were always served for Christmas Eve dinner in my home and I can discern a good one on the first bite. I harbor great respect for dumpling makers because a good cook can make these tiny stuffed (cabbage, potatoes, cheese, ground meat, fruit of the season) envelopes of dough sublime, while a bad cook will produce dumplings hardly edible. I began to dream about dumplings filled with cherries and slathered with sugared cream, of savory dumplings of cabbage and onion floating on a pool of melted butter, of dumplings filled with crumbled potatoes and bits of farmer's cheese served with crisply fried onions. I hoped that dumplings would appear at the next meal, but they never did, or would. So much for old cookbooks, I said to myself. But then we were invited to the feast in Zariche, and a day or two before we leave Lviv, Martha Stasiuk invites us to a dinner party celebrating her husband Roman's fortieth birthday. To my surprise and delight, a number of the dishes I remember from my grandmother's cookbook are served. I wish Katia and my mother had come with me, but my mother remained in the hotel in bed and Katia wanted to spend the evening with Mirka.

Roman is dark, jovial, and more relaxed than his wife. As he greets me, he tells me he loves every kind of banquet, but especially a family feast. The party is at the lunchroom of the Lviv Polytechnic Institute, where Martha and Roman teach in the mathematics department. I learn that the lunchroom was chosen because no one in their families has an apartment big enough to accommodate sixty guests. The women in Roman's family must have begun planning the feast a month earlier and must have cooked for a week, if not more. They also found time to transform the cavernous lunchroom into a disco with flashing red and blue lights that pulsate to the beat of the rock tunes pouring out of the loudspeaker. There is no cocktail hour or dillydallying before the main event. Arriving guests are seated immediately at two long tables on the far side of the dance floor. The tables are covered with platters that brim over with tempting zakuski. Everything, I learn, was prepared at home, then shuttled by trolley and private car to the lunchroom.

We begin to eat. First, we are served several kinds of robust, garlicky sausages and platters of golden cheese. These are followed by cold salads. Some are made from cooked vegetables with bits of herring for unexpected piquancy. Other salads tremble with aspic. One of these encases knobs of pig's feet and pale cloves of garlic. I remember how my father loved this dish and I wipe my eyes with the back of my hand. Soon come platters of stuffed fish dressed with dill and cucumbers. The fish course is followed by a meat course that offers pink slices of beef surrounded by a pungent salad of julienned beets sprinkled with grated horseradish.

I am seated near the head of the table, to the right and a seat or two down from Roman, who keeps repeating that he loves good parties and this one is going to be the best. Roman has assigned me to his cousin, Dmytro, who plies me with stories and vodka. Dmytro is thin, with a pale, monastic face and a level gaze, but with an appetite that is at odds with his thin, lanky frame.

I know that good manners require that I sample food from every platter that comes my way, even if only a morsel. I also know that I am being observed, for later comment on the manners of Americans. Eventually, Dmytro nods in approval. I am stuffed, but I am still eating. Dmytro offers this anecdote:

"Ivan Ivanovich, a man with a prodigious appetite, was invited to a feast. He piled his plate high and ate everything in sight. 'Ivan Ivanovich,' the host said, turning to him, 'how do you like the pickled pig's feet?'

"'First rate, I haven't had better.'

"'And the *pelmeni?*'

"'I'm on my second one.'

"'Second one! You've already eaten a dozen.'"

I laugh. I know exactly what Dmytro means.

Dmytro says that zakuski—the term is the same in both Russian and Ukrainian—was developed by the Russian nobility in the eighteenth and nineteenth centuries. It grew out of the necessity to give sustenance quickly to people traveling to far-flung estates and arriving at ungodly hours of day and night. A selection of cold meats, aspics, salads, and canapés was a practical way of keeping the guests happy until real food was served.

Dmytro says disparagingly, "The Communists adopted zakuski because it's an ideal way to hide the fact that you have been unable to buy as much as you want of one food, particularly meat. Instead you serve the meat as a zakuska, while the main course is *kasha* [buckwheat] or cabbage."

I grin and nod. We are getting on famously. Dmytro tells another story while filling my tumbler to the brim with vodka. Is he filling my glass a second or a third time?

"A millennium ago, Volodymyr the Great [Grand Prince Vladimir in Russian history], the Kyiv prince who brought Christianity to the Slavs, was drawn to Islam and not to Christianity. He had sought a husband for one of his daughters in the Christian court in Constantinople and found the princes devious and pompous. What he learned about the more simplistic rituals of Islam pleased him until he heard about Islam's prohibition of alcohol.

"Vodka, of course, had been invented by then and Volodymyr was not one to pass up a chalice filled with the honey-flavored mead he favored.

"'You're certain that Islam forbids my mead?' he asked.

"'Certain, my lord,' was the reply.

"Volodymyr considered the problem. Then he said, 'I'll give up our idols. I'll build grand churches. I'm even willing to donate one tenth of my wealth to the faith, but I'm not going to give up drinking.'

"And so, the people of Kyiv were baptized."

I am feeling tipsy and mellow. Dmytro passes another platter to me and I eat stuffed cabbage drizzled with a tangy tomato sauce. A ragout called hunter's stew that is combination of sausage, pork, and game follows.

When the desserts come, I regret that I have eaten so heartily. The tortes are as monumental as I had expected, the layered breads golden and delicate, their fillings sugared memories of succulent ripe fruit.

I admire these creations and lament my limited capacity. Next to me, Dmytro is serving himself and me with gusto. I protest only to myself when he places a huge chunk of torte on my plate. With a stuffed, carefully arranged smile, I listen to a dark-haired woman, whose hair is braided into a severe, old-fashioned coiffure, lean across the table and elaborate on Dmytro's vodka story.

"Russians will tell you that vodka was introduced in the fourteenth century in Moscow as a medicine, but of course they are wrong," she says with a smile.

I stay late, but even so the feasting is not quite over by the time I leave. My face is flushed with too much vodka and too much food. I walk with a spring in my steps, certain that I have partaken twice in one week of feasts prepared by cooks who cherish their copies of my grandmother's cookbook. Not once, but twice, I have dined at the ancestral table and it was a memorable event. I know that the ancestral cuisine is still being practiced and that, as an adult, I have eaten with my "ancestors."

My mother gave my grandmother's cookbook away a long time ago to show her displeasure with me. She told me this in a moment of lucid spitefulness. "You married an American. You don't use Ukrainian in your home, so why should you have a Ukrainian cookbook?" she asked. Today, I no longer rue as keenly the loss of my grandmother's cookbook as I did before our trip to Ukraine.

That evening in Lviv at the Dnister Hotel, I find my mother standing at the window, waiting. "We're in Lviv, aren't we?" she asks.

I nod.

"I've been standing here for a while," she says, "remembering." From her eyes and from her voice I know her thoughts are clear and lucid.

"What are you remembering?" I ask, expecting her to speak of Father Zenon or Archbishop Sterniuk. But she is remembering the war.

"I was visiting Katia," she says, "when the war began. The planes darkened the sky like flocks of birds. They bombed the railroad and factories and huge plumes of black smoke rose into the air."

She pauses. "Russians entered the city two weeks later. They were mostly peasant boys who had never been to a city before. They bought up everything, especially the food in the confectioneries on Akademik Street." She pauses again. "By mid-October, Russian officers came with their families. The women would go shopping at the finest stores. They would walk in and buy silk negligees from France. Money was no obstacle." I can see in her eyes that she is seeing an image from many years ago. She smiles and her eyes flash as she says:

"Katia and I went to the opera one evening. As we stood in the foyer, we saw these Russian women strolling in on their husbands' arms. They were all dressed up, their hair done up. And do you know what they were wearing? The French negligees. They didn't know the difference between a negligee and an evening costume." She shakes her head. "We laughed and didn't take them seriously, and look what they have done."

Her face is now contorted with sadness and the light dies in her eyes. I realize what malaise has afflicted her during our stay in Lviv: under the drabness and the dust, she has not been able to find the city she once told me was called "Little Paris."

Perhaps I do it on purpose, but I don't go sightseeing again in Lviv. We soon depart the weary, seven-hundred-year-old city for bustling, cocksure, very male Kyiv. Do I leave Lviv with places left unseen as a form of insurance that will make me come back someday and reconsider the city? I don't know the answer.

Chapter 8

GOLDEN-DOMED KYIV AND BABI YAR

Volodymyr Kanash, looking both anxious and disapproving, is standing on the narrow, concrete platform as our train glides into Kyiv's main station. A giant bouquet of flowers in Volodia's arms hides his graying walrus mustache. Next to him stands a taller, fair-haired man who looks ill at ease.

"I don't know what's happening any more," Volodia says without preamble as he thrusts the flowers into my arms. "Trains used to run like clockwork. You're an hour late."

"We sat on the outskirts for a long time," I say. I look around quickly. The day is cold and clammy, bone-chilling weather. I'm glad I'm wearing my red parka.

Wearing this same parka, I met Volodia the year before on an ascent in the Sangre de Cristo Mountains in southwestern Colorado. The climb brought together members of the Colorado Mountain Club, including myself, and a group of Ukrainians and Russians, whose trip was sponsored by the Pacifica Foundation. Although not a mountaineer as were most of the other men and women in the Soviet group, Volodia, a short, spry man in middle age, came on the climb because he thought it would be an interesting experience. We became friends during the six-hour ascent of Mount Lindsey. He was behind me when I slipped on an icy stretch and slid down ten feet or so. He was ahead of me as we negotiated a narrow chimney on our descent. By the time we reached camp, he was saying he would arrange for me to work and teach in Ukraine the following year.

Joining Volodia on the train platform is Valery Hruzyn, the quietly reserved deputy editor at *News from Ukraine*. I introduce my mother and Katia and pass the flowers into my mother's arms; she examines them carefully while we deal with the luggage. The drizzle turns into fine rain.

I hunch my head between my shoulders and reach behind me for the parka's hood. The train platform has no overhang and is stained with grease and sputum that make the soles of our shoes slide. As soon as Mother and Katia are settled at the Kyiv Hotel and Valery is dispatched to return the borrowed van, Volodia, ignoring the rain, takes me sightseeing.

I do not know what to expect since for me Kyiv is a legend, a New Jerusalem, to which, my mother used to promise, we would return when Ukraine had thrown off the Soviet yoke. I know too much about Kyiv and too little. I know the legend about Kyiv's founding. It was named after Kyi, the eldest of three brothers (Shchek and Khoryv being the younger ones) who built a trading center on the Dnipro. A little river, a tributary of the great Dnipro, winds its way through the hills and is named Lebed (swan), after the sister of the three brothers. But I am surprised to discover that Kyiv's streets are as steep as San Francisco's, so steep that some are broad steps hewn into the rock; and I did not know that the earliest town is separated from the later one by soaring palisades. The city's architecture also surprises me. It is an amalgam of the old and decaying, and the new and ostentatious. The center of town exudes an Old World flavor, but like the antiquity of many cities in Central and Eastern Europe, this patina is something of a sham. I learn that at the end of World War II, 80 percent of Kyiv lay in ruins, destroyed in the savage battles between the Red and German armies for control of the Dnipro River. Volodia and I walk down Khreshchatyk, the principal boulevard in Kyiv—its Champs Elysées—where buildings that remained after the war blend with the tall, curved apartment blocks that Stalin built. The postwar buildings are adorned with a hammer and sickle or the standards of the battle regiments that fought for control of the Dnipro River. Although grand on the outside, the interiors of these buildings, I will discover in the months ahead, are cramped and starkly utilitarian.

But the war was not the only spoiler of gracious, old Kyiv. The destruction began in the 1920s with the Bolsheviks. A map I purchased shows the sites of 254 buildings and monuments of Old Kyiv that were leveled by Stalin and his successors.

The Dnipro River, which is not quite as wide as the Mississippi, bisects Kyiv. It is visible from the summits of several of Kyiv's hills. A greenbelt of chestnut, linden, and poplar parks stretches along the Dnipro, and Volodia leads me into the park despite the cold drizzle. I huddle more deeply into my red parka and do not reprimand myself—

as I have now done several times since Slavske—for bringing such an "unsuitable" garment with me.

We climb the steps of Volodymyr Hill to the giant statue of Grand Prince Volodymyr, after whom Volodymyr was named, the same Prince Volodymyr who figured in the story Dmytro related at Roman Stasiuk's birthday party in Lviv. In 988 A.D., Prince Volodymyr ordered the ancient Slavs baptized by the expedient and highly effective method of driving his subjects into the Dnipro to get wet. The prince practiced his new religion with gusto. He built some three hundred churches in Kyiv, a few of which survived into this century, only to be dynamited on Stalin's orders in the 1930s. Only two clusters of onion domes are visible through the rain: St. Sophia's to the northwest and the domes at the Monastery of the Caves to the south.

Volodia stops, turns to face the Dnipro River, and assures me that on a good day the view from the hill is beautiful and panoramic. Some two hundred feet below flows the great, gray river. The opposite bank is veiled in mist, although I know that it marks the beginning of the great flat plain known as the steppe. What I see through the haze is called Darnitsa, a Soviet-style bedroom suburb of high-rise apartment buildings. Volodia says Darnitsa extends east for many miles, and I nod.

Volodia says eleven bridges connect Old Kiev with Darnitsa and the Left Bank, but because of the mist, I can barely make out two or three. As we descend from the hill, I discover Volodia's passion: the Kyiv Dynamo soccer team. The rain is coming down hard now; both of us are thoroughly wet, our noses red and drippy, but Volodia leads me to a monument commemorating Dynamo soccer players. The Nazis shot the entire team after the players refused to throw a game to the German Luftwaffe team in 1941. Volodia gives me a quick rundown of Dynamo's chances for making the playoffs for the European Cup. I nod and wonder if we will ever find shelter. I fantasize that perhaps we'll stop at a museum and dry out a bit.

We walk north past an amphitheater with a concrete stage. This stadium will soon become the favorite site for gospel rock concerts and sermons by American television preachers. Rain is trickling down my cheeks and dripping from Volodia's mustache, and since no museum appears to be on our itinerary, I am ready to postpone the rest of the tour to a more clement day, but Volodia dismisses my timid suggestion.

Kyiv is a "hero city," an appellation the Soviet regime gave to cities that fought valiantly against the Germans. The preeminent "hero city" is, of course, Leningrad, now St. Petersburg, which withstood a nine-hundred-day siege by the German Army. After the war, hero cities were granted special rewards, among them an array of new government buildings. Volodia and I stop before two of these.

Above us loom two enormous façades that are overblown copies of some classical building, perhaps the Parthenon. Fat columns with elaborate Corinthian entablatures hold up the flat roof of the portico, while massive Doric pedestals and arched and gated entrances announce that this is the way into the interior. The architecture means to awe, to intimidate, to display arrogant power. It does. Above us surges an arch so huge that I, gazing upward, feel puny, an ant. Volodia, who is about my height, is frowning and looking even sterner than usual. This, he says, is the regional government of the Kyiv *oblast* (province). What do I think of it?

I say I don't like buildings that are of a scale that reduces people to the size of ants. He asks whether America indulges in such architectural excesses. I say yes, America does.

"I agree," he says. "I think our two countries influenced each other both in their antagonisms and their aspirations." He visited Washington, D.C., during his 1990 trip, and had been shown the Pentagon.

These semicircular buildings come to encapsulate for me the dichotomy of Kyiv: the abiding heavy hand of a master who celebrates himself in grandiose architecture while condemning his subjects to tiny, tight, and overcrowded apartments piled one upon another in gray ungainly buildings that stretch for mile after mile in stultifying anonymity. Kyiv is pockmarked with such out-of-scale monoliths. One of the worst towers beyond the graceful domes of the Monastery of the Caves. This monument consists of a granite wall of stern profiles and jutting heroic breasts that commemorate the battles for the Dnipro during World War II. Here, again, I encounter the Mount Rushmores of Soviet heroism. Beyond this wall of heroes rises a giant statue, a monstrous Mother Ukraine welcoming her sons and daughters. Her lance pokes at the sky. A shield, protecting her armor-clad body, wards off an invisible enemy. This graceless monolith is derisively called the "Iron Baba," and Volodia wisely leaves it to someone else to take me to gaze at her. Instead, we walk farther north, then down one of the steep, stepped streets into Podil.

Podil is the core of the old, charming Kyiv. The buildings here are as ancient as is Orthodoxy. Their façades are of buff-colored stucco or stone, or sometimes of brick, human in scale and unpretentious. The churches are whitewashed, with small, unadorned cupolas. The plazas and piazzas hark back to a time when European towns were built on intersecting trade routes that invited travelers, trade, and barter. Podil will become one of my favorite haunts and a week will not go by without my coming down here from the upper city on the palisades. I will find a cloister where I will observe a nun filling a pail with water from a stone well, and I will listen to the Sabbath chant in the walled courtyard of a recently reopened synagogue.

As Volodia and I stroll through a city I believed would be off limits during my lifetime, I am cold and wet, but also very happy. I want to pinch myself to make sure I am awake and not dreaming, and then I reprimand myself for being childish. I forget the drizzle and the cold while trying to comprehend the reality not only of being in Kyiv but also of knowing that I will live here. I even forget that I am wearing a red coat that stands out like a streak of blood in the hurrying, colorless crowd.

Volodia halts in front of the Mohyla Academy, named after Metropolitan Petro Mohyla, who in 1632 established a school that became the largest center of scholarship and education in Eastern Europe in that century and the next. But in 1817, the academy, by then a ward of the Russian czar, was closed. After almost 175 years, the school is about to reopen. The academy's buff buildings surmounted by red-tile roofs are our last stop. Volodia, as if finally realizing that it is raining, heads for a café, where we stand in an interminable line to buy a cup of Turkish coffee, a drink that I do not take to immediately, but which Volodia considers a culinary tour de force.

My mother's unhappiness vanishes in Kyiv. She likes the hotel and the glimpses her window offers of the sultry Dnipro River. She also likes the fact that Mirka has stayed behind in Lviv and is no longer a rival for Katia's attention.

One day, my mother asks Katia to buy her a street map of Kyiv, and for the week they stay in the city, the map does not leave her side. Katia and I joke about her devotion to the map, but the one time I borrow it and do not return it immediately, my mother becomes angry and weeps.

I wonder about her attachment to the map. And I also wonder if she is remembering, or has the disease spread? She never speaks of Zariche or any of the places we have visited. It is as if each evening the slate of her memory is being wiped clean.

The bad weather passes and late September is singularly beautiful in Kyiv. The shimmering heat we encountered in Lviv gives way to dry sunny days and cloudless skies, perfect weather for sightseeing. The days hang like the ripe apples on bent boughs we saw in Slavske, soon to detach and fall. The sun's rays glance off the glowing, amber domes of the Cave Monastery, while the smooth waters of the Dnipro, faded to a pale blue, mirror the sky. One morning, as we are walking down Khreshchatyk and admiring the banners and flags, my mother stops and says, "When I was a young woman, I thought Lviv was a beautiful, cosmopolitan city, but it's faded and provincial."

I do not know what to say. I had thought so too, but was afraid that if I said anything critical I would hurt my mother's and Katia's feelings.

Mother's comment echoes in my mind all that day. Eventually, I begin to understand what she meant. She spent the second half of her life telling stories of a lost, idyllic life. In these tales, the weather was always sunny, the countryside enchanting, the cities were cosmopolitan, and the people friendly. Until I saw Lviv and Zariche, I did not realize that her stories had portrayed a world bathed in a glowing light that erased all blemishes and rough edges. Yet, for my mother, these stories were not only real but, with time, created invisible enclosures, boundaries beyond which she was reluctant to explore or see.

She never learned or understood the pragmatism of America. If you were born poor or came to the United States poor, it was no lasting shame. You could work your way up from washing the floor in an office on Wall Street—which she did for two years when we lived in Brooklyn—to running the enterprise. If you were poor, your child would be the first in line for scholarships, as I was. You came to be judged—and admired—for what you became in America, and not for what or who you had been before you were processed at Ellis Island. This, of course, was the American model of success, not the European one. No one in America cared a whit how narrowly you could define your lineage back to a Cossack who had a head of thick hair and was therefore called Chubaty.

At some point in every exile's life comes a time to make a choice: to remain frozen in the woes of the exile or to use the opportunities the new world offers. My mother chose not to adopt and adapt to America. She could not find a meaningful role for herself, and perhaps that is why America inspired a lifelong critique—it was too brash, too disrespectful, too uncultured. Then again, it seems, in retrospect, that my mother was always displeased with her life, with all her friends, with me, with my father, with her circumstances. Something was always missing. Something was always vulgar. Something was always not what she had expected it to be.

Yet, exile and the experience of living in the West had worked on her subconscious. Whether she knew it or not, her expectations on her return were far more sophisticated than those of the twenty-seven-year-old provincial woman going into exile. She had lived in or visited New York, Miami, San Francisco, Paris, Rome, Tokyo, and these, as well as other cities, had left their impact. In the weeks immediately preceding our arrival in Lviv, she had been to Frankfurt, Prague, Munich, and Warsaw.

In Lviv she recognized that her memories could not be reconciled with reality. This made her anxious because she knew instinctively that something had gone awry. The tragedy, of course, was that by then, she had lost her cognitive power to comprehend fully what was happening. Lviv betrayed her. Zariche was foreign territory. In the Carpathian Mountains, the vistas looked the same, but the people had not wanted to talk to her or her sister. She was a stranger, an alien in a land she had called her own her entire life. She had no relatives and no friends—as Katia had Mirka—who could have welcomed her back and helped her make the transition.

No wonder she liked Kyiv. She harbored no expectations that the present-day city could shatter. The map she clutched in her hand was a concrete, tangible reminder that she was in Kyiv. Being in Kyiv was, in fact, a dream from her girlhood that was coming true.

With Katia, it was the opposite. She preferred Lviv, where she had connected with Mirka, and talked about stopping there again when she and my mother began their return journey to America. She said that she had to see Mirka's husband, who was helping her with her petition for the restoration of her ownership of the house. I recalled how one day in Lviv, I met Katia and Mirka walking arm in arm toward our hotel. They were chatting and did not notice me at first, so I had time to observe them. Had it not been for the lines on their cheeks, and the silver in their hair, they could have been mistaken for young women enjoying an afternoon stroll in their beloved city. When Katia stayed with Mirka, she was welcomed into the circle of Mirka's friends. Katia had returned, and had reconnected. My mother had not.

When my mother began to succumb to Alzheimer's, I had a bad case of remorse. I couldn't forgive myself for asking her so little, for knowing so little about her inner life, for losing her. It was probably this remorse that had made me suggest that she accompany me to Ukraine. How unfair life was, I thought. At the very moment when her homeland was becoming free, at the moment when she could return and even make a new life for herself there, she lost not only the ability to do so but also the power to understand the changes taking place. Let me explain this in a different way: My mother looked upon her life as a long journey leading her far away from home, on and on, farther and farther. And when the time came to return, when it became possible to do so, she was powerless to make her dream come true. What a rich conclusion to her life she could have had, and what pitiful scraps she ended up with. Sometimes I find it unbearable that she lost her mind precisely when she needed it most to make her happy.

I muse about such things as we wander through Kyiv's museums and churches, buy tickets for the philharmonic and books in the many bookstores in the city. The weather continues to be warm and lovely and the mood of the people is upbeat. The crowds on the streets are smiling and cordial. There are many tourists and foreigners and we blend into the crowds on Khreshchatyk, by the fountain on the Square of Independence, and at the philharmonic.

Euphoria fills the Indian summer air. Ukraine is getting ready for its first-ever democratic election of a president, and Kyiv is leading the way toward independence from Moscow. My mother's dream of visiting a sovereign Kyiv is coming true, and I know that inside her heart she instinctively knows this. That is why she clutches the map. It's tangible proof that she is living her dream.

Lenin's exhortations to workers flutter on buildings even though a construction crane is dismembering his enormous statue on Khreshchatyk. A red-on-white streamer proclaims: "The victory of the proletariat is inevitable." A black-on-white banner says: "Bread is the life of the earth." A third: "Marx's teachings are invincible because they are true." One day, new, multicolored pennants join the old ones. They announce the fiftieth anniversary of the start of the killings at Babi Yar (or Babyn Yar, in Ukrainian), one of the most infamous places of the Holocaust. I take trolleybus number 16 to the Babi Yar park for a memorial ceremony, while Katia and my mother stroll along Khreshchatyk.

Trolleybuses, as the name suggests, are a hybrid of trolleys and buses. Overhead electric cables power them, but instead of running on tracks, trolleybuses ride on tires. A trolleybus is a low-slung, long, often articulated coach with hard seats and several pneumatic doors. Printed above the seats is a notice stating that seats are reserved for old people, invalids, and women with children.

Kyiv trolleybuses offer a microcosm of city life. Kerchiefed babushkas struggle in with plucked hens and farm produce in enormous sacks, while office workers, clasping briefcases and holding their breath, edge their way past. Schoolchildren, clutching books held together by frayed leather belts, congregate in the back, while the occasional young mother with a baby in her arms climbs in at the front, where she is assured a seat, if not through the courtesy of another passenger then on the insistence of the bus driver, who patrols the teeming mass of humanity through an enormous rearview mirror.

The natural way to behave on a trolleybus is to sit or stand stone-faced, an attitude very similar to the one Americans adopt in office-building elevators. Riding is based on the honor system and there are no conductors to collect or punch tickets. Riders purchase tickets from a seller at the stop, then board the bus and punch the tickets themselves at one of several machines on board. However, inspectors appear now and again to check passengers for tickets and whether these have been punched.

I must look foreign and apprehensive because as soon as I sit down (this is the first stop of trolleybus number 16, and the coach is practically empty), a grim, Stalinist-type woman inspector in a blue serge uniform hails me and asks to see my ticket. I fish it out of my pocket.

I notice that many of the passengers boarding number 16 are carrying flowers. As the trolleybus lumbers northward, most of the new passengers also carry bouquets, usually red carnations. Although Communism and Lenin have been thrown into the trash bin of history, as the *International Herald Tribune* will proclaim, the flower of choice remains the blood-red carnation, Lenin's favorite. Half an hour into the trip, the trolleybus smells like an Irish wake.

By then, the crowd is so thick that I have to tuck my legs sideways and under the seat in order not to get my toes stepped on. An old woman, profusely sweating, has pushed her way to the corner where I sit. I get up and offer her my seat. She sinks down gratefully and we exchange smiles.

We travel for a long time. We pass a modern office complex where the centerpiece is a sprawling three-story white, marble-clad building. A high wrought-iron fence with pickets ending in sharp points surrounds it. To the left of the white building, a ten-story building is under construction, while a little beyond it rises a completed building of about eight floors.

"The Higher Party School," someone mumbles and spits through the open window.

We travel farther north. Then the loudspeaker is turned on and the driver booms, "Babi Yar." The trolleybus empties into the Indian summer sunshine.

I wait for the woman to whom I yielded my seat. I fall into step with her and introduce myself. She says her name is Angelina Nikolaevna. I stay at her side as we slowly make our way up the street, following the surging crowds. The buildings yield to cemeteries on the right and on the left. Only later will I discover that we exited the bus at the same spot where the Jews of Kyiv were told to gather. According to historian Nora Levin, about two thousand notices with the following legend were posted in Kyiv:

> All Jews of the city of Kiev and its environs must appear on the corner of Melnikov and Dokhtura Streets (beside the cemetery) at 8 A.M. on September 29, 1941. They must bring with them their documents, money, valuables, warm clothing, etc.
>
> Jews who fail to obey this order and are found elsewhere will be shot. All who enter apartments left by Jews and take their property will be shot.

"My parents are buried here, but not my husband," Angelina Nikolaevna volunteers as we pass the cemeteries. "We were married for such a short time before they took him off to the war. He never came back. On the way back, I'll stop by my parents' graves to tidy up."

Angelina Nikolaevna is in her seventies, born in Kyiv, where she has lived her whole life. She is dressed in the uniform of the babushkas: a black, heavy scarf on her head, a shapeless black coat on her back, and sturdy, ugly shoes on her feet. She has a long nose and a downturned mouth, but her skin is rosy and smooth. Her eyes are clear, blue and young.

"I remember when they started taking the Jews to Babi Yar. I was working out this way then," she says. "There wasn't much out here—fields, cemeteries, and a few enterprises. I worked in a sewing factory as a pattern cutter. We made gloves."

According to Levin, "for two days, September 29–30, 1941, over 33,000 Jews were killed in the ravine Babi Yar—a greater killing rate than that of the gas chambers of Auschwitz at their murderous peak."

Angelina Nikolaevna is continuing her story. "Whenever I heard a commotion on the street, I would run to the window and look out. Several times a day, men, women, children were driven like cattle up the street. It wasn't paved then."

Flowers in front of the Babi Yar monument during the fiftieth-year commemoration. Photograph by Ania Savage.

"Did you know?"

"Yes and no," Angelina Nikolaevna replies. "These people never came back. They went only in one direction—north.

"I had a friend, a Jewess, who lived in the same apartment building as I did. One day when I came home from work, she was gone. They had found her and taken her away. She's up here," and Angelina Nikolaevna gestures to what lies ahead of us. "I can't forget."

"Babi Yar was a gully, wasn't it?" I ask.

"Oh, yes. As I said, this was open country. A wild, uncultivated place. The gully was deep, deep." She runs the back of her hand across her eyes. "You'll see. It's flat now. Flat like the palm of my hand." She extends her hand and turns it palm up to demonstrate. Her palm is large and callused.

Altogether, between sixty thousand and ninety thousand Jews perished at Babi Yar. Later, several thousand Ukrainians and Russians were also shot at the gully. Several thousand young Russian sailors taken as POWs when German armies captured Odessa also died at Babi Yar.

Olena Teliha, a Ukrainian activist and poet, died at Babi Yar on February 21, 1942. She was thirty-five, a pretty woman with dark hair cut into a bob and a Clara Bow mouth. She was arrested by the Gestapo for organizing underground resistance. Although she was tortured, she did not betray her co-conspirators. She was kept in cell number 34 in a jail on Korolenko Street, where she scratched on the wall the Ukrainian trident the night before she was taken to be shot at Babi Yar.

Several days before the anniversary, Kyiv newspapers began writing about Babi Yar. The stories said that corpses of at least one hundred thousand persons filled the gully. I cannot grasp the magnitude of the tragedy because the numbers are so fantastic: the dead at Slavske multiplied fifty times. Perhaps that is why I am on my way to Babi Yar.

Angelina Nikolaevna and I are now walking in silence. I notice her side-glances. Finally she says, "You can get flowers at the monument. Someone's bound to be selling flowers up there. But they'll cost more." She is carrying a bouquet of red carnations.

She falls silent again. I can tell she is thinking about something. "Did you see that program on television last night? The one with the survivor?" she eventually asks.

I say I did. "That's one of the reasons I came."

"The Jewess I was telling you about, she was blond like that survivor. She had blue eyes like mine. That's how we became friends. We both had blue eyes. She could have been saved. I lived alone by then. Both of my parents died in the bombings. I could have taken her in. No problem. I had plenty of room." She sighs again.

The woman who had appeared on morning TV was Raisa Dashkovskaya. She had said, "I never spoke about what had happened. For forty-eight years I lived without my name and my nationality." Her three-year-old son, her sisters, and her parents were shot and killed on September 29, 1941, the first day of the killings. She crawled from under the dead bodies and took refuge with non-Jewish friends. She changed her name from Rebecca to Raisa, and when she eventually remarried, she hid her identity from her husband.

Angelina Nikolaevna has stopped to catch her breath and to wipe her eyes with the back of her hand. Around us, the crowd is slowing down also. There are thousands of people ahead of us, at our sides, behind us. In the distance looms a large monument.

Angelina Nikolaevna says, "The figures on the monument represent the people who died here. There's a woman, a boy, a sailor. I don't remember who else. One hundred thousand innocents," she adds, repeating the published statistic.

We halt because a wall of people blocks the way, all pressing forward toward the monument, where a stage has been erected.

"Go ahead," Angelina Nikolaevna says. "I can't push my way through. And don't forget to get flowers."

We say good-bye and she pats my arm. I will not see her again.

I edge my way forward, see a babushka selling red carnations, and buy a bunch.

Some two hundred or three hundred feet before reaching the base of the monument, the crowd divides to the right and to the left. I reach an enormous catafalque heaped high with bouquets. Some are wrapped in transparent cellophane, which glints and ripples in the breeze and makes a soft swishing sound. As new arrivals approach the median, they add their flowers to those already there. I do likewise. There is a mountain of carnations, gladioli, and chrysanthemums. Thousands upon thousands of bouquets.

I push my way farther to the front until there is no room to move. On my right, a gray-haired man with a yarmulke on his head holds a sepia photograph of a young woman. As the ceremonies begin, he raises the photograph as if to offer it to the heavens. Tears roll down his cheeks into his thinning beard. He weeps through the speeches, the a capella singing, the brief theatrical dialogues by actors representing each group of people killed at Babi Yar. When the ceremonies are over and the crowds begin to disperse, the old man does not move. He gazes at the sepia photograph of the young woman and weeps quietly. The photograph shows that her hair was light, like the hair of the Jewess Angelina Nikolaevna had not saved.

According to Levin, when the Red Army recaptured Kyiv on November 8, 1943, Moscow radio reported that "only one Jew was found alive in Kyiv," a city that had a prewar Jewish population of 140,000. One day, a Jew who survived Babi Yar would seek me out.

Chapter 9

TELEFONNOYE PRAVO AT WORK

My aunt has brought a number of letters from America (since no one in the diaspora trusts the Soviet mail system), and, first in Lviv and now in Kyiv, people have come to the hotel to pick them up after receiving a telephone call from her. Toward the end of the week, a handsome and charming dark-haired man comes to our hotel to get his letter. His name is Oleksander Oleksanderovych and he is wearing a well-made dark blue suit, striped red and navy tie, and blue shirt. His black shoes are polished to a gloss and a large gold watch gleams on his left wrist. He clicks his heels in the best tradition of prewar etiquette, bends over my aunt's extended hand, and plants a light kiss.

Katia is charmed. He repeats the greeting with my mother and me. We also are charmed.

Oleksander Oleksanderovych is solicitous and seems to know everyone. When he hears about the difficulty Katia and my mother are having in obtaining first-class berths on the train for Budapest, he says he can help. When he hears about my difficulties in renting an apartment, he cocks his head and says he has a solution. Would I come with him? He has a taxi waiting outside the hotel. We will first stop at the train *kassa* on Shevchenko Boulevard to settle the matter of the Budapest tickets. It will not take more than a moment. Of course it takes more than a moment—an hour, in fact—but eventually he emerges triumphantly brandishing two tickets in his manicured fingers.

Our next stop will be the ideal place for me to live in Kyiv. It isn't exactly in the center, Oleksander Oleksanderovych says, but it is on the trolleybus line and the accommodations are first-class. In a few minutes, the taxi stops in front of a beautiful white marble building. My mouth falls open. This is the building I admired on my way to Babi Yar. This is the Higher Party School. Oleksander Oleksanderovych sees my expression and hastens to reassure me. "It's not what you think. This is where I have my offices. A new enterprise called the Ukrainian Center for Market and Entrepreneurship has taken over the premises."

Following my return from Babi Yar, I had asked Volodia about the sumptuous white marble building on Melnikova and he told me what he knew, which wasn't much.

"It used to be a school for Communist Party members before they were sent to the West?" I ask Oleksander Oleksanderovych, repeating Volodia's information, although I do not add that Volodia said that this was the place where Soviet spies were "introduced to the living standards common in the West."

For the first and only time that day, Oleksander Oleksanderovych looks pained. "It used to be a school for diplomats," he corrects me.

We climb the broad, white marble steps of Melnikova 36 to the entrance of glass doors. The *dezhurna* greets Oleksander Oleksanderovych by name. A friend of his does not need to check with security. Will I just sign in? We enter a three-story atrium, the walls and floor alternating between cream-colored marble and honey-colored travertine. Far above, clerestory windows flood the atrium with sunshine. The balconies and staircases are edged with gleaming brass handrails. Oleksander Oleksanderovych's office is equally well appointed, large, light with two handsome desks.

He says he must make a phone call. For the first time I witness the so-called *telefonnoye pravo* (the law of the telephone) in action. This law has been one of the pillars of the Soviet system: the higher-up official calls the one below him and issues instructions. The subordinate says *"Da,"* and carries out the order, often by calling the man below him. Such a system ensures no paper trail. The man on the other end of the telephone must have said "Da," because Oleksander Oleksanderovych replaces the telephone receiver with a broad smile.

"I think this is the perfect place for you," he says.

We ride in a carpeted elevator to the second floor and walk down a long hallway on springy red plush carpet. Oleksander Oleksanderovych knocks on a closed door.

A smiling man wearing an Ivy League professor's tweed jacket, complete with elbow patches and an unlit briar pipe in the breast pocket, opens the door. He says, "How do you do?" in English.

He introduces himself as Oleksander Antonovych, a good friend of Oleksander Oleksanderovych. Oleksander Antonovych speaks passable English but has not been to the West and "does not know the ropes."

"That's the right expression?" Oleksander Antonovych inquires with a grin.

The conversation that follows is hardly believable. Oleksander Antonovych says he is delighted I am a professor. He assures me I've come in the nick of time and he considers himself very lucky. He explains that he has been given the task of teaching Western business methods, but he knows so little since he has never been to the West. On the other hand, I, who grew up in the West, must assuredly be an expert. I would do him an enormous favor if I would agree to teach a course here at the center. Of course, I will be paid for my trouble. And, Oleksander Antonovych continues, Oleksander Oleksanderovych had mentioned that I am looking for a place to live. Would I consider looking at a room in the hostel next door? "It's not your Waldorf Astoria," Oleksander Antonovych sums up, "but it's not bad. We have other Americans living here. You won't get lonely for a family." He laughs.

I don't quite know whether he is being serious or if this gush of words is some kind of joke that I don't understand. Before I can respond, Oleksander Antonovych excuses himself to make a phone call. I watch telefonnoye pravo at work again. I even catch the loud, enthusiastic "Da," on the other end of the line. Both Oleksanders escort me to the hostel, more a Motel 6 than the Waldorf. A different dezhurna jumps up, snatches a key from the rack behind her, and leads us upstairs. As we ride in the elevator, I am torn between relief that I may finally have found a place to live and, still not quite believing Oleksander Antonovych, a curious reluctance to see the room in the event that I will be horribly disappointed. I want the elevator to stop, the doors to open, the four of us to walk down the hall to the room, yet at the same time I want to postpone the moment of denouement.

The room is of a decent size, probably about nine feet wide and twelve feet long. It has a balcony that looks into a gully obscured by a tangle of unpruned shrubs and trees. But most important, I will have my own, private bathroom. It is located right inside the room, a cubicle on the left wall. The dezhurna points out, as if on cue, that only eight rooms in the entire hostel have private baths. I smile and nod, but don't bother to turn on the light in the bathroom to examine the fixtures. I can imagine the loose ceramic tile, the toilet without a seat, the shower stall with uneven walls. I will take any private bathroom. I move farther into the room, the two Oleksanders and the dezhurna behind me. The room is furnished simply, but adequately. A narrow bed stands against the wall on the left, while a desk, with a bookcase above it, occupies the right wall. The built-in wardrobe is against the bathroom wall, so it will muffle some of the plumbing noises.

"How much will it cost to rent?" I ask.

"Oh, a mere detail," Oleksander Antonovych assures me. "I'm sure we can work something out to everyone's satisfaction. The important question is 'Do you like it?' Yes? Then it's settled. Here's the key."

He stretches his hand to the dezhurna, who, beaming, places the key in his hand. He transfers the key into my palm. There's nothing like telefonnoye pravo.

Volodia is shocked that I've chosen to move to such disreputable quarters, but I assure him I will be fine. I have become reconciled to the fact that there is someone watching, that I am not simply paranoid. Thus far the watching has been benign, if the disappearance of the plastic bag of exposed film canisters is overlooked. I need a place to live, and the hostel room with its private bath is more than adequate. Also, I am getting homesick and the promise that I will be living in close proximity to several Americans—although I have yet to meet them—cheers me.

I have no idea of how much I will pay in rent, or how much I will be paid for teaching a course at the center. Volodia warns that, for the time being, I should tell no one where I live. "People might misunderstand," he says.

The day of my mother's and Katia's departure has arrived. I take them to the train and we find their seats. They have first-class tickets and a two-berth coupe all to themselves. This will keep them safe, I think, and blink back tears. I don't want them to leave, but I realize that they have to—and need to. We have been traveling for many weeks, and they both are tired.

"These are the very best seats," I say, trying to smile. "And in Lviv, you'll be staying again at the Dnister Hotel and you'll see Mirka."

I bend down and kiss my mother on the cheek. She looks up and there is no smile on her face. She is staring past me and her eyes are unreadable. Katia takes out her handkerchief and blows her nose. I also kiss her on the cheek.

"Then from Lviv you have tickets to Budapest, and from there to Frankfurt, where you'll get the plane," I repeat information that we all know and have gone over several times. "No need to find a taxi like we did with Yan in Przemysl," I say, trying to make a joke.

It falls flat. Mother is still looking out of the window and Katia is dabbing at her eyes with the crumpled handkerchief.

"I'd better be going," I say to my mother. "I'm moving today to my new room and I'll have to make two trips on the trolleybus."

"That's nice," she says and looks out of the window.

I don't think she understands that she is returning to America, while I am staying behind, or that we are parting for a long time. Katia blows her nose again.

"Good-bye," I say and hug them again before I step out into the corridor and close the roomette's door. I take a few steps and then wipe my eyes with the sleeve of my red parka. I had put it on because it is raining. I feel lonely and lost. Who is going to be my guide in the months ahead?

Chapter 10

RUKH AND THE TOPPLING OF LENIN

Newspapers are carrying news that can hardly be believed. They trumpet the end of the Soviet Union and the Soviet system. I find a kiosk that sells the *International Herald Tribune* and marvel at the stories pouring out of Moscow. In Kyiv, in the meantime, it seems that the continuing disintegration of the Soviet Empire is being viewed as an anticlimax to the events of August 23–25.

I go to the headquarters of Rukh, the democratic grassroots organization that elected several national deputies the year before, and meet Irene Jarosewich, a Ukrainian American, not unlike myself, who has returned to work in the public information section of Rukh.

Vivacious and energetic, she tells me that she was at the Verkhovna Rada on August 24, 1991, the day the deputies ratified a resolution declaring Ukrainian independence. Her eyes glow with the memory as she says, "I remember one phrase that preceded the vote. It was uttered during the meeting in the auditorium that was presided over by Stanislav Hurenko, the leader of the Communist Party of Ukraine. He said *'Nam bude bida.'*"

The phrase means "We'll be in trouble." He was saying that Ukrainian Communists would be in trouble if they failed to support independence.

"His words stunned me," Irene continues. "They meant that the Communists were capitulating. I remember the total silence that followed his words. I remember sitting in the back, barely breathing."

On the following day, I make my way to the headquarters of Ukraine's Communist Party, which loom on the hill behind the enormous statue of Lenin being dismantled on Khreshchatyk. The building is unnaturally quiet. I'm drawn to it like a moth to a flame and manage to finagle my way inside, past the guard, a gorilla of a man, a New York City night-

*Dismantling of a statue
of Lenin on Khreshchatyk.
Photograph by Valentyn
Bondarenko.*

club bouncer. In the hushed, dimly lit halls, I walk noiselessly. Every door is closed; many are upholstered in tufted leather (to muffle the cries of brutal interrogations?). I shiver. I listen again, but there are no sounds — no creak of chairs, no staccato of typewriters, no one-sided telephone conversations. The offices are silent, unoccupied. The corridors are empty wherever I go. They are carpeted in runners that are plush and blood-red, soft under my hesitant footfalls. The runners are identical to the red carpeting at Melnikova 36. In one corridor, I come across chairs stacked in untidy heaps. Next to them are desks heaped one on the other. Is someone moving in or out? Where is everyone?

On Khreshchatyk, where Lenin is now losing an arm, now a piece of his flapping overcoat, politics and history dominate the discourse. I find myself joining a group of passersby who have paused to listen to an impassioned orator. Everyone wants to examine the past and understand it. The rising voices carry such an intensity that you must stop and listen. People are publicly articulating their stories for the first time in their lives. As I join the knots of people talking, arguing, listening, I don't get a sense of individuals telling individual stories but of many people telling the same story. The dams of silence are crumbling, as is the statue of Lenin across the street. The hum that rises above the street, above Kyiv itself, is that of newfound voices, of recovered memories, of eagerness

The Square of Independence, Kyiv. Photograph by Viktor Marustschenko.

to search for understanding and to understand. The orators on the Square of Independence are recovering their—and Ukraine's—history.

I understand the urgency the orators must feel when they stand on their soapboxes to deliver their version of the truth. I, too, have felt the compulsion to define myself, to define my and my family's roots, to differentiate my heritage, in the many instances in my life when I said to someone that I was Ukrainian and the person asked me if I meant I was Russian. Even Russians I met who were not xenophobic regarded me not as a foreigner but rather as a prodigal daughter of the *rodina*, the great Russian family, and were puzzled by my insistence on drawing a distinction between them and myself.

I am walking through the metro tube under Khreshchatyk and suddenly I am at a dead halt. People jostle me, some run into me, but I am not budging. I am standing in front of a poster on the tiled wall that is announcing a public meeting of "Ukrainian nationalists" two days hence. I am drawn to that meeting as I was drawn to the headquarters of the Communist Party. Ironically, the meeting is being held kitty-corner to the Communist Party headquarters, in a once-pretty yellow-and-white villa that became the headquarters of the Ukrainian Writers' Union after the October Revolution.

I am drawn to this meeting because of the audacity of its organizers. Even as late as 1990, to say you were a nationalist in Kyiv was to invite scorn. A nationalist, sometimes called a Banderite (i.e., a follower of Stepan Bandera, the principal leader of the Organization of Ukrainian Nationalists), was the ultimate dirty word in the Soviet Union. A nationalist was a fascist, an anti-Semite, the enemy the Soviet Union defeated in the great Patriotic War (World War II).

The night is cold and rainy. The bus is late and my feet get wet as I step into a puddle on the uneven sidewalk. I carry no umbrella and my hair drips rain down my back as I slosh into the Writers' Union building. A woman, who is collecting donations, says the meeting is in the second floor meeting room, then studies me with interest as I climb the once elegant staircase. I see only one other woman in the audience, which numbers perhaps a hundred young men. This woman is big and burly. She reminds me of the distaff side of the Politburo couple we encountered in Slavske. I realize almost immediately that this is not a meeting of the Organization of Ukrainian Nationalists, which was founded in the late 1920s and later organized the UPA into a guerrilla army. The young man who takes the podium delivers a tirade against the "old nationalists," who, he says, sold out to the government. This young man has a closely shaven head and wears army fatigues, including army boots. He is a Ukrainian skinhead. The second speaker raises his fist and slowly clenches it into a vise. "That's what this country needs," he shouts. "It needs an iron fist."

Other young men spring up from their seats and salute him. The salute is suspiciously similar to the Nazi salute.

What am I doing here?

The speaker launches into another tirade, but someone in the back interrupts him. The speaker and the heckler exchange several shouts. The first speaker steps to the podium and invites the heckler to step outside. A broad-shouldered man climbs over chairs and people to get to the door. The speaker resumes his tirade. Suddenly there is a loud grunt outside the meeting room on the staircase landing. It is followed by a thud. The speaker pauses as the scuffle escalates. Someone snarls an epithet; there's another heavy thud. The audience sits transfixed. No one moves. Then the speaker resumes in a louder voice. I get up to go to the door, but a man behind me puts both of his hands on my shoulders and says, "Sit down."

I sit down. During a break, I gather my belongings and go downstairs. "What happened here earlier?" I ask the woman who had been collecting donations.

"A drunk came in and we had to throw him out," she says.

Chapter 11

KYIV STATE UNIVERSITY

Andriy Kulykov looks solemn and somewhat ecclesiastical because of his black, flowing beard, although he says early on in our acquaintance that he is an atheist. His eyes are a startling bright blue. He has a deep, resonant voice that a year later will get him a job with BBC in London. But at the time of our first meeting, that deep voice is at odds with his painful thinness, which is made that much more noticeable by his unusual height. He is well over six feet tall, the tallest man I will meet in Ukraine. I remember Volodia saying that Andriy, the second deputy editor at *News from Ukraine,* has been gravely ill and is only now returning to work.

First impressions turn out to be correct. Andriy is reserved, polite, proud, and stoic. He is too polite to be visibly put off by my Western ways, and, if anything, they amuse him. This first time, he invites me to accompany him to a press conference Lev Lukianenko, the head of the Ukrainian Republican Party, is holding in half an hour. I go eagerly, curious about Ukraine's new breed of politicians. The press conference is in a run-down, dimly lit building off Khreshchatyk. About ten journalists, all male and all looking bored, have gathered.

The press conference has been called to announce Lukianenko's candidacy for the presidency of Ukraine. Lukianenko is an intellectual, a dissident and a lawyer, who spent twenty-seven years in prison and Siberian labor camps for proposing a method by which Ukraine could secede from the Soviet Union through constitutional means. His party stresses national identity as a reason for separatism, a moderate nationalist agenda coupled with the decolonization of the Soviet Empire. He is perceived as a moderate nationalist, but that word *nationalist* remains troubling, and his strongest support is among Western Ukrainians, followed by liberals from central Ukraine.

"I would have thought that his announcement would merit state television coverage," I say.

"You can censor by not covering an event," Andriy says.

Lukianenko makes a sincere but lackluster announcement. His remarks are measured, far from sensational, and his gray walrus mustache bobs up and down. His platform is forthright: Ukraine wants to do it alone. It's time to get rid of Moscow once and for all.

Someone asks a question. Another follows, but without much enthusiasm. Then the room falls silent. I decide to ask a question, because I am curious how Lukianenko plans to present his candidacy in the populous eastern Ukraine, which traditionally has not objected to Russian hegemony.

I am the only woman at the press conference. The men sitting in front turn around to stare. Lukianenko says that, contrary to what the media has published, he enjoys support in the eastern provinces. Soon thereafter, the press conference ends. One of the journalists comes up to me and asks where I am from.

I say, "America."

"Aha," he says and walks away.

Andriy and I converse in Ukrainian, although he is Russian. I have learned by now that Russians born and raised in Ukraine invariably do not know Ukrainian. I ask why he speaks Ukrainian. He says his father was a young recruit in the Red Army during World War II and after the war ended, he married a local girl and settled in Kyiv. Andriy learned Ukrainian from his maternal grandmother, who told him fairy tales in Ukrainian. (I have heard that Gorbachev, who speaks excellent Ukrainian, also learned it while listening to his grandmother's fairy tales.)

"What was the language in your home?"

"Russian."

"Then why . . . ?"

"If you live in a country you should know its language," he says and I look at him with renewed interest.

Andriy married a Ukrainian and the language in his home is Ukrainian. He and Olia send their daughter Nina to a lyceum where instruction is in Ukrainian, not Russian.

Andriy suggests that we stop for a cup of coffee while he fills me in on the journalism faculty at Kyiv State University, where I have an appointment with the dean the following day. I learn that I will be paid not only by *News from Ukraine* but also by Kyiv State University. "I doubt what you will receive in two salaries will match what you earn in one salary in America," Andriy says with a sardonic smile. "You will be paid, of course, in rubles."

I also learn that not everyone at the university was happy to have a Western journalist lecture there. "It took a while; there are many people who like the old ways better," Andriy says.

I ask if that means I will not be able to talk freely in class. He says, "It's just that you're going to be an oddity like you were at the press conference today."

We have reached a café on a side street off Khreshchatyk. No light shines through the grimy window and a padlock hangs on the door. Andriy looks chagrined. "It was open yesterday," he says.

We try another café, but it is out of coffee beans.

"By the way," Andriy asks, "What name will you use in class?"

I have no idea what he means, and say so.

"What was your father's name?" he asks.

"Ivan," I reply.

"Tomorrow, mention to the dean that you would like to be called Anna Ivanovna. That'll make everyone feel better—Ania's just too informal," he adds by way of explanation, "and I don't think you want to be called Comrade Savage."

I discover later that the name Anna Ivanovna wields a double-edged sword. It's the name of Czarina Anna Ivanovna, Russian empress from 1730 to 1740. That's nice, but what Anna did to Ukraine isn't. She reduced Ukraine's autonomy from Moscow even further by forbidding the election of a new *hetman* (commander in chief) of the Dnipro Cossacks. During Anna's reign the Cossacks were divided according to wealth into the privileged "elect Cossacks" and the less fortunate "Cossack helpers." Were my Chubaty ancestors affected by Anna's rule?

Andriy and I have reached a third café. The interior is dark and empty, but a clerk lurks behind the counter. I glance sideways at my companion and see that he is genuinely pleased by the small victory of finding an open café. The clerk pours two tiny cups of coffee and Andriy carries them to a table.

I take an experimental sip, while he watches.

The coffee is thick and bitter, the same Turkish coffee I sampled with Volodia when we went sightseeing. "Sugar?" Andriy asks.

I nod and look around for a sugar bowl.

"By the cashier," he says.

I carry the cup to the counter and ask the clerk for a spoon in order to remove a cube of sugar from a sugar bowl at her elbow.

She points to a chain dangling from the cash register.

I say I don't understand.

"The spoon's at the end of the chain," she says irritably.

I pick up the spoon and examine it. It was washed a long time ago. I let the spoon drop.

"Look at it closely," Andriy says behind me. I pick the spoon up again and study it. A hole has been drilled through the shallow bowl of the utensil.

"Why?" I ask. I do not know whether to laugh or be outraged.

"People steal. A hole makes it less useful, so it may not get stolen."

"But it's already attached to a chain."

"No matter," Andriy says.

Rector (Dean) Anatoly Moskalenko is wearing an embroidered Ukrainian folk shirt under his dark businessman's jacket. He invites me into his office, but instead of sitting at his desk, we sit across from each other at a polished, oblong table. His secretary serves us Turkish coffee in tiny cups stamped with an embroidery pattern that seems to match that on the stand-up collar of his shirt. Every time I turn the conversation to my teaching assignment, he regales me with another story. He used to be a newspaper correspondent in Siberia. He is a stocky, dark-haired man with a deceptively jovial manner but dark keen eyes that miss and reveal nothing. His in-law is Leonid Kravchuk, also a deceptively soft-spoken man, a former Communist, who is the leading contender for the presidency of Ukraine.

Rector Moskalenko speaks to me in Ukrainian but answers his telephone in Russian. When a student comes in for a moment to drop off a packet, the conversation is also in Russian. A month or so later, the media, raising the question of Kravchuk's commitment to Ukrainian, will ask him what language he uses in private conversations. Kravchuk, whose nickname is "the silver fox," because of both his striking mane of silver hair and his political adroitness, will say he uses "the language appropriate for the occasion." Rector Moskalenko must feel the same way. If Moskalenko were ever to run for office, he might be dubbed the "black fox."

"So what do you propose to teach?" he asks at last.

For a moment I think I have misunderstood him. Then it dawns on me that I am here not because someone has decided I have something worthwhile to offer but because at this point in time, having an immigrant Ukrainian lecture in the journalism department is to be on the

Kyiv State University. Photograph by Ania Savage.

cutting edge of reform. I say I want to lecture on the methods used in the West to gather and report news. I say I have brought several textbooks on the development of Western journalism and its theories, and I plan to use them as the basis for my lectures.

"May I have them when you're finished with them?" he asks.

I am in a quandary because Volodia has made the same request and I have promised the textbooks to him.

"Of course," I say.

The interview lasts perhaps half an hour. At our parting, Rector Moskalenko plants a fleeting kiss on my extended hand in the gallant Austro-Hungarian, pre-both-world-wars manner. I blush. He laughs. He escorts me to his secretary's desk and says she will organize a classroom and the students.

I'll be teaching two courses, he says, and again I'm caught off balance. One course, taught in Ukrainian, will have an open enrollment. The second course will be a seminar for handpicked senior students specializing in international media studies. I will conduct that course in English and assignments will be written in English. The Ukrainian course will be in a large upstairs classroom. Moskalenko pauses and considers. "Perhaps that small room next to the office for the seminar. It's available, isn't it?" he asks, pointing toward the hall. The secretary, who has been murmuring her acknowledgment of the instructions while taking notes, stops, raises her head, and objects. She says there are no lightbulbs in the small room. Since the conversation is being conducted in Russian, I think I have misheard. But no, the secretary repeats the word. She is asking Rector Moskalenko where she will get lightbulbs for the room since the class will be held at six in the evening.

Rector Moskalenko ignores her question. He turns to me and says, "By the way, would you please drop off a syllabus tomorrow. Leave it with my deputy."

As I leave, I hear them resume talking about lightbulbs.

The first session of the class in Ukrainian attracts a standing room audience. Fewer students come to the second and third classes, and the attendance settles at about twenty-five students. After the first couple of weeks and several visits by professors who drop in unannounced, I think I have passed scrutiny. Seven students are in the seminar and they attend faithfully. At first, those in the lecture class hesitate to ask questions, while in the seminar, perhaps because the atmosphere is more intimate, discussion flows freely. In both classes we discuss the difference between Western and Soviet newspapers, and I point out that there are only two mass circulation newspapers in the United States that are owned by a political party or a religious group. All others are independent, for-profit enterprises. This fact surprises my students. How can a newspaper not be the organ of a political party?

"American publishers want to sell as many copies of their newspapers as possible and thus they strive to attract the largest possible audience by presenting a variety of viewpoints on their editorial pages," I counter.

Maria, a student who has been listening with a deepening crease between her black eyebrows, speaks up. "But, Anna Ivanovna, we learn that, by definition, newspapers are political organs."

"Not in the United States," I say. "Newspapers in the West are written and edited to appeal to the widest possible audience. Newspapers and TV shows are treated like products—not organs of ideology."

The students are astounded.

"But a newspaper must have an ideology," Evgeniy, the Afghanistan war veteran, insists.

"In theory, and to a large extent in practice, news stories, which comprise the bulk of articles in a newspaper, are written without the reporter's opinion. Comment is reserved for special pages called editorial pages."

I pull out my notes and say, "Mark Twain and Jack London are two

American authors most of you have read. This is how Mark Twain described American newspapers: 'A newspaper is a nation talking to itself.' An American newspaper has many voices."

"Preposterous," Evgeniy says. "People need to be told what's right and what's wrong."

This becomes an ongoing argument in class. I say in one class, "In America I teach that there are three fundamental canons in American journalism, and reporters who violate them flagrantly lose their jobs: accuracy in reporting facts, fairness in presenting facts, and balance in presenting various opinions about the facts."

"Preposterous," Evgeniy snorts.

Eventually, reports of our discussions reach the dean's office. Viktor Y. Myronchenko, the deputy dean of the journalism faculty, summons me. He asks how the class is progressing.

I say, "Fine."

He suggests that I discuss in class how "American newspapers build a national consensus" and how "we can adopt your techniques here."

I am beginning to see why I have been summoned. Mustering my American journalist persona, I say: "That's not the job of a free press. The job of a free press is to serve as a conduit of information, information of all kinds and of all persuasions."

He looks at me in disappointment. I leave him puzzled and dissatisfied.

Back in class, Evgeniy shakes his head and insists, "Anna Ivanovna, *nyet. Nyet.* People are too stupid to make up their own minds. A journalist must sift through the information and tell the reader what the truth is."

When I point out that this approach does not differ much from the former practice of printing what the Communist Party said was the truth, Evgeniy decries my "naïve trust" in human nature.

One day I ask how many of the students work on newspapers after school. Nearly all raise their hands. I ask whether they have ever been offered "a gift" in return for writing a favorable article.

"It happens all the time," says Ivan, who works at an evening newspaper in Kyiv.

"What are you offered?"

"Not much. Sometimes something that is scarce in the stores. What I really want is a cassette recorder, but no one has offered me one yet."

Others are nodding in agreement.

"Would you take it?" I ask the class.

"Yes," they answer in a chorus.

"But wouldn't you be compromising your integrity as journalists?"

Evgeniy speaks up, "Anna Ivanovna," he says, "you are very naïve. Accepting gifts is part of life."

A professor who is considered progressive in his teaching methods and his outlook asks me to lecture before his journalism class. This is a large introductory class and the students sit tightly packed and facing the front along one side of long narrow tables. Instead of standing at the podium in the front of the room, I decide to walk in the center aisle between the narrow tables that serve as desks.

The students stare at me in confusion and I return to the podium. I lecture on Western media practices, then ask for questions.

There is a long, uncomfortable silence. Finally, the professor clears his throat. "Anna Ivanovna, we are not used to taking such liberties with professors," he says.

I consult Volodia and Andriy. I am apparently creating a minor scandal by asking students to comment and argue in class.

"You must understand," Volodia instructs, "that the system we have today has its roots in the Russian Empire. To believe otherwise is an illusion. Russian education has always been rigidly structured. The teacher was the lecturer; the students had to be obedient. You are advocating a revolution in the classroom." Volodia smiles, sips his Turkish coffee, and adds, "I'll tell you an anecdote I heard long ago when I approached one of my teachers with an idea on how to change a lesson.

"Alexander I came to a lyceum where Pushkin and others were studying. He asked to see the good students. Pushkin was brought forth, but was waved away after answering a question in a way that could have been construed as brash. Alexander I pointed at a student who was standing at attention and who had said nothing. The czar said, 'This is the kind I want. This is a real Russian student.'"

Knowledge, Volodia says, is the ability to regurgitate lessons learned from the textbook. The opportunity for creative input from both teachers and students is minimal.

"This is how it was under the czars and this is how it was under Communism," he says. "The only thing that changed was the picture on the wall. Instead of the czar's we had Lenin's."

The material poverty of the university is startling. The two principal classroom buildings, one with a red façade and the other with a yellow façade, look imposing on the exterior but are poorly lit, poorly furnished, and indifferently kept on the interior. The lightbulbs in the ceiling fixture in the classroom where I lecture in Ukrainian have burned out. Although I notice this at once, I don't report the need for new lightbulbs because I assume they will be changed soon by a janitor. Also, since it is early October, the lack of electric light is a minor inconvenience; but in the second half of the month, as the days grow noticeably shorter, it begins to be a nuisance. By five in the afternoon, it is twilight outside and dark inside. I go down to the dean's office to ask for new lightbulbs. Another week passes, but nothing happens.

Because the seminar class begins at six, the light fixture in that room has been supplied with a solitary lightbulb. But one day, the light switch does not work. One of the students props the door open so that the hall light illuminates the room's interior and we see that someone has unscrewed the lightbulb from the fixture. We bring our chairs out into the hall and begin the class. The next day, I arrive early and wait until Rector Moskalenko comes out into the outer office. I tell him about the absence of electric light in both classrooms. The next day both classrooms have lightbulbs, but I am told to get a guard to unlock and lock the seminar room door before and after each class because the light fixture is on the wall and can be easily reached.

The lecture class has a blackboard but no chalk or eraser. I bring my own chalk to class and I am given a rag with which to wipe the board. One or another of the female students, but never a male student, offers to go to the bathroom to wet the rag so that the board can be erased. The water from the rag sometimes drips into my sleeve as I move the rag across the blackboard. Desks are very old and dark and some of the seats are broken. There are few typewriters and no computers in any of the offices in the journalism department that I visit.

One day one of my students, who has just been hired as a reporter by one of the daily newspapers, stops me in the hall. Maxym is grinning ear to ear. I ask him why he is so pleased.

"I love American journalism. I love advertisements," he says.

His editor had sent him to report on Western firms exhibiting at an electronics trade fair. Not only did Maxym get an exclusive interview with one of the biggest exhibitors, he also sold the exhibitor advertising space in the newspaper.

"Isn't that against the journalistic ethics of your newspaper?" I ask.

"Oh, no," Maxym says. "My editor said that if I sold an advertisement, I would get a ten percent commission."

I look for Maxym's story in the newspaper. When it appears, it contains a sentence referring the reader to an ad the firm has placed on the back page. If he was paid his commission, as I assume he was, then Maxym has enough money to buy the tape recorder he and the other students so covet.

Chapter 12

THE MEAGER CIRCUMSTANCES
OF THE PRESS

The headquarters of the Ukraina Society are in a handsome building that was once a private residence. The building is on a side street between the Golden Gate, a remnant of the fortifications built by Yaroslav the Wise in the eleventh century, and St. Sophia's, which was also built by Yaroslav and contains some of the earliest Christian frescoes.

The offices of *News from Ukraine* are clear across town from the association's headquarters, but like the association's, they also occupy what was once a private residence and are on a dead-end side street. The building is about halfway between Melnikova 36 and the city center on the number 16 trolleybus line.

News from Ukraine is a weekly newspaper published in English for export to the West. My job is to read and edit articles so that they are grammatically and stylistically correct. About half of the articles are prepared by the newspaper's staff of reporters and editors, while the remainder are written by freelancers or stringers or are clipped from the myriad of newspapers available in Kyiv and included, with attribution, in a "digest." There are no wire services similar to those in the West, supplying information by teletype or by computer. With the exception of Andriy, who writes in English, everyone else writes in Russian, sometimes in Ukrainian. Four or five translators who occupy the largest room on the second floor translate articles. I see the articles after they are translated. To facilitate the smooth movement of stories from translators to a final copyedit, I am given a desk next door to the translators. Except for Volodia, no one on the staff has ever been to the United States and the use of American idiom, which for some reason is preferred to British English (perhaps because most of the staff watches CNN?), is sometimes far-fetched. My corrections are scrutinized and often the translator who has worked on the article will come in to have a phrase explained. After I use the word *chocoholic* in a feature story, all the translators crowd around my desk as I explain that this is a relatively new idiom, combining "chocolate" and "alcohol" to describe someone addicted to that sweet. The matter goes all the way up to Volodia, who tells me the translators are wary of using a word that does not appear in any of their dictionaries.

All of the translators are men. All of the editors are men. All the reporters are men, although there is a young woman who is an intern and helps in the coverage of the Parliament. Volodia's secretary is a woman. There are no computers. The two best typewriters, both manual, are in the anteroom outside Volodia's office on the third floor. Andriy's office is down the hall from Volodia's. The only bathroom in the building that I find is on the third floor. The sole photographer's studio and lab are on the first floor behind a glass-walled cubicle occupied by a *dezhurna* or *dezhurnyi,* a female or male guard, who won't let you climb up the stairs without checking your ID. I usually come in about eight in the morning and work until one o'clock in the afternoon, when I go back to Melnikova 36 for the big meal served at midday. I return in the afternoon and work until it is time to go to the university. On slow days, I spend an hour or so in midafternoon drinking Turkish coffee with Volodia and talking journalism and politics.

Andriy obtains press credentials that enable me to attend sessions of Parliament whenever I hear something interesting is planned. Some years back, I was accredited to the New Jersey State Legislature and have reported on the New York legislative assembly's sessions in Albany as well, so I think I am on familiar ground. I soon realize that the Ukrainian Parliament is a different animal. The proceedings are significantly less decorous than those I am used to, although I do not witness a deputy punch another in the nose, as would happen in the Russian Duma in Moscow. Speakers seek recognition by the chair but are often booed, interrupted, and subjected to catcalls. There are two main blocs: the reformers, led by Rukh, and the conservatives, led by the Socialist Party. The socialists took up the banner of the Communist Party when it was outlawed following the failed August coup. Within each bloc are numerous smaller parties and factions that cannot always be depended on since each has its own agenda.

I also write political stories, about one every two weeks, on the upcoming election, or sometimes a feature story on something that strikes my fancy. One of these features describes the national convention of the Socialist Party, which I attend. The delegates are square-shouldered, grim-faced men and women who debate motions, but the votes are invariably unanimous. Whenever Mikhail Gorbachev's name is mentioned, some one shouts "Shame!" and then the delegates pick up the word and chant it. A bust of Lenin dominates the stage and blood-red carnations lie scattered at its base. It seems as if we were back in the 1970s, or even earlier.

I meet Oleksander Moroz, Parliament deputy, outspoken Communist, and organizer and head of the newly formed Socialist Party. He is one of the most skillful politicians I have ever observed firsthand. He runs the convention with an iron fist sheathed in a velvet glove. I have the opportunity to speak to him during an intermission and come away marveling at his virtuosity in doublespeak. His pale eyes are round and sincere as he asserts that he himself is in the forefront of modernization, yet he cannot fathom why the Communist Party is in disgrace since the Soviet Union, nay, the entire world, has benefited from the socialist ideal.

"He may very well be Ukraine's next president, after Kravchuk," Andriy predicts, as I protest that Moroz has picked a losing cause. Within three years, Moroz will become the president of the Ukrainian Parliament, a respected politician and statesman. He is often mentioned as the strongest "conservative" candidate in the 1999 presidential election, although in 1995 he will yield to Leonid Kuchma, who succeeds Leonid Kravchuk.

News from Ukraine has fewer resources for news gathering than any newspaper I have ever been associated with, yet its offices and equipment are first-rate when compared to the miserable conditions at *Donetskii Vechir (Donetske Evening News),* which I visit in November. *Donetskii Vechir* is one of the largest newspapers in the heavily industrialized, populous Donetske region of Eastern Ukraine, where more than a million people live. Although a daily, the newspaper has no wire services from which it can draw timely news stories from outside its immediate area. Two or three reporters crammed into tiny offices share one telephone.

Valeriy Gerlanec, a black-haired man with the soulful eyes of a basset hound, is the cultural reporter. He says he writes his articles in longhand because there is only one ancient typewriter in the department and the department secretary has first claim on it. He says the lead time for a story is a minimum of twenty-four hours because the newspaper uses hot type to set print. The newspaper has one photographer, who has a single camera.

At both *Donetskii Vechir* and *News from Ukraine,* stories are duplicated with carbons because neither newspaper owns a photocopying machine. Even if *News from Ukraine* were to get one, the perpetual paper shortage would keep the machine idle, Volodia points out. The paper shortage, which began when the Baltic states and their paper mills left the Soviet Union, has never been solved. There is also a shortage of typewriter ribbons, and to prevent theft, some reporters remove their ribbons once they are finished typing their stories.

You cannot leave a ballpoint pen lying around anywhere. It disappears instantly. I had brought a box of Bic ballpoints. By the second month, every single pen was gone. I ask Andriy why the petty thievery.

His answer, as always, is laconic. "Have you tried one of our ballpoints?"

"No," I say.

The next time I am editing at *News from Ukraine,* he presents me with a locally made pen. The pen runs out of ink before the week is out.

Because electronic news gathering, writing, and printing are still in the future, and because government subsidies of newsprint and publishing have disappeared, newspapers, including the big ones in Moscow, are not usually on the forefront of reporting news. That role has been mostly usurped by television, especially the evening news program *Vremya,* and to some degree by radio. Both media continue to be subsidized by the government. Newspapers fall back on the role of analysis and comment and experimentation. For a while, a tabloid called *Koza (Goat)* appears in Kyiv. It publishes muckraking stories full of moral indignation. One concerns the explosive growth of prostitution. Yet this story loses much of its journalistic punch because of the accompanying photos, including one of a stark-naked woman lounging on a narrow bed, a latter-day odalisque. I go out of my way to find *Koza* at the newsstands since it sells out quickly. Neither Volodia nor Andriy can fathom my interest in *Koza* since the concept of muckraking is utterly foreign to them.

When our conversation turns to politics, the usually mild-mannered Volodia becomes a tiger. "You expect us instantly to be a nation?" he demands when I complain that the Ukrainian Parliament wastes its time on points of order and bickering instead of tackling the myriad of problems facing the country.

"Where were we to learn how to govern?" he asks. "We've been 'the little brother' since before the time of Peter the Great."

Yet, Volodia's life is politics. He writes a weekly column of political analysis. His radio is always tuned to a live broadcast of the proceedings of the Parliament. At his home, his Hitachi television set, which he purchased in New York the year before, is on whenever I visit. If it isn't tuned to CNN, it is on channel 1 so that he won't miss the *Vremya* broadcast from Moscow.

Andriy also writes about politics, including commentaries on the Parliament, although he himself was a candidate for the parliamentary seat from his district. Neither he nor Volodia sees any conflict of interest in a journalist running for political office and also writing about that office. But that is the norm. The owner of *Vechirnii Kyiv*, the afternoon daily, is a Parliament deputy, and Vyacheslav Chornovil, the head of Rukh, started his career as a journalist before becoming a dissident, a politician, and a presidential candidate.

Volodia invites me to his home regularly to talk politics while his wife Alla cooks and serves meals that can easily feed four or six people. They live in a tiny flat on the Left Bank on a street called "The Street of Enthusiasts." Volodia and Alla have to take a bus, the metro, and a second bus to get to work on the Right Bank. Alla also works as an editor.

A pink neon slogan pulsates at night from the roof of the bloc of apartments in which they live. The slogan exhorts the enthusiasts to work harder.

The first time I visit, I cannot find their flat. I have learned from other visits to other apartment blocs to bring a pencil flashlight with which to read apartment numbers. More often than not, the hallways are in semi-darkness because of the lightbulb shortage. If a lightbulb is replaced in the morning, it is gone by the next morning, if not sooner, Volodia says.

The evening of my first visit, I cannot find the right building, let alone the right apartment, because lightbulbs are missing from the light posts outside the buildings, too. Although my Russian has improved dramatically, I speak a slow, accented Russian. In a strange place, especially at night, I am reluctant to ask directions. I do not want to reveal that a foreigner is looking for a Ukrainian editor. I arrive half an hour late. Volodia is so relieved at my appearance that he fails to introduce me to Alla, who has come out of the kitchen.

Alla is blond and her virtuosity as a cook is a source of pride for Volodia and wonderful culinary surprises for a guest. She is Russian, but she was born and raised in Georgia. She prepares spicy Georgian dishes pungent with herbs and laced with nuts and dried fruit. Volodia and Alla converse in Russian, but when I am there, they talk in a mixture of Ukrainian and Russian. Alla invariably sets the table with more food than the three of us can possibly eat. In fact, Volodia and I eat and talk politics while Alla picks at her food and jumps up to replenish a plate as soon as we make inroads into it. She tells me that in Georgia, women do not eat with the men when there are guests, even female guests.

As the conversation on what the country needs heats up, Volodia's mustache quivers with indignation. "We became a nation without possessing the elementary things that distinguish a nation," he says, leaving his fork stranded in the air. "Borders? They were Soviet borders until a little while ago. Army? We spent precious time trying to convince the officers to exchange the red star for the trident. Banking? We don't even have a decent currency." At this juncture, Volodia flushes in consternation. "Our money looks like the play money you use in your game Monopoly."

Over Turkish coffee, which he—not Alla—prepares with the skill of a connoisseur, he adds: "What can you expect if you have a Parliament that's composed of poets and dissidents? Where were they supposed to have learned how to rule?"

Then Alla says, "Under Stalin you would have been shot for talking like this. Under Brezhnev you would have gone to jail. There's been progress."

The day after elections, I will visit the editor of one of Kyiv's important newspapers, *Demokratychna Ukraina (Democratic Ukraine),* to see first-hand the compiling of election stories. Since the election is on a Sunday and no one works or publishes on Sundays, I know the stories will be prepared on Monday for a Tuesday, or even a Wednesday, publication. The managing editor has a problem. There are no photographs available to illustrate the election results. He asks the editor in chief if it's all right to use the graphic he is holding in his hand. The drawing shows a young man and a young woman in three-quarter profile. Their chests are thrust forward, their heads are held high, veritable Mount Rushmores. Between the figures and slightly behind them hovers a portrait of a benevolent, bearded Taras Shevchenko, the bard of Ukraine and a national hero.

"Yes, that will do fine," the editor says and resumes our conversation, not about journalism and the election but about the shortage and expense of newsprint, the disappearance of government subsidies, the need for advertisements to offset costs. "They tell me, 'You're now independent. Find your own way to pay the bills,'" the editor complains.

When the issue comes out, Volodia fumes. "You know what they did?"

he asks, jabbing at the graphic of the two young people. "They removed Lenin and pasted in Shevchenko. And you tell me things are changing? I guarantee they've kept a copy of the original, just in case."

I read Ukrainian and Russian newspapers voraciously. Stopping at a newspaper kiosk is like being in a candy store. There are so many publications to sample. Unlike American cities, which have one or two daily newspapers and perhaps two or three weeklies, Kyiv has a half-dozen newspapers that appear regularly, plus there are the Russian newspapers and several monthlies to choose from. One day I see a newspaper I have not seen before, a Lviv-based weekly called *Poklyk Sumlinia (Dictate of Conscience)*. On the front page are photographs of an open mass grave containing three skeletons and a close-up of a skull. The headline says "Slavske." The report is not a news article but a letter to the editor signed by Andriy Farion, a member of the education section of Memorial. Formed during glasnost, Memorial has the mission of safeguarding and reviving Ukrainian history as well as uncovering and reporting crimes perpetrated during the Soviet regime. At first, the two-year-old *Poklyk Sumlinia* was printed in the Baltic states and smuggled into Ukraine to avoid being confiscated. Now it is published freely and mailed to subscribers. A subscription box gives yearly and six-month rates.

Farion writes that he requested Slavske's town council to furnish a bulldozer to assist in the excavations of the roadside ditch. The machinery was promised but never provided. He mentions a handful of names of local residents who helped with the excavations, adding that many people feared that opening the mass grave would bring on an outbreak of infectious diseases such as cholera and typhus. Other people, especially visitors, who, he says, constitute 70 percent of the day-to-day population, do not care one way or the other. He does not mention Irena Sen or the two men who accompanied her or the two young gravediggers.

Reading the letter a second time, I realize that we were in Slavske about two weeks into the digging, which, according to Farion, had been under way for more than a month at the time he wrote the letter. He says that twenty-five skeletons have been recovered, including one of an adolescent boy and one of a woman. The woman had had a door hinge nailed to her breastbone.

Chapter 13

THE UKRAINIZATION OF A
UKRAINIAN AMERICAN

It takes me some weeks to shed my American self outwardly. The change occurs on several levels. I am determined to become self-sufficient. This means I will not be defeated by the food lines, the overcrowding in the trolleybuses, and the differences between the language I speak and the one spoken on the streets of Kyiv. I acquire a vocabulary of Ukraino-Russian words that are not in use among emigrants of the diaspora in the West. For example, the Ukrainian word for store is *sklep* or *kramnycia,* the first a borrowing from Polish. I consciously drop *sklep* from my vocabulary because no one in Kyiv uses that word. I acquire *magazin,* the Russian word in general use.

The language has its entertainments. It's spawning expressions to meet the changing times. I tune in on the word *biznisman,* which means many things, from entrepreneur to capitalist to shyster. It is usually said with a mild disparagement in the voice, followed by a deprecating shrug. I focus on Volodia's use of the word *bukval'no,* which literally means "by the book." He uses it to underscore the exactness or veracity of a statement or claim. I next realize that *bukval'no* is used in Ukraine as we use "you know" in America. It's slang. I try using it but am not able to carry it off, as I still cannot carry off some American slang, such as the phrase "go it alone."

This examination of slang reminds me of how I learned English. English was my third language. I had already spent first, second, and third grades in a German elementary school where the nuns whacked you with a thick ruler for any, and all, infractions or lessons not well learned. The nuns at the Catholic parochial school where my parents enrolled me after we arrived in the United States used a laissez-faire approach. They put me back in first grade and waited. As soon as the teacher nun felt I had mastered enough of "See Jane run," I was advanced to the next class, until I reached the grade that corresponded to my age. Since my parents spoke even less English than I did and since I had no friends and was too shy to ask a nun to explain a phrase, it took several years before I comprehended two American slogans of the 1950s. The first one concerned Morton's salt. I still remember puzzling over a poster of a little girl carrying an umbrella and a box of Morton's salt. The poster shows that the box is open and the salt is pouring out. The slogan read "When it rains, it pours." I had no idea what that meant, since I thought the phrase referred to the rain and not to the salt. The other slogan was "You auto buy now." It took me some time to comprehend that the message was urging a consumer to buy a Ford or a Chevy.

Just as I asked my mother in the 1950s to cut off my braids so that I would not look different from my American classmates, in the 1990s in Ukraine I consciously begin to dress like local women. I stop wearing my red parka and the pearl earrings I brought for evenings out. Both invariably attract attention on the trolleybus or in the metro. I seldom wear jeans and I have replaced my leather walking shoes with a pair of Soviet bloc–made, plasticized shoes from Bulgaria. I wear my new Reeboks when it rains and pretty soon they become scuffed and old look-ing. Because of the absence of dry cleaners, washing machines, and good detergent, my clothing acquires that slightly grimy look that character-izes everyone else's clothing. I buy a handmade sweater in a sedate shade of olive green at the weekend flea market. And as winter approaches, I invest in a *shapka,* a fur hat.

I congratulate myself the first time a passerby stops me on Khresh-chatyk and asks for directions. I become indignant when a Russian woman takes me for an ignorant peasant fresh from the countryside and pushes herself into the queue ahead of me.

It happens when I am killing time at the trolleybus stop. I missed the trolleybus by seconds and know that another one is not due for fifteen minutes. On a nearby street corner, a farmer has set up a makeshift stand and is hawking tomatoes. I eye the queue mistrustfully, but count only a dozen people. I cross the street and get in line. Minutes pass. I stand in line, torn by doubts. On the one hand, what will I do with a bag of tomatoes? I have no refrigerator to prevent them from overripening and rotting. On the other hand, I've already invested five minutes. Why let those minutes go to waste? I crane my neck to see what is going on. I soon realize that several people ahead of me are stand-ins; that is, they are holding a place—not for one but for several people shopping at other nearby stands. Three spots ahead of me, a balding, hawk-faced man is a stand-in for two other men who are in the vodka line down the street. They exchange shouts now and again.

More minutes tick by. The hawk-faced man and one of his friends who has switched lines are about finished buying tomatoes. It is almost my turn. Just as I am about to place my order, a henna-haired woman with a pug nose, big lips, and dangling earrings steps in front of me and places an order for two kilos. "It's my turn," I say in Ukrainian. She is worming her way in without queuing, an unforgivable crime. Yet no one behind me is protesting, no one is standing up for my rights as a member of the queue.

She acknowledges my protestation by sticking her right elbow into my chest, while with her left hand she extends a wad of money to the farmer.

"It's my turn," I insist, but to no avail. The farmer is taking her order. Unconsciously I sense that I am particularly vulnerable because of my limited experience with queues. I summon my Russian. "It's my turn." I yell at her in Russian. She looks right through me. She raises her string *sumka* and the farmer dutifully pours the tomatoes into it.

Behind me the line quivers like a serpent as people crane their necks to see what is going on. Across the street, my trolleybus has arrived and is unloading its passengers. It will begin loading and leave in moments. The farmer stares at me in amazement when I ask for three tomatoes. At the last moment, when the hennaed woman leaves, triumphantly carrying her two kilos of tomatoes, I realize that the farmer is not providing bags and I have no receptacle except my purse. As I trot toward the trolleybus, I hear the farmer's admonition behind me: "Speak Russian in town."

I also learn to walk like a local.

"The problem is that we shuffle our feet and you don't," one of the female students tells me. "When you walk into the classroom, you don't act like a woman. You stride in, swinging your arms." She is tactful enough to stop short of saying that my stride is unladylike.

There are other things I learn by trial and error. I am invited to people's homes almost every weekend, and I realize after two such invitations that I must go on an empty stomach. Whatever time of day it might be, the kitchen or dining room table will be set with food. From shopping occasionally in the stores on Khreshchatyk or at the Bessarabian produce market, I know that these "impromptu" meals have taken a great

A queue for vodka in Kyiv. Photograph by Valentyn Bondarenko.

deal of time to assemble. To express my gratitude, I bring gifts. I stop at Kashtan, the hard-currency store, to buy whiskey or wine or Swiss chocolates or sometimes imported fruit, items my host and hostess cannot readily afford.

A Georgian proverb says: "Cooks never die of starvation," and nowhere does it seem more applicable than at the buffets and dining halls at Melnikova 36. The women who work there are hefty, with big, hamlike arms and wide, solid bodies.

The buffets are akin to luncheonettes, but instead of sitting down at a counter or in a booth, customers stand at elevated, chest-high, round bistrolike tables. There are three such buffets, one each on the second and third floors in the white marble classroom and office building and one on the ground floor of the eight-story hostel. The clerks in the luncheonettes are not only large; they are also friendly. Only the waitress in the dining room is skinny, but she is mean.

If I come alone to eat, she ignores me until she has taken orders from all the male diners in the room, whether they arrived before or after me. If I eat with Oleksander Antonovych, she takes his order first, and after a pause, she turns her hostile eyes on me, as if she has just noticed my presence. I gather she does not trust or like foreigners, especially capitalist American women who should be home raising a family. Once, I try to give her a tip, but she smirks in my face. I pocket the ruble.

I try to make friends with the diners to make eating a more congenial experience. My overtures do not work at all. The men—and the clientele consists mostly of men—want to eat by themselves and talk business. The women come in tight groups that leave no room for outsiders.

It is a curious arrangement, this dining room. A long table against the right wall, which is the wall nearest the kitchen, is set with tiny plates on which lie two or three different zakuski and some not-too-clean tumblers filled with two or three varieties of beverages. You can select one zakuska plate but two beverages.

The zakuski are invariably either coleslaw made from sauerkraut or shredded pickled beets topped with a sliver of herring. The beverages are unusual. A yellowish liquid, which looks like a combination of weak tea and watered-down orange juice, turns out to be the juice from stewed dried fruits. As the week progresses, the fruit juice grows paler and paler. I learn that the dried fruits are restewed each morning. Sometimes a plump raisin floats in a glass, but this happens only at the beginning of the week.

The clear liquid that appears occasionally is birch juice. I am told it is made from birch bark. It tastes sweet and medicinal. The third beverage is not a beverage in the true sense of the word. It is called *kefir* and is semiliquid yogurt that is drunk instead of eaten with a spoon. It is very sour and leaves a fat mustache on your upper lip. If I want to drink water, I have to bring a bottle of it with me and ask the waitress for a glass. She will sometimes bring me one, and sometimes she will ignore my request.

Occasionally, there is soup. If it is borscht, I order it. It is served with a dollop of sour cream. I always ask that the sour cream be omitted, but without fail the borscht arrives with the cream spreading a white circle that changes the color of the soup from red to pink. The other soup is a pale, anemic broth, suspiciously similar to the fish soup we were served in Slavske. In the three months I live at Melnikova 36, I never try it. The main course alternates between meat-stuffed dumplings *(pelmeni)* and "mystery meat." The origin of the meat is the subject of lively discussions at several tables at each meal.

Napkins are occasionally available at the tables. Sometimes the knives disappear for a day or two. When this happens, I order the pelmeni. A stack of sliced bread is available at each table, as is butter. When she tallies the bill, the waitress invariably knows how many slices of bread you have eaten and how many pats of butter you have used and charges you accordingly.

The best thing about the meal is its price. It costs about a dime.

Melnikova 36 continues to be subsidized by the government. I learn that the same wholesaler who supplies the dining room at the Parliament also supplies Melnikova 36. After all, this used to be the Higher Party School.

The meal I am describing is called *obeyd,* which means dinner, although it is served in the middle of the day. If I happen to miss it, that's that. No evening meal is available. I begin to rely on the luncheonettes, which carry excellent ham and sausages as well as a variety of sweet breads. The problem is that the luncheonettes keep erratic hours. Besides, if I happen to arrive late, most of the food is gone.

I am losing weight rapidly. The luncheonette ladies notice. Nina, a round-faced stocky woman, takes pity on me. She and I became friends earlier. Nina once stopped at the table where I was gulping down an open-faced sandwich and casually asked if I ever visited the Kashtan stores where purchases can only be made with Western currency. I said I occasionally shopped at Kashtan. She said she had a daughter whose birthday was coming up and she wanted to get her a pair of Western stockings. I said, "No problem." The next day, I motioned to Nina. When she came to my table, I started to pull out the Hanes pantyhose I had brought with me, but she grabbed me by the elbow and pulled me to a dark corner of the luncheonette. Only then did she accept the package, and I watched her hide it under her apron. She wanted to pay, but I shook my head. Since then, Nina has saved packages of food for me, which I pick up after I return in the evening from the university.

Nina intrigues me. She is very unattractive. She has no husband, but she is not a widow. Her daughter has a child but also no husband. I surmise that Nina is about sixty. I ask her where she grew up. She says "in Western Ukraine." I ask how her family lived through the war and she turns pale.

"They took me to Germany," she whispers into my ear. "I was barely old enough."

"How did you get back?" I cry, knowing that most of those who were deported by the Nazis to work in wartime factories chose to stay in the West. Those who returned were arrested and often sent to Siberia. Stalin decreed that these people "had seen the West and had been contaminated."

"Shh!" Nina whispers ferociously. "Don't ask. I don't talk about such things."

I never learn the rest of her story.

Oleksander Antonovych loses his cool only twice.

One morning around seven, fierce banging on the door wakes me up. I run to open it, expecting that a transatlantic phone call I had ordered the night before has finally been patched through. I open the door and Oleksander Antonovych strides in. His face is flushed.

Would I please get dressed immediately, he says. His boss wants to see me at eight sharp. He, Oleksander Antonovych, will be back five minutes before the appointed hour to escort me. As I dress, I worry. I have been living at Melnikova 36 for more than a month and have not been asked either to pay for lodging or give a lecture or teach a class. When I ask, Oleksander Antonovych says a "new module" will begin soon and I will have my hands full.

He returns precisely at five minutes to eight and escorts me into the marble office building. He is formal and nervous. After waiting a few minutes, I am ushered into the huge, beautifully furnished office of Vladimir P. Cherevan, the director of the Ukrainian Center for Market and Entrepreneurship. He is a short, intense, dark-haired man. After we are introduced, he says he is an economist by training. We converse in Russian because he says he has not had the time to learn Ukrainian, although his mother is Ukrainian.

"How do you like living in the hostel?" he asks.

"I like it very much," I say. "It's convenient to work and it also gives me privacy."

He considers me for a moment, then says, "A new module is about to begin. I don't know if Oleksander Antonovych has mentioned this to you, but our program has been very successful. We have received many more applications than we can accept."

Oh, dear. So, Oleksander Antonovych was telling the truth. I ask who the applicants are as my mind works furiously on what to do next. Cherevan says the applications are coming from managers of collective farms, the kolkhozes, who want to learn the basics of goods production and distribution in a market economy. He pauses for emphasis, then adds, satisfaction and pride discernible in his voice, "Seventeen thousand people have applied. Of course, we can accommodate only eight hundred in several two-week modules."

I'm both impressed and disheartened as I realize that by tomorrow I might be out on my ear in the middle of Melnikova.

"I would like to stay," I say, "but I understand your situation. Oleksander Antonovych suggested that I teach a class in Western business methods when the new term begins."

Cherevan begins to say something, then changes his mind. He picks up a copy of *Izvestia* lying on the polished cherry table where he is conducting the interview. He points to a story that says the United States is promising aid to the newly independent republics of the Soviet Union.

"Food? Grain?" Cherevan says, his voice contemptuous. "We will survive without them. Remember, you can send food forever and nothing new will happen. There won't be a reason for anything to happen. But if you send experts, men who will show us how to increase our production, if you send us technical assistance, such as tractors, which will improve our harvests, then there will be progress."

I say: "I can't show you how to improve your harvests, but when Oleksander Antonovych offered me a teaching position at the center, I contacted the United States and next week I'm expecting several textbooks on Western office management and business correspondence.

"I certainly can teach classes in writing business documents," I said.

For the first time, Cherevan smiles.

"So you're a journalist," he says. "We are doing heroic work here. We are trying to pull all these people up by the bootstraps. We need to have our name recognized in the West."

With a straight face, I reply: "May I come back when you have more time and interview you for an article?"

I interview him a few days later and am impressed by his vision and his confidence that the post-Soviet society can succeed as long as it is given the tools to do so. I also stay at Melnikova 36.

A few months later when I am back home, I read about the various proposals on sending food to Russia in the event there is a famine. I take out my notes from my interview with Cherevan and write an essay about the economic conditions I had observed and quote Cherevan's ideas. The essay is published as a "Comment" piece in *USA Today*.

After I return to my room, I make myself a cup of coffee using a heating coil, then go upstairs to see Doug and Frieda Nicol. Well-meaning and optimistic, they volunteered through the Soros Foundation, which sponsors educational and entrepreneurial projects in Eastern Europe, to teach English at the high school and college levels in Kyiv. Neither Doug nor Frieda knows Russian or Ukrainian, but both hold degrees in teaching English as a foreign language. They left their oldest son, a college student, at home in Arlington, Washington, and brought with them Amber, eight years old, and eleven-year-old Kahlil. Kahlil, a gregarious young man, is adjusting well, but Amber is shy and refuses to learn even the basics of a new language. I met the Nicols shortly after I moved to Melnikova 36. I act as their interpreter.

Frieda, a big, blond, excitable woman, is in a state. They, too, have been given an eviction notice. She is on her way to the Soros Foundation to straighten the matter out.

Since the day is Friday, Frieda plans to go shopping at the open produce markets downtown and invites me to dinner. The food-shopping excursion is a typical end-of-the-week activity for the Nicols, one the children usually enjoy. On Saturdays and Sundays, Frieda prepares meals in the hostel's communal kitchen on the second floor, and I always look forward to the smells of familiar food cooking. Besides, on the weekends, the dining room in the marble building is closed.

The textbooks arrive together with a five-pound jar of Skippy peanut butter. My uncle Michael, my father's younger brother, is making his first trip to Ukraine and has agreed to bring them to Lviv. From Lviv, a friend transports the packages to Kyiv. I now not only have sandwich makings for the next month and a half but also the materials for a course for the kolkhoz workers turned businessmen.

Ten days later, Uncle Michael calls to say good-bye. "You know, if I were a younger man, I would come back to live here and start a business," he says. "What this country needs are plumbers who know what they're doing. The bathrooms here are a disgrace."

Although he's calling long-distance, I cannot refrain from relating an anecdote I recently heard on the state of the country's plumbing: A tourist group is driven into the countryside to a wonderful historic site. All goes well and the tourists are amazed at the cultural richness and antiquity of what they see. They agree there is nothing similar back home and they envy their Russian hosts who live in such proximity to history. At the close of the day, many of the tourists need to use the toilet. The Russian hosts take them to a public toilet and the tourists file inside. When they bolt from the toilet a few moments later, they say they are ready to go home. No, they demand that they go home immediately because they still need to use a toilet.

Uncle Michael laughs. I laugh, although sadly. There is nothing in the West to prepare a Westerner for the so-called Turkish toilets in Ukraine or Russia. The Turkish toilet is simply a hole in the floor surrounded by a tin flange that goes unwashed. That is it. The stink is suffocating since bathrooms have no windows, and if there is an occasional window, it is barred and locked. Of course there are no exhaust fans. Fans? What an unheard-of luxury!

At Melnikova 36, I fight an arduous battle to get a toilet seat for the toilet in my bathroom. "You Americans are so spoiled," the matron in charge of the hostel says when I make my request. "You have a sink, a shower, a toilet, a full private bathroom. What else do you want?"

"A toilet seat."

She clucks disapprovingly. A few days later I drop in at her office with a package of Hanes pantyhose. I say I have extras and thought she might have a daughter or a sister who could use the hose. She accepts the gift, but I do not get a toilet seat. I then purchase a bottle of vodka and present it. That does the trick. Toward the end of the week, I have a toilet seat.

Living at the former Higher Party School has its disadvantages. I begin to avoid telling people where I live because they tend to do one of two things when they find out: They either grow cool and watch what they say to me, or they become more interested in where I live than in what I am saying to them. Some suspect that not much has changed, despite the change in regime and school name.

One foggy afternoon, a man gets off the trolleybus with me. As I head for the wrought-iron gate, he stops me and asks, "Is this the Higher Party School?"

"Well, yes and no."

"They keep the KGB records here, the ones they say they'll be opening to the public?"

I know something about these records since I tried—unsuccessfully—to obtain access to the records upon my arrival in Kyiv. I am convinced that these archives contain information about the mass grave in Slavske. After two weeks of evasions, I am told the records will remain sealed.

"No," I say to the man who stopped me. "Those are still in the KGB building on Lesia Ukraine Square. I was told they will be moved to the national archives, but that will take some time."

The man is looking skeptically at me.

"But this *is* the Higher Party School?" he insists.

"It was," I begin, but he is not interested in my explanations and walks away.

Also, I do not talk about teaching a class in the marble building. When I mentioned the arrangement to Volodia, he looked at me silently for a moment, then blurted out, "What can you possibly teach them?"

I wonder that myself, as I wait for Oleksander Antonovych to assign me a class. As soon as the books arrived and I showed them to him, he borrowed them and I have not seen them again. Then, one afternoon, Oleksander Antonovych says he has scheduled a lecture that I will deliver. He suggests that I dress as "an American businesswoman" and talk about American office etiquette.

I prepare the lecture and dress as instructed. I wash and curl my hair. I put on my dark business suit, my pearl earrings, and my white silk blouse, which has not been worn and therefore is still white. I wear sheer stockings and high heels. As I walked down the hall to class, people stop and stare.

About forty students attend the lecture, most of them men in their thirties. At the end of the lecture, the questions focus on business lunches and credit cards. Someone asks me the ingredients of a martini and what a "three martini lunch" is. A man in the back of the lecture hall calls out to ask whether women are permitted to use credit cards. Others begin to hoot and clap.

When I say women use credit cards, he raises his voice and challenges: "Show us yours."

The hooting and clapping grow louder.

I can play a game of one-upmanship also. I call back to him: "Which one?"

The class breaks out into loud laughter. Someone finally calls out, "How about the blue one, American Express."

I say: "I don't have a blue one, but a gold one," and explain the difference.

The students file past the podium to examine the gold American Express card. One of them places it in his mouth and bites on it. "That's how you make sure gold is gold," he says with a grin.

He asks me if my ring is gold. It is, but I lie. He raises my hand as if to plant the fleeting Austro-Hungarian kiss, then bites the ring. He smiles and congratulates me on having the wit to tell a lie.

I wonder what the next lecture will bring.

Most of my communications with home are either by telephone or by fax. I had briefly nurtured the fantasy of calling home about once a week. I once managed to reach the long-distance operator through sheer persistence but was told it would take four hours to get a connection. Fax became the more expedient alternative, since Oleksander Antonovych has told me it won't be "any problem" for me to use the center's fax machine to send and receive messages.

A week passes, then ten days, and I have not received a fax. Whenever I stop at the office, Olga Petrovna, Cherevan's blond, cheerful secretary, sympathizes and asks rhetorically how can I bear to be parted from my boys for such a long time. In her eyes I am as much of a curiosity as a woman in one of those Western soap operas on state television who sacrifices a happy home for a career. Incomprehensible.

One afternoon, I have an hour to kill before the luncheonettes open and I drop in to chat with Olga. She is brusque. It takes me a few minutes to realize that Olga is very nervous and that she wants me to leave. Surprised and a little hurt, I get up to leave. At that moment, Cherevan walks in, and asks Olga where Oleksander Antonovych is.

Olga flushes and points to the closed door to Cherevan's office. Cherevan opens the door. I see Oleksander Antonovych bent over the table on which a long fax is spread out. An English-Russian dictionary is in his hands. Our eyes meet and he flushes deeply. As I leave the office, Cherevan's and Olga's faces are as expressionless as those on mannequins in Bloomingdale's windows. The next day, I get my fax.

After I realize that my mail is being read, I make it a point to see less of Oleksander Antonovych and the other people who work in the marble building. One Monday, Oleksander Antonovych stops me in the hall and says, "What did you do yesterday?"

Since it was Sunday, I had gone to mass in a Podil church and, after the service, went sightseeing. I say as much.

"You were at the Pechersky Monastery," he says, his voice accusing me of being vague.

"Oh, yes," I say. "Why didn't you say hello?"

He studies me silently for a moment. Then he asks, "Who were you with?"

"A friend," I say, taken aback by the baldness of the question and annoyed.

"What friend?" he insists.

"A friend," I say and walk away.

Paranoia and reality merge. My spirits plummet. I have begun to mind that this is the longest I have ever been separated from my family. Perhaps that is why I am so sad, and not because I now know I am being watched. I had thought that they would leave me alone if I lived at Melnikova 36 and let them keep an eye on me.

Chapter 14

FIRE AT CHERNOBYL

On Saturday or sometimes on a Sunday after attending Catholic mass in a courtyard outside an Orthodox church (the Orthodox priest refuses to let the Catholic priest celebrate Sunday services inside his church), I take the trolleybus or the metro to the flea market at the Dynamo stadium.

Black-shrouded, dark-skinned women with flashing black eyes are selling beluga caviar, which I adore. They pull the blue- or red-lidded jars from vast black sacks, while teenage punks in Levi's and leather jackets hawk pirated Madonna tapes, which they stack in the open trunks of cars. Afghanistan war veterans peddle wristwatches with Red Army stars on their faces; buxom matrons sell pantyhose made in Western Europe or, occasionally, Playtex bras, which they hold up to their bosoms so that a passing shopper can judge the bra's size. You can buy everything and anything at the flea market. All you need is money, preferably dollars. You can also become one with the crowd, which puts aside its inhibitions and cares for a few hours.

Rain or bitter cold, the file of sellers takes shape in the early hours, before the flea market opens at nine sharp. The file, in the form of two facing rows of sellers, begins at the metro stop, snakes its way to the entrance to the stadium, then forms up again on the concrete apron at the foot of the steps leading into the bleachers. The sellers stand shoulder to shoulder, not unlike a gauntlet in an earlier century, when individuals sentenced to punishment were made to run between a double file of men brandishing clubs or other weapons with which they beat the victims as they ran past. Except that here, on these overcast November mornings, the people in the double line stomp their boots in the cold and hold in their reddened hands not weapons but articles they want to sell. Those passing between the facing lines do not run, but stroll while examining the goods, and stop only if the price is right or the item desirable. Before the fall of the Soviet Union, the sellers would have been called *spekulianty*—speculators—a cherished term for abuse and oppression by the regime. But these spekulianty are hardly big-time crooks. For the most part, they are small-time peddlers buying tiny quantities of goods in one place and selling them elsewhere for a slight profit. At the Dynamo stadium, they are babushkas, minor clerks, housewives with children to clothe and feed. They come to sell the extra tin of red caviar they received from a son in Vladivostok, or a pair of boots they found at a kiosk, or a bottle of vodka for which they waited half a day in line at a government store. Outside the gauntlet, other sellers, who have more than one item to offer, display their wares on the ground. Kittens and puppies fall out of baskets covered with cloth, wine from Georgia and Crimea and bottles of homemade vodka crowd yellowing newspapers spread on the ground or sink into the semifrozen mud. A Fisher-Price toy train, scuffed but intact, sits in solitary splendor on an empty crate. An icon cut from a church *iconostasis* lies on a filthy rag. Every item gets a cursory glance; a few, such as embroidered pantyhose, have a way of freezing a passerby to the spot. Everyone feels obliged to offer advice—requested or not—to a potential buyer. "I saw one just like it over there," a bystander whispers to a buyer, inclining the head in one direction or the other, "for less."

Handmade sweaters no longer tempt me. The one I bought was fine until I washed it. It matted and smelled like wet dog. When I mentioned this to one of the women at the hostel, she said that much of the yarn was being made from dog hair. I gave the sweater away.

The weekend flea market is the largest gathering of people in Kyiv. The place is a cacophony of competing sounds. Loudspeakers blare out prices. Western rock thunders from loudspeakers on cars with trunks gaping open to show hundreds of cassettes. Vendors stroll through the crowds, hawking pretzels and hot sausages. Everywhere there is a pressing horde of buyers and sellers, gawkers, hangers-on. Two blocks away, a government store is open, but its shelves are nearly bare of merchandise and it has no customers.

This seller is a plump, round-faced woman with a white kerchief hiding her hair. She has spread her blanket at the base of the stadium steps, where the gauntlet of sellers widens to adjust to the broad set of staircases. She has a pair of worn shoes, a cotton housedress, a teacup without its handle or saucer, and a few other pieces of cracked pottery lined up on an old *Pravda*. She also has an icon. It is pale, with much of the paint worn off. Portrayed is the journey of Joseph and Mary to Bethlehem to register for the census.

I pick up the icon to examine it. The seller has been talking to a neighboring seller, but now her attention rivets on me. The price is stiff for a local, but not for a foreigner. We barter for a few minutes, but she never loses her cool. She knows she has a sale. Other women nearby follow our discussion with keen interest.

When we agree on a price, I do a quick calculation, adjust the price a bit, and offer to pay her in hard currency. Five American dollars, I say. The sellers around us fall silent. Here is someone with *valiuta*. The seller is so delighted that she rushes off to find a friend who has brought brown wrapping paper. As I wait, one of the neighboring sellers comes up to me.

"Please buy something from me," she asks.

I walk over to her hoard. She has a tube of German toothpaste, dark children's socks, and a pack of Kents and some clothing. I shake my head.

"Please," she begs.

I reach into my pocket to pull out a dollar bill, which I place in her hand. She yelps with joy and does a little jig around her items. She then unfolds the dollar bill and raises it to her face. She plants a resounding kiss on George Washington's portrait.

"Fire has broken out at Chernobyl," I write in my journal, after listening to the early news on Kyiv radio, something I do every morning. No one speaks about the fire on the trolleybus, but many people, including me, study the sky and the air, as if radioactive isotopes could be discerned by the naked eye. At *News from Ukraine*, Volodia and Andriy have more information.

"I heard the roof's on fire in one of the generating rooms," Andriy says. He has a friend at Slavutych, the city that was built outside the zone of contamination for workers employed in Chernobyl's remaining three power stations.

Volodia, who religiously watches CNN, says he heard that there is no danger of a release of radiation, then adds, "Isn't it a shame that we have to learn the news about ourselves on CNN?"

Neither Volodia nor Andriy appears worried, or perhaps they, like most other Kyiv residents, have resigned themselves. What can be worse than what had transpired on April 26, 1986, when the Number 4 reactor exploded, spewing radiation, and no one knew about it for three whole days? Neither *Izvestia* nor *Komsomolskaya Pravda* carries any news about the fire that's burning now. Channel 1, the principal television channel, does not interrupt its normal programming to report the fire. Andriy tries calling the Chernobyl cleanup office, but the telephone goes unanswered. The information being doled out is coming from a spokesperson at the Chernobyl station. There are no journalists or mobile television cameras on the scene to tell us what is really going on.

Over a cup of Turkish coffee, Volodia points out that at Chernobyl (or Chornobyl, in Ukrainian), Mikhail Gorbachev's government played the old socialist game of "I know nothing. I hear nothing, and I'll say nothing." In the Soviet Union there was—and is—a cult of lies, Volodia says, his mustache quivering. There are "lies for the sake of a greater good," "lies that save," even "sacred lies."

We spend a listless morning, talking about Chernobyl and assuring each other that, with the new freedoms, we would be told if there was danger of an another explosion. Eventually, I go to my desk to do some work, but my thoughts keep returning to what Volodia said. I can think of one "sacred lie." Lenin, on his way back from Western Europe to take charge of the Bolshevik Revolution, did not arrive openly in triumph as Soviet history books maintain. He sneaked across the Finnish border into St. Petersburg in a red wig, disguised as a sailor.

The day is overcast and still, with no breeze blowing, which everyone agrees is a plus. I think of breathing an invisible poison, of my flesh being bombarded with invisible atoms that kill. On the way to Melnikova 36 for *obeyd,* I cover my mouth with a handkerchief because everyone else is doing it.

A week or so later, Andriy gives me *Vechirnii Kyiv,* the capital's evening newspaper. I glance at the paper, thinking there's an update on the fire, but can't find a Chernobyl article.

He sees my bewilderment and says: "Look at the photographs."

Only then do I recognize myself in one of them. From then on I see myself in other photos that appear in newspapers. I see myself in the broad Slavic cheeks, the high and too wide foreheads, the small mouths dominated by longish noses and underscored by pointed chins. Although outlook and experiences separate me from all these people, I recognize my mother, Katia, and myself in them. I think about the origins we share, about genetic and cultural ties that can be traced to the horsemen of the Ukrainian steppe. Although separated from them for most of our lives, we are tied to these people by hidden bonds, the way underground rivers link and flow below us and we do not realize their existence until a spring erupts to the surface. I begin to understand more fully my mother's lifetime longing to return from exile and I begin to feel more at home.

Poets are celebrities in Russia. When Volodia and Alla ask if I want to accompany them to an appearance by Yevgeny Yevtushenko, I jump at the chance, although I worry about my Russian. "I'll translate important passages," Volodia promises.

Tall, slim, and wearing a well-tailored gray suit and a pale blue shirt, Yevtushenko strides onto the stage and I immediately think of Gary Cooper. Yevtushenko is handsome in the rugged, Marlboro-man way. He is also relaxed, urbane, and in complete control of the adoring audience. People are applauding his mastery of language even before he recites a verse. Unfortunately, when he does begin to recite, my Russian fails me. His recitation is monotonous, with no inflections, yet musical, which is a tradition in Russian poetry readings but does not foster comprehension. Someone calls out for him to recite "Babi Yar," the poem that made him famous in the West, and since I know it, I follow his recital.

Yevtushenko says that when he wrote "Babi Yar" thirty years earlier—thereby lifting the official silence about the killings—the Communist Party forbade him to visit Kyiv. He wrote the poem from a sense of guilt for keeping silent. He is back in Kyiv to screen a movie he wrote and directed. It is called *Stalin's Funeral*. The movie was born of this same sense of guilt.

Yevtushenko then leaves the stage, a screen is lowered over the curtain, and the lights dim. *Stalin's Funeral* is in color, but is not like the slick, seamless movies in the West. Perhaps this is due to technique, or the position of the camera—or perhaps the method used is intentional. It seems that I am looking at raw footage made by a camera that does not roll on wheels but is carried on the shoulder of a man who is sprinting or filming from the window of a careening car. The story deals with the spread of news about Stalin's death and his funeral. As I watch, I cannot, for the life of me, fathom a series of scenes in a huge room where several women are cooking while shooing children away from the stove, where babies crawl on the floor or are being bathed in tin tubs, and where men lounge against the room's walls, smoking and talking idly. I finally nudge Volodia and whisper, "Where's this taking place?" He looks distractedly at me and says, *"Komunalka."* I am no wiser than before.

Throughout the film, one actor reappears in a variety of roles as Yevtushenko uses his face and figure as a refrain of evil. The man is a KGB operative, an informer in a labor camp and an anonymous man lurking in a store or on the street. In vignettes piled upon more vignettes, Yevtushenko evokes the animal fear of being arrested, the servile Russian acceptance of authority, the stupid cruelties perpetrated by adults with power against children, old people, and anyone perceived as a weakling. The fear and the horror grow as people begin to stream to see Stalin's corpse. At first, they go in orderly groups, such as the group of people from the komunalka. Then the groups become crowds that grow larger and larger. They push and shove and soon turn into an angry, spiteful mob that surges headlong toward its dead idol, trampling the weak, the old, the children who get in its way. The face of the man playing multiple roles looms on the screen whenever something horrible is about to happen.

In his autobiography, published in the early 1960s, when Stalin no longer was idolized, Yevtushenko described how he was part of the mob he recreated on film thirty years later:

> The stream of people drove me ahead. Suddenly, I felt something soft under my feet. In a moment, it dawned on me that it was a human body. Horror-stricken, I tucked my legs under me and the crowd pushed me along. . . .
>
> With one of the fellows who was in charge of keeping order, I began making my way home. On the way, we bought a bottle of vodka.
>
> "Have you seen Stalin?" my mother asked.
>
> "Yes, I have seen him," I answered and we hastily tossed down a drink.
>
> I wasn't lying to my mother. That day I saw the true Stalin. He was in the bloody chaos of his funeral.

On the way home on the metro, I ask what a komunalka is. Both Volodia and Alla are astounded that I do not know. Both grew up in one. A komunalka was a communal apartment. After the fall of czarist Russia, the large apartments of the merchant class and of the nobility were not divided into smaller units. Instead, families were given a room apiece in these large apartments, while everyone shared the apartment's kitchen and the toilet. What had been recreated in the film was the kitchen of a large komunalka apartment.

A year later, I will watch in Crimea a wildly successful TV series entitled "Komunalka," which follows the lives of several characters living in a communal apartment. The horrid, cramped existence in a komunalka during the reign of Communism now inspires a Russian soap opera.

Two months later, I visit one of the remaining komunalkas in use in Kyiv. Under Brezhnev, they began to disappear, as blocks of apartment buildings were built in the suburbs. The city komunalkas were broken up and divided into smaller units to which bathrooms and kitchens were added. I think Andriy lives in a former komunalka, but I never ask. From the apartment's awkward layout and from its location in a fine, old building, it appears to have been carved out of a much larger apartment.

The komunalka I visit is also in a building with a beautiful Old World façade. But the interior is as dim and grubby as in any of the new apartment buildings on the Left Bank. A metal cage takes us up. An eye stares at us through a peephole in the apartment door before it opens a crack. This visit takes place late in the evening of election day and I have obtained permission to accompany an election official whose job is to seek out old people and invalids who have not come to the polling place to vote. The official explains who he is and shows the suspicious man blocking the door the voting box, a wooden rectangle with a lid that has a slot. The lid is padlocked to the box. The suspicious man steps aside and lets us pass. We enter a small foyer. To the left stretches a long hall with several closed doors. We proceed to one such door, the official knocks, and we enter a high-ceilinged, well-proportioned room with brass candelabra on the walls. A frail old woman sits on a bed tucked against one wall. Behind us, the suspicious man remains standing in the open doorway. Behind him other people are forming a curious crowd. Everyone watches the old woman mark her ballot and drop it into the voting box. Then the suspicious man and the curious crowd escort us back to the front door.

Tina Shermel, my Russian teacher in Denver, spent several miserable years in a komunalka as a girl. Tina earned distinction as a singer with the Moscow Opera before she and her mother immigrated to Israel, and later to the United States. One day when we were talking about living conditions in Moscow, Tina described how her family was assigned to a komunalka, but the other residents would not tolerate Jews living and cooking among them. Eventually, a compromise was arrived at. The Shermel family was given a room that Tina described as a space not unlike our idea of a mud room: the cubicle opened onto the metal fire escape. The Shermels lived, slept, and cooked in these cold and cramped surroundings for several years.

To this day Tina lives as if she were about to move.

Chapter 15

HORROR IN THE HOSPITAL

The Nicols, the American family living at the hostel, were shopping in the Bessarabian Market on Khreshchatyk when their daughter Amber complained she was not feeling well. On the way back to the hostel in a crowded trolleybus, Amber, a slim child with no extra fat on her bird-like frame, turned pale and weak. She slept the rest of the afternoon and, by evening, her temperature had skyrocketed to 104.4 degrees. A dinner that Frieda, Doug, and I had planned to have together was canceled.

The following day was Thursday, the day I left for an excursion into south-central Ukraine. As Frieda recalled later, Amber complained that her "tummy hurt" when she woke up on Thursday morning. In the afternoon, Frieda, frightened by Amber's rising temperature, asked the dezhurna to summon an outside doctor. The dezhurna said that she would try.

A doctor came Friday. She examined Amber and said Amber probably had eaten something spoiled. She left several charcoal tablets, which, she said, would cleanse Amber's intestinal tract. She also showed Frieda how to brew herbal tea from dried chamomile blossoms. The medications did not help.

Amber remained feverish on Saturday and Sunday. She was refusing all food. Frieda turned to her own home remedies. She fed Amber fluids and gave her cold compresses. She thought Amber had a bad case of the flu, which had started going around Kyiv when the weather turned cold. Frieda was reluctant to give Amber any of the antibiotics for adults she had brought from the United States.

On Sunday evening, Amber began to have severe diarrhea. She vomited all food, including fluids. A man staying in the hostel heard about Amber's illness and offered to "lay hands on her," a technique he said he had been trained in. Frieda was desperate enough by then to try anything. She described the procedure later: "He made several passes over Amber's abdomen and said, 'She'll be better in the morning.' Amber wasn't."

Monday went by, but Amber did not get better. On Tuesday, six days after Amber fell ill, the hostel's doctor came to see her.

By then, I am back and I do the interpreting. The doctor agrees with the original diagnosis that Amber ate something that did not agree with her. He gives Amber more chamomile tea, some tablets that Frieda and I decide are antibiotics, and an antihistamine to combat any reaction to the antibiotics. Amber is a very sick child. She is lying prostrate on the bed, hardly moving, uninterested in her surroundings. She does not eat or drink. Diarrhea convulses her thin little body. She is losing weight so rapidly that we can see her bones sticking out more and more as the day progresses. Frieda and Doug are frantic. I call my acquaintances, but they assure me the hostel's doctor has a good reputation and we should listen to his advice.

On Wednesday, seven days after Amber fell ill, the hostel doctor becomes alarmed and sends for a pediatric specialist. The specialist examines Amber, says that she is dehydrated, and orders Frieda to feed her fluids, even if they have to be force-fed. Amber begins to vomit bile. That evening, when I return from teaching, Frieda is weeping. Amber is delirious. Doug and I go down to the dezhurna and ask her to call an ambulance.

A young, arrogant doctor arrives first. We dislike him instantly. When he pokes Amber's abdomen, she screams. He says she has either food poisoning or acute appendicitis. He says he will place her in a children's hospital. He fills a syringe with liquid from a vial and injects the medication into Amber's buttocks. The commotion has attracted a half dozen people. Everyone is offering advice. Frieda asks me to find out what the injection was.

"It's what you call Demerol in America," the doctor says. "The child won't cry."

The doctor leaves, saying he is too busy to wait for the ambulance.

Frieda, on the verge of hysterics, sits by Amber's bed and strokes the little girl's burning forehead. Doug returns to the dezhurna's desk to use the hostel's solitary telephone to call the U.S. Consulate for help. He comes back with assurances that Amber will be taken to the best hospital in Kyiv. Frieda, frightened by the callousness of the last doctor, vows that she will not leave her baby's side.

The ambulance arrives at ten o'clock in the evening. Frieda carries

Amber through the cold and the rain to the ambulance, which is parked
in the hostel's driveway. The driver refuses to let Doug or me ride with
Frieda and Amber.

We assume that Amber is being taken downtown to Polyclinic Number 1, where the U.S. officials predicted Amber would go. This is the
hospital that treated the Communist Party hierarchy. Later, Frieda will
tell us that the ambulance traveled only a short distance. "This worried
me," she would recall. "When the driver stopped at an entrance, the
gate was locked. The yard beyond was dark. It didn't look like a regular
hospital."

Frieda tries to communicate with the driver, but cannot, since neither knows the other's language. He drives to another entrance and a
guard lets them in.

Frieda would remember noticing in the beam of the headlights that
the driveway is unpaved and is littered with garbage.

The ambulance stops in front of a compound of two-story, poorly
kept buildings. Frieda is told to carry Amber up a staircase to a small
examining room where she lays Amber down on a cot covered with a
dirty sheet.

The ambulance driver leaves, and Frieda and Amber are alone. They
wait for several minutes. Down the hall Frieda can hear a child wailing
and someone reprimanding in a loud, rough voice.

The ambulance driver returns with a doctor. The doctor motions to
the driver to take Frieda by the arm and escort her out. Frieda refuses to
budge. The doctor scowls and says, "*Nyet,* Mama." But Frieda only shakes
her head and holds her ground. Exasperated, the doctor storms out of
the room. A few minutes later, the doctor returns with a second doctor,
who speaks a little English. He explains to Frieda that parents are not
allowed to stay in the hospital. Amber will be treated and the doctor
will call Frieda in a few days. Frieda says she will not leave Amber alone.

"You must go," the doctor cajoles. "The child is infectious and must
stay at least five to seven days."

Frieda is beside herself. "Infectious?" she asks. "What kind of hospital is this, anyway?"

"This is a hospital for infectious diseases among children. Diphthe-
ria. Tuberculosis," the doctor says. "That is why you must leave. If you
stay, you could be infected or infect others when you leave."

"My God," Frieda cries. "Amber has the flu. I don't want her to be
treated here."

The doctors tell Frieda to put Amber's coat back on. She follows them to what she thinks is the exit. But when they step out into the rainy night, she is led around the corner to another battered building. The English-speaking doctor unlocks a metal door and ushers Frieda inside.

I would see the room later. It is a small, dirty hovel. Two metal beds with metal springs are pushed against the walls on either side. A small scratched table is the only other piece of furniture. The wall is chipped and loose paint flakes in sheets from the ceiling. Two windows to the outside are covered with metal grating that is fastened with large locks to the windowsills. A bathroom with a toilet without a seat and a plat-form with a makeshift hose for taking showers is visible through an open door. The sink is dirty, as is the floor, which is covered with broken lino-leum tiles. Frieda will remember that cockroaches scurried into a drain when she turned on the bathroom light. The third door of the room opens into a hallway. Next to the door is an interior observation win-dow through which nurses can see into the room.

Some minutes pass before Frieda realizes that the doctor who spoke broken English had not understood that she wanted to take Amber to a different hospital, not a different room. She tries to explain, but a lab technician comes in to take a sample of Amber's blood. The technician also takes a sample from Frieda. When Frieda asks why, the doctor says, "in the event you are also infectious."

The doctor tries to reassure Frieda by saying that the syringes used are "single-use-only needles," but Frieda sees that the syringes are not disposable. She suspects they are rinsed between uses. Frieda's determi-nation to leave is crumbling. She asks that Amber be given intravenous feeding or fluids. No one seems to hear or understand her. The doctor says good-bye and Frieda suspects that he is going home. After some minutes, a nurse brings Frieda a cup of strong tea and warns that not a sip be given to Amber. Frieda looks down at her watch. An hour has passed, yet Amber has not been given either fluids or medicine. The nurse leaves, closing the door behind her. Amber is fidgety and frightened. She begins to whimper. She has another violent attack of diarrhea and has to be carried to the toilet.

Midnight passes. Somewhere down the hall, children are sobbing quietly. At two o'clock in the morning, Frieda realizes that no one will come until morning to treat Amber. Since there is no bell or call system, Frieda decides to summon the nurse by going to the nursing station. This is when she discovers that she and Amber are locked in.

Frieda takes Amber's temperature with the thermometer she brought with her. Amber's temperature is 104.2. Frieda gives Amber two Tylenol pills she finds in her purse and a sip of tea. A few minutes later, Amber vomits the pills. Frantic with worry, Frieda begins banging on the locked door. A night clerk comes and yells through the locked door, "*Nyet,* Mama."

Frieda is now convinced that she has to get Amber out of this hospital and seek help elsewhere. She tries the metal door to the outside. It is locked. She tries to remove the metal grating, but cannot jimmy the locks. Time creeps by. Amber is no longer responding to Frieda's words. Drops of blood appear on her lips. Her skin has turned chalky. Frieda prays. She is terrified. Amber's death becomes a horrible possibility.

By dawn, Frieda knows what she must do: Get Amber out of the hospital and fly her either to Moscow or to a hospital in Western Europe. She will remembers thinking, "I have my buck knife in my purse. If they don't let us go, I'll take a hostage to force them to release us."

Sometime later, Frieda hears doctors making rounds. At about eight in the morning, a team of doctors and nurses unlocks the door. The doctor, who speaks English, informs Frieda that Amber will have to stay in the hospital for at least a week. The blood sample showed that her white cell blood count was high. She has an infection.

Amber cries out in pain when one of the doctors probes her abdomen. Frieda has noticed that none of the doctors or nurses had washed their hands before examining Amber. She is horrified. Frieda demands that she and Amber be permitted to leave.

"*Nyet,* Mama," the doctor says.

The doctors leave and breakfast arrives. It is a bowl of porridge. No fluids are brought for Amber. Frieda demands to see the doctor. When he arrives, she tells him she has to call her husband. To her surprise, the doctor agrees. He unlocks the door and leads Frieda down the hall to a phone. The clerk at the hostel answers immediately and calls Doug, then me, to the phone. While she is waiting, Frieda realizes she does not know the name of the hospital or where it is located.

An orderly is passing in the hall and Frieda grabs her. After talking to Frieda, Doug hands the receiver to me. I find out from the orderly that Frieda and Amber are at Polyclinic Infectious Diseases Pediatric Hospital Number 12, a few stops on the trolleybus from the hostel. Doug and I say we will come to the hospital at once.

The orderly tells me that Amber has been diagnosed as having botulism. Doug and I discuss this diagnosis on our way to the hospital. We agree that Amber's illness has been misdiagnosed. Botulism kills in a matter of hours, and Amber has been ill for more than a week.

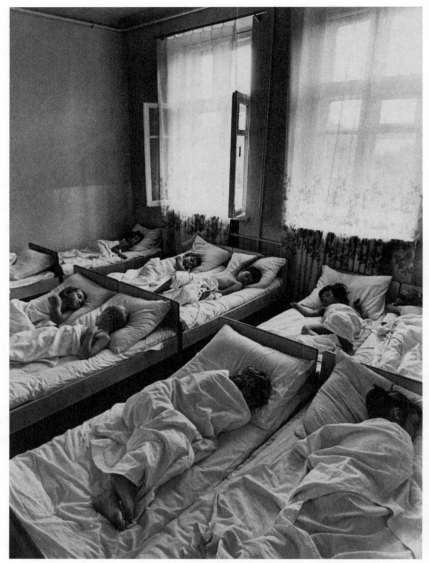

A Ukrainian children's hospital ward. Photograph by Viktor Marustschenko.

Meanwhile, Frieda refuses to let go of the telephone. She calls the U.S. Consulate and is assured that she and Amber will be removed from the hospital at once.

Her worry subsiding, Frieda walks back to the room where Amber is. As she passes rooms, she glances inside through the observation windows. Children, covered by thin, sheetlike blankets, lie inert on narrow cots, several children to a small room. Every room is bare, with no toys, no colors. As nurses walk in and out of rooms, they lock the doors behind them. A child begins screaming down the hall, but the nurses pay no attention. Frieda turns and runs to the child in distress.

Through the observation window she sees a girl of about twelve pummeling a child, about seven. Another child, about four, sits passively on the bed, watching. Frieda pounds on the window. The twelve-year-old shoves the seven-year-old into a corner. Frieda tries to get a nurse to go in, but the nurse shakes her head.

Frieda finds Amber squatting over a chamber pot. A nurse has given her an enema and is waiting for a stool sample. The nurse tries to give Amber an injection in the buttocks but Amber refuses to roll over. Soon, the English-speaking doctor, much agitated, returns.

Frieda demands that Amber be released. The doctor says no, storms out and locks the door behind him.

"Mommy, I'm going to die," Amber whispers.

Frieda weeps as she cradles Amber in her arms.

When a nurse brings a clear liquid for Amber to drink, Frieda asks again to be allowed to use the telephone. She calls the U.S. Consulate again and is assured that everything possible is being done to get Amber released.

On the way back to the room, Frieda sees a child sitting on the floor opening vials from an unlocked cupboard and drinking the contents. Frieda calls a nurse who takes the child and leads her to another room where the little girl is locked without being examined first.

Amber has dozed off.

A nurse looks into the room, closes the door and locks it.

Frieda sits next to Amber, stroking the child's pale hair. Once, the little girl wakes up and smiles weakly at her mother as tears roll down her flushed cheeks. In a soft voice and trying to hide her anguish, Frieda tells Amber her favorite fairy tales. She does not know whether Amber hears or understands, but the child's face softens and she falls asleep again.

Suddenly, there is a commotion in the hallway. The door is unlocked. An orderly comes in and with hand signs tells Frieda to dress Amber because a car has arrived to fetch them. The orderly then unlocks the outside metal door. Frieda hurriedly dresses Amber and, with the half-conscious child in her arms, steps into the cold November morning.

Frieda stops in confusion. There is no car. But she is outside, away from the hospital. Frieda quickly walks toward the corner of the building and around it, afraid someone will drag her and Amber back. This is when Doug and I, coming from the opposite direction, nearly collide with her. I run back inside the building to fetch Amber's ski cap, which Frieda has forgotten.

We return to the hostel on the trolleybus. The car that supposedly was sent to fetch Frieda and Amber never arrives.

At the hostel, Frieda and I pool our supply of antibiotics. Among them is a powerful broad-spectrum drug. The first time, Amber vomits up the pill. Frieda tries again a little later. Amber manages to keep the medicine down. Frieda begins feeding Amber boiled sugar water, a sip at a time, through the afternoon and evening. When she takes Amber's tempera-ture, it has dropped to 101. Frieda also gives Amber an antidiarrhea drug for adults, which she had hesitated to give earlier.

By evening, Amber is responding. She smiles weakly and her eyes no longer look glassy. She asks to listen to the Red Grammar tape "Teach-ing Peace," one of her favorites.

Amber takes American antibiotics every four hours. At eleven that night, Amber's fever breaks. At four o'clock the next morning, Amber wakes Frieda, who is sleeping in the chair next to her, and says, "Mommy, I'm better."

She adds, "Can we go home?"

A month later, the Nicols leave Kyiv. Before their departure, a health inspector visits Frieda and Doug. He says that a diagnosis of Amber's illness has been made. She had salmonella poisoning. Frieda will specu-late that Amber was infected by a chicken that the Nicols had purchased at the market.

Chapter 16

CONVERSATIONS WITH RUSSIAN GERMAN EXILES

Most mornings are damp and foggy. And the temperature hovers near freezing. During the day, the fog clears a little, but not enough for the sun to break through the mist. I decide this is a good time for a trip to Eastern Ukraine. When Volodia learns I will be traveling *platzkart,* he is aghast. I cannot possibly go third class.

"Why not?"

"You just can't. You're not used to our conditions," he says.

The art of travel—of adventure—is to know when to give in and when not to. I go anyway. The third-class sleeping berth ticket is the only one I was able to buy to Donetske, the coal-producing city near the Russian border and the Sea of Azov. Aleksandr Artumovych Dinges (Sasha), a Russian German who was the only one in his family to survive deportation to Kazakhstan during Stalin's reign, has invited me to meet him and other Russian Germans to hear their stories.

Kyiv's main railway station is bursting with jostling, angry, and anxious crowds. Several people approach me to offer to buy my ticket for twice to five times what I paid for it. Third class cannot be that bad. In the large dimly lit corridors, people are pressed one against the other. They sit silently or are asleep, their belongings clutched tightly to their chests. To reach the platform, I climb over lumpy bags, old women wrapped in shawls, and children with pale, exhausted faces. I skirt men drunk on *samohon,* the homemade whiskey, who, in their stupor, assume strange catatonic positions. Once on the platform, I pick out the first-class coaches and ask each attendant about empty berths. I drop hints that I will pay in Western currency, but none of the granite-face matrons swallows the bait.

A fearsome matron takes my ticket and leads me into the third-class wagon. My first impression is of being in a dormitory on wheels. Eighty bunks in all stages of disarray line the train car's walls or create doorless cubicles. The first bunk is at about seat height, a second looms above it, and on the long walls there is a third-level bunk, seemingly inches from the ceiling. Bed sheets, blankets, hard pillows, and thin, lumpy mattresses dangle every which way from the upper bunks.

Volodia had wrung his hands and predicted that I would be immediately spotted as a foreigner and robbed once I dozed off.

The fearsome matron stops in front of bunk number 25, one-third of the way into the wagon. This is my berth, one of the two lower bunks in a cubicle, a plus. I thank the matron and examine the passengers with whom I will spend the night. One is a bespectacled middle-aged man, who looks like a professor. The other man is young and handsome with a shock of strawberry blond hair. The fourth occupant of our little cubicle has yet to arrive. The two parallel berths across the aisle are empty. The young man gets up, lifts the hinged seat, and I drop my small bag into the storage area. So far I have said little, except for "Thank you" and "Hello" in Russian. I do not attract the curiosity of the two men and they resume the conversation my arrival has interrupted.

The third-class car fills quickly. A young, very nervous, and nicely dressed girl takes one of the bunks across the aisle. An unshaven man, who looks as if he has just come from a job in a factory, climbs into the upper bunk. The third-level bunk near the ceiling as well as the one across from me remain empty. As the train lurches forward, there is an enormous commotion at the door. In another moment, a middle-aged woman swathed in a voluminous black skirt, a black shawl, and a black kerchief and carting two black sacks, one slung over her shoulder and the other one in her hands, stumbles into our cubicle and falls exhausted into the remaining seat. The fearsome matron yells at her for being late and nearly missing the train. The woman yells back at the matron, cursing government inefficiency and Aeroflot, which had curtailed its flights. I am staring in horror at one of her sacks, which has fallen open to reveal a partially plucked turkey. The professor-type jumps up and he and the woman lift the hinged seat. Only one of her bags will fit into the space. The dead turkey remains on her lap. It's time to act. I offer the space under me for the turkey. She accepts, but my offer focuses the attention of the other passengers on me. My Russian is different. The kerchiefed woman comes to my rescue. "Aha, you must be from Poland," she says. "You speak with a Polish accent."

I say I have come from Poland and that my family is a mixture of Poles and Ukrainians, both comments true when interpreted broadly. But I volunteer nothing of the narrower truth because of Volodia's warnings. Besides, I feel the urge to be like these people in the bedroomlike intimacy of the third-class sleeping coach, not someone foreign and frightening.

It is just as well that I am circumspect. Once I am pigeonholed, they lose interest in me and I begin to relax. The professor opens a book. The young man stares out of the window. The young girl bites her lower lip nervously, while the laborer takes out a bottle of vodka. The kerchiefed woman sighs.

We do not talk again until about an hour into the journey, when, as if on cue, everyone whips out a lunch bag. I have brought nothing with me except a sweet roll. The others are dumbfounded when they see my meager dinner. The professor offers me sausage; the kerchiefed woman, black bread, and the young man has some extra *salo,* which he slices with his pocketknife.

We start talking. The young man, who will sleep in the bunk above me, is a military policeman on leave from a unit patrolling Chernobyl. The professor, who will chivalrously yield his lower bunk to the kerchiefed woman, is exactly that—a scientist on his way to take methane samples in one of the coal mines in Donetske for a study he is doing. The woman is a villager who farms a large and fertile plot and is taking produce and meat clear across the country to her son's family in Donetske. The young woman says she is a university student, and the laborer-type does not introduce himself. As we eat, the young policeman tells us about people who are ignoring the posted warnings and are drifting back to the villages contaminated by radiation from the Chernobyl explosion. He says they can be spotted at night because their hair glows in the dark. The professor-scientist, who is employed by the Academy of Sciences, tells us that coal production in Donetske mines is suffering because of the lack of steel and timber to shore up new tunnels. He also says that safety measures are being consistently ignored in the mines because Ukraine is in desperate need of coal to generate electric power. And Maria Stepanova, who is from Lutzk, weeps as she relates how she tried in vain to get a plane to Donetske to be on time for the induction of her grandson into the army. The military policeman gives her detailed instructions on how to find out where the draftees are being kept and to see her grandson. Eventually, my turn comes, but I am careful not to develop my Polish persona too far. I appeal to the caution I know each of them has learned and practiced when speaking on politi-

cally sensitive subjects. In a lowered, confidential voice, I say I am going to visit people returning from exile in Kazakhstan. Everyone nods
sagely. They understand that I am bound by discretion. The laborer-type,
who has volunteered nothing about himself, but who has been following our conversation, clears his throat and says, "A lot of people are coming back now that the regime's changed. There'll be more, mark my
words."

The young student blushes crimson, looks even more frightened, and
averts her gaze from ours.

The fearsome matron strides down the aisle yelling that it is time to
make up the bunks and interrupts our conversation. The men climb up
and hand down the mattresses, sheets, and pillows. There are no blankets, but the air in wagon has grown warm and stuffy. The customs of
train travel are rigid. Whether you are traveling first class or third, men
and women travel together. When the time comes to make up the bunks,
women do their beds first and change, while men go out on the tiny
platforms on either end of the railcar to smoke. I was told that flannel
pajamas used to be the popular evening attire on the train, but now West-
ern-style sweat suits are appropriate. Since I have neither, I plan to spend
the night in my street clothes. None of my companions changes either,
although the men remove their jackets or cardigan sweaters and unbut-
ton their shirts at the throat. Precisely at ten o'clock, the lights go out.

Sometime during the night I wake up to hear Maria Stepanova crying. I sit up and we begin talking.

She is well off by local standards. She keeps a flock of geese and chickens, a cow, and several pigs. Her three children attended the university
and hold good jobs in the city. I noticed earlier that she is well read and
is versed in the current political situation.

"My life has not been all that bad," she says, tears trickling down her
mottled cheeks. She wipes them away with her large, callused hand. She
smiles sadly and, in the dim night light, her many metal-capped teeth
glint between her lips. She sees in my face that I have noticed.

"I was handsome once," she says. "I had good strong teeth. If it were
not for my daughter who is a dentist, I would have no teeth at all."

The awful truth is that Maria Stepanova's husband beats her regularly and brutally.

"He's a tractor driver at the collective farm," she says. "On pay day he
gets drunk. He weaves his way home on the tractor and falls out of the
seat at the door. I drag him in. When he comes around and something
doesn't suit him, he beats me up."

"Why don't you call the police?" I ask. "Or lock him out until he sobers up?"

She gazes at me strangely and remains silent for some time, thinking over what I've said.

"It's his house and he could have me evicted," she says, then adds, "And what will the neighbors think?"

Her question epitomizes that rigorous habit of privacy regarding all family matters that was instilled in me at home and which I discover is part of the greater Slavic heritage. In the sixteenth century, a Russian monk wrote *Domostroi* (Law of the Home), which was distributed at the order of Ivan the Terrible. The book ordered wives to remain silent about all domestic matters, including abuse. Today, such silence not only raises a formidable barrier for psychologists and social workers but also prevents women from seeking either escape or help.

The city is gray like iron, while the sky is opaque like buttermilk. The day is bitter cold. Donetske is the center of Ukrainian coal mining and I was warned that I would find mounds of coal slag lying on the streets. I don't see any, but the blocks of gray apartment buildings that stretch for kilometers in every direction give the impression that Donetske is a huge housing project. A tall building in the city center is shrouded in a milky mist bearing the odor of coal smoke. Donetske burns the coal it extracts from beneath itself, and chokes on it.

Sasha is in his fifties, red-haired and red-bearded, soft-spoken and with bright intelligent eyes. He was born in 1938 and spent his childhood and young adulthood in Kazakhstan. During glasnost, Sasha joined the Russian German Society. He says he is going to write the history of the Russian Germans.

Germans started to settle in Russia and parts of Ukraine during the reign of Catherine the Great, who was German and who invited her countrymen to follow her east. Some Germans stopped when they reached the fertile land in the bend of the Dnipro, while others went on to the vast steppes Catherine won from the Moslem khans. These Germans became extremely successful farmers. They worked hard, but they also were the only free peasants in an empire of serfs.

During the civil war following the October Revolution, several all-German units fought on the Red side. In 1918, Germans living in the Volga steppes were permitted to set up the Volga German Autonomous Republic. In 1942, the republic was dissolved and approximately one million people of German extraction were exiled to Siberia and

Kazakhstan. Stalin accused them of collaborating with Hitler. Their language and their Protestant and Catholic faiths were outlawed. They were not permitted to leave exile until 1976, and then, in one of those meannesses in which the government excelled, they were barred from returning to their ancestral lands.

My godmother was German. When my mother finished primary school she went to live in town with "Angela" so that she could continue her education at a gymnasium. Angela (my mother pronounced the "g" as in "good" and placed the stress on the second syllable, making the name sound quite different from the way it is said in the United States) was married to a doctor, my mother's distant relation, who was a Ukrainian. My mother enjoyed living with him and Angela. They had an adopted son, younger than my mother by ten or so years, but no natural children. Angela, described by my mother as a handsome and forthright woman, became a surrogate mother to the young girl from the village.

Angela never gave up her German citizenship and traveled back and forth during the 1930s and continued to do so during the German occupation of Ukraine. In 1944 she obtained good papers for my mother, Katia, and Roma, which enabled the family to get berths in a railcar heading for Czechoslovakia. After the war, Angela lived in Austria while we lived in the American Zone in Bavaria. I think my mother visited or corresponded with Angela, because I remember being told that she was ill and, later, that she had died. I have no memory of Angela except as a character in my mother's stories. The story of what happened to her family has always puzzled me. The doctor died during the war. The boy somehow ended up in an American-run orphanage and was brought to America right after the war. He lived with a family who made him work in the family's saloon as a janitor. How this came about, I don't know. I heard later that he had a talent for languages and was with the CIA. I met him at the funeral of Katia's husband. He drank a lot and became garrulous, although he still spoke carefully about himself. That evening, Katia's older daughter Christine and I drove him to the railroad station in Trenton, New Jersey, so that he could board the Metroliner to Washington, where he lived. He is now retired and we exchange Christmas cards.

I must have been six or seven when I saw one of the identity cards Angela obtained for us. I was already attending German school and could read German. The identity card belonged to my mother and said that she was of German extraction. With blond hair and pale eyes, I blended well with the other children in school and my mother must have shown that card when enrolling me. I still speak a little German. When I met Sasha, I mentioned that my godmother was German. I don't know whether he misunderstood what I said, but in Donetske he introduces me as "one of us."

"There's no more to tell," the middle-aged, henna-haired woman repeats softly every few sentences. She stops and stares at the floor. She sits perched on the edge of a chair, her thin legs sideways under her and crossed at the ankles, across the room from Sasha and me, to whom she has yielded the sofa upon our arrival. She lives in a fussy flat where the walls are papered with a wine-colored, flocked wallpaper, and portieres trimmed with a reddish ball fringe hang on windows as well as doors. She is an ethnic German, but few people know this. After a pause, she picks up the threads of her story once again. She has tried to forget, she says, because it is better that way. Although she is divorced, she kept her husband's name because her family name is "too German." Eventually, she goes back to the very beginning. She tells us how she and her family were loaded "in one of the cattle cars General Sorov sent for us." She relates how her infant brother died while suckling at her mother's dry breast during the long, cold, hungry trip east. Her father was taken away to work in the gold mines in Siberia, and she never saw him again. Her mother raised her and her three sisters on a kolkhoz.

"We would dig for potatoes in the frozen earth in the middle of the night, or sell what was left of our possessions for a little bag of grain," she says. For many years there was hardly anything to eat, and at the end of each winter her belly would swell because of starvation.

Sonia Petrovna is a frail, birdlike woman. She possesses a certain short-ness of stature and thinness of arms and legs that I begin to recognize as physical characteristics of adults who were children during the war and had little to eat. As mentioned, Volodia is short of stature and narrow of frame. Only once did he refer to his height. One day, I noticed an athletic bag in his office at *News from Ukraine*—it may have been a Nike or an Adidas bag—and asked him if he belonged to a club. He said he did, adding, "If things had been different and I had had more to eat as a child, I would have been a good athlete." He never told me the details of his childhood, but I gathered over time that it was spent somewhere in the east, although he had been born in Ukraine.

Sonia Petrovna says that life is better than death, and that survival is the most important lesson of life. Since her marriage, no one ostracizes her, unless someone finds out she is an ethnic German. She is glad she has a nice apartment and a good salary, but she cannot forgive a regime and a society that killed her family and made her suffer so.

Would she consider immigrating to Germany, an option Sasha and I have discussed, since the German government is offering full citizenship to ethnic Germans living in the Soviet Union? Yes and no. How will she manage in Germany? She grew up speaking Russian because German was forbidden. Isn't it ironic, she whispers through her tears, that she would have to learn German although she has spent her entire life suffering because she is German?

Sonia Petrovna is the first of several ethnic Germans Sasha takes me to see. Why do they talk to me? I think because I am an audience—guaranteed safe by Sasha—for whom their stories are new and fascinating. And I have told them that in Kansas and eastern Colorado there are many settlements of Germans from Russia who immigrated in the nineteenth century. I can be a conduit of their stories back to their ethnic brethren.

As I listen, the hairs on my neck begin to bristle, a reaction similar to the one I had when I read the UPA accounts. I turn afraid. Do I possess the words to tell others about these poor people? I have no true concept of the depth of suffering and depredations these men and women endured, and, as I think of this, I am fervently grateful that my parents immigrated and that I did not grow up with the suffering I hear being described. But since I do not comprehend the magnitude of the degradations this woman has endured, how, then, can I capture the agony of her remembering? She seems to shrink back into the chair as she talks, a tiny, red-haired woman, twisted sideways as if ready to scuttle away if she perceives danger. In her gossamer hands lies a crumpled handkerchief, which she raises to her eyes to dab at the tears left by a half-century of indignities.

The next day I meet Josef, who does not want to reveal even his patronymic and speaks on the condition that nothing about him be identified. He is a tiny man and his voice is a birdlike twitter. He sits behind his vast, walnut desk in one of Donetske's government offices. It is Sunday afternoon, and no one is around. He does not want me to know where he lives. He says very few people know that he is of German extraction, and he wants to keep it that way. An enormous oil painting of Lenin, bent industriously over a desk lit only by a small candle, dominates the wall behind Josef.

Ghosts and secrets haunt him. Josef lost his father during the deportation and his mother raised him and his sister. Two other children died.

His mother earned bread by doing the chores no one else wanted to do in the barracks where they lived "in tiny stalls with paper-thin partitions." Like Sonia Petrovna, Josef remembers stealing frozen potatoes from a field in a kolkhoz and running the risk of being shot on the spot. "They succeeded," he says bitterly, "in reducing us to animals digging with our bare hands in the earth to survive."

He does not realize that years later he continues to be furtive.

"We were caught between two warring powers," he says. "It was a cruel fate."

For Josef, as for Sonia Petrovna, Germany is far off, unfamiliar, and potentially hostile. As long as his neighbors and coworkers do not know about his ethnicity, he can blend into the society, remain safe.

During this time, a man called Aleksandr Grep, an ethnic German whose family had been deported to Asia, was trying to take a group of German families back to the Volga region. He made an exploratory trip to the steppes and was told by local people that Germans were not wanted there. His trip made headlines and when Josef mentions it, he shakes his head in sadness. "No one wants us."

I spend four days among people like Josef and Sonia Petrovna, who were not only abandoned and forgotten for a generation but are still reviled. I think about growing up ashamed of who you are, of hiding or denying your identity, and I am overcome by a feeling of horror. Would this have happened to me if my parents had not fled west? Could I, like these people, turn the other cheek over and over again? Would I have the courage to climb out of the vast grave of shame dug for me by my country?

The moment comes to say good-bye. On the evening of the fourth day, Sasha takes me to the train. Suddenly, I am not able to say anything, but shake his hand with tears in my eyes. He envelops me in a great big bear hug. I return to Kyiv in splendid comfort. Sasha had searched assiduously until he found a second-class coupe seat for me. My companions are a babushka who shares her cold dumplings with me, a man who offers me a slice of salo, and a handsome youth, who sleeps through the entire journey. The babushka pulls the window shade down; I cannot see Ukraine unfolding outside the window. I say nothing because I don't want them to know I am a foreigner, although I notice that the babushka has kind eyes. I realize that I would probably tell her who I am, if the men were not present. I think women who are alone feel safer with other women.

Chapter 17

THE HARD LIFE OF WOMEN

A few days later in Kyiv's Bessarabian Market, I bump into Lidia Mazur, editor in chief of *Zhinka,* a women's magazine with a million and a half readers. She examines my bulging string bag and the equally fat plastic bag I am carrying—one in each hand—and laughs. "You're looking more and more like a local woman," she says. I laugh too, knowing she is right. The desire to eat fresh vegetables and fruit is making me overcome my aversion to long queues and rude vendors.

I met Lidia a few weeks earlier and she has asked me to write a series of articles on family life in America. I agreed readily for two reasons. Lidia has promised to send me the issues in which my articles will appear and I plan to give them to my mother to make her feel proud of me. She has lost the ability to read what I write in English. I know that I will encounter some difficulties in writing in Ukrainian since I never attended Ukrainian school. My mother taught me grammar, history, and literature during Saturday afternoon lessons that continued all the way through high school. The second reason why I write these articles is because in payment for them, Lidia has agreed to spend two afternoons with me discussing Ukrainian women and their concerns.

Lidia is a dark-haired, handsome, and well-dressed woman. She is wearing a blue wool dress and has artfully draped a coordinating scarf around her neckline. When we begin our conversation, I ask her to describe the life and circumstances of a typical reader of *Zhinka*. She considers the question for a moment, then laughs, but not in amusement. "What's a typical woman's life? Not very exciting. A girl gets married at seventeen or eighteen to a boy a year or two older. That's our norm. Children come almost immediately since the couple has no information on family planning and contraceptives are not available, or beyond their means. The girl quickly becomes a woman steeped in her responsibilities."

Lidia cocks her head to the side and examines in her mind's eye the image she has drawn, then elaborates: "The children, the job, and the home consume all available time. Once she has a family, our young woman ceases to have the time to take care of herself. After thirty-five, she grows old quickly."

I noticed this rapid aging in Zariche, where a woman who said she had been my mother's student looked as old as my mother, although she must have been closer to my age. As I got to know more women and listened to what they said, I came to realize that both the state and tradition are conspiring to keep a Slavic woman's focus centered on the home. In Ukraine, there is the ancient cult of Berehynia (Protectress), who was the goddess of the home, the keeper of the family and the nation. The continued existence of this cult restricts—and largely negates—the freedoms and rights a woman in the West takes for granted. Moreover, the cult of the woman as mother and keeper was historically the ideological basis of most women's organizations, including such radical ones as the Committee of Mothers of the Soldiers of Ukraine. In August, 1990, this group staged a mass meeting not to demand feminist rights but to call for better conditions for soldiers—their sons. Tradition assumes that a woman will be a wife and mother first, always.

A young woman, Lidia says, as she continues to refine the portrait of her reader, lives at home, even if she has a job, until she is married. Then she goes from her father's house to her husband's house, at least for a time. Invariably there are no available apartments and the young couple must place their names on a waiting list. Because housing is scarce, it is not unusual for a young couple to wait as long as five years to get a home of their own. In the meantime, the husband and the in-laws have the right to decide whether the bride will be listed as a legal occupant of the in-laws' apartment. If they choose not to list her, she will have no legal right to the flat in the event of a divorce. Divorce is rare and, consequently, joint custody of children and alimony don't exist. A divorced woman has few options. Often, she and the children move back in with her parents. Very, very few women live alone. A woman in Ukraine, but also in Russia, leads a regimented and a restricted life.

"What do women aspire to?" I ask Lidia.

Lidia has the answer ready: "If she's a young mother, she will tell you her dream is to stay home, take care of the children, and cook." That is, the Berehynia cult fulfilled.

I put the same question to Tamara Suplyna, then the president of the Ukrainian Charitable Federation of Business Women. Tamara, a brusque, red-haired woman, is an accountant and has held a job her entire adult life. She shrugs off the "stay-at-home" mentality and the Slavic woman's espousal of the Berehynia cult. Miserable conditions in the shops and factories where most women work make women yearn to get out. "Give her a chance to earn money with dignity, and she will not opt to stay shut away at home," Tamara says.

Shortly after that conversation I come across this government statistic: "In our kolkhozes, 90 percent of the milkers and swineherds are women." But the government has no statistics on women in government or on the wages women earn.

When I ask the women I meet how they feel about their lives, invariably they shrug. The shrug says: "Since there are no alternatives, why should I waste my time dreaming? A woman's life is what it is." These women are convinced that perhaps their daughters will lead different lives, but not they themselves. The eloquent shrug says everything.

Not long after my conversations with Lidia, I accompany Andriy to a ministry conference. Five people sit on the stage behind a wooden table. I ask him to identify them. "Well, you have two former apparatchiks who are members of Parliament, a representative of the peasantry, a university student representing 'new blood,' and the woman."

"Who is she?" I ask.

He shrugs. "There's always a woman."

I watch her throughout the meeting and, in the following weeks, watch other women in similar situations at other meetings and events. These women seldom speak and seldom are consulted. They are deferential to the men. They are the ones who refill the pitcher with water and, after the meeting, they are the ones who collect the tumblers and papers. I consult Lidia when I deliver my articles.

Lidia laughs dryly. "I do the same thing," she says. "I clean up and keep quiet."

I ask her to describe the future of women in her country. She says, "We need to learn not to be so passive. Now that political barriers have come down, we must learn from you, women like you in the West, how to create our own fate."

Sometime later, I encounter one nascent women's group. I am invited to attend the weekly meeting of the Kyiv Women's Union. The meeting is an informal affair, held in the evening in a basement. The space consists of two small rooms. There are a telephone, a desk, and several chairs, but not enough for everyone to have a seat. Some women stand, leaning against the lumpy concrete wall, while others sit on the stone floor. About twenty women attend.

These women have come together not because of ideology but because they wish to control their destinies. All work and many know one another through their jobs. As economic conditions worsened during and following the breakup of the Soviet Union, these women discovered that their jobs were threatened. Women are the first to be given indefinite leaves of absence, to have salaries cut, to be laid off.

One woman says: "Our boss keeps the men, but lays off the women, even if they have seniority."

Olena Zamostian, at that time the president of the Kyiv group, explains that many layoffs have a sinister side. Employees who are let go stand to lose their rights to obtain shares in a business once it is privatized. "It is in the boss's interest to shrink the labor force to as few people as possible because then the shares can be divided among fewer people," she explains. "I know women who are being left with nothing. It's happening everywhere."

At the Women's Union, women given a pink slip seek help from other women. In one flagrant case, a boss fired all women workers and hired his cronies in their place. Shortly thereafter, the agency privatized and the shares were distributed among the new workers. Subsequently, several women banded together and sued, an unheard of move. The Women's Union found a lawyer for them. The case will take several years to decide, but there may be a chance that the adverse publicity would force the boss to rehire the women he let go.

Chapter 18

MOSCOW AND ZAGORSK

Tania Smirnova, who does occasional secretarial work for Oleksander Oleksanderovych, offers to help when she learns that I want to go to Moscow. She is a plump woman with strawberry-blond hair, a big smile, excellent English, red talons for fingernails, and friends everywhere. I have a choice of going by train or flying. Tania considers, then asks if I have a visa for Russia. I don't. "The train," she says.

A few days later, she presents me with two first-class seats on the overnight train to Moscow and back. Since I had given her more money than the tickets cost, she explains with that big smile of hers: *"Ne pomazhesh, ne pojedesh."* This proverb translates roughly as: "If you don't grease (the wheel), you'll go nowhere." I laugh with her since I don't mind at all. She also arranges for me to stay with her best friend in Moscow, Lyuda Kuraeva, and mentions, with an offhand gesture of her beautifully manicured hands, that the friendship dates to the time they spent in Cuba.

I feel a sense of great anticipation. In my mind, Moscow is not only the center of the penal colony I have feared all my life but also the place where the metamorphosis of the penal colony began three months earlier. As I pack, I anticipate the extraordinary.

A mean, cold drizzle chills Moscow's opaque air. It's eight o'clock in the morning, but it's barely dawn. No one is waiting for me at the train platform. I make my way upstairs to the cavernous waiting room, but at this hour it is deserted. I go outside. Across the square, a snaking queue of black umbrellas juts out into an expanse of cobblestones. As I consider the possibility of hailing a cab, I see hurrying toward me a woman carrying three unwrapped, golden loaves of white, French baguette-type bread.

"You look exactly like Tania said you would," the woman says. "Only foreigners wear red."

Lyuda is a true "Moskvichka": dark reddish hair, a pert nose, a thin-lipped broad smile showing prominent teeth and a gold-capped molar. She is in high spirits because she has bought the bread without having to wait in a line. She says it is from a small, private bakery not far from the train station. The loaves cost five times the price of the heavy rye bread at the government bakery down the block where the queue of umbrellas undulates. From Lyuda's purchase, her gray-and-white-check wool coat with its modish flared skirt and fur collar, and her high-heeled leather boots, also trimmed with fur, I surmise that she is well off, although she is a divorcee, a combination rare in Russia. Tania told me about the divorce so that I wouldn't put my foot in my mouth by asking Lyuda the whereabouts of her husband. He apparently ran off with a young woman and any mention of him pitches Lyuda into a depression.

Before my departure, Tania also explained the Cuba connection. The two women met in Cuba in the 1970s when they accompanied their husbands, who were "advisers" helping Fidel Castro. The two families lived next door to each other in a Russian compound. Tania used to baby-sit Lyuda's son, Timofey, when he was a baby.

"You *lived* in Florida?" Lyuda marvels, her voice full of wonder, as we compare the subtropical Caribbean weather to Moscow's. We are in a car—an early 1960s Chevrolet with fins for taillights and a pair of fuzzy dice dangling from the rearview mirror—driven by one of Lyuda's neighbors. He says nothing, but watches us in the mirror as we leave Moscow's center for the suburbs. "We used to sit on the beach in Cuba and look toward Miami and imagine how it would be to go there just for a day," Lyuda says. "Is it rich and beautiful?"

Before my return to Kyiv, Lyuda will tell me another Cuba story: One sunny January afternoon, she and several other Russians were on the beach sunning and swimming. A helicopter circled over them, then landed. A tall man dressed in army fatigues got out. The women recognized Fidel Castro. He saw them from the air and stopped to find out who swam in the ocean in the middle of winter. "He was very nice. He posed for a photograph with us."

Lyuda lives in one of the anonymous high-rise suburbs that ring Moscow. Each of the apartment clusters is a village, with its own cinema, post office, food stores, and bakery. It is too early for the cinema to be open, but the dairy store is selling milk. About forty people are queued outside. They are dressed in heavy shapeless coats and clunky boots. None of the aura of the urban sophisticate that exudes from Lyuda is present in the long, unhappy queue. The sociologist Pitirim Sorokin

describes these inhabitants of the high-rise villages as the urban peasantry, transported into cities during Stalin's industrialization and unable
ever to go back because the village no longer exists, having been replaced
by the kolkhoz.

Lyuda's apartment is on the eleventh floor in a building that looks
like a dreary tenement. The entry door does not close, the lobby walls
are grimy with years of palm prints and dirt, and the elevator smells of
urine. Lyuda's apartment, however, is a middle-class haven—clean, well
furnished, and cozy. It is one of three apartments serviced by a small,
private vestibule. A heavy door, padded in red fake leather and always
kept locked, separates the vestibule from the grungy public hallway.

The apartment has a small central foyer from which all rooms radi-
ate. To the left is the bathroom, partitioned into two cubicles, one for
the toilet, the other for the bathtub and sink. Next to the bathroom is
the kitchen, which is large enough to serve also as a dining room. A good-
sized, rectangular room that is furnished in what I have learned is middle-
class Russian décor is next to the kitchen. A dark, flocked wallpaper covers
the walls. A heavy, dark wooden sideboard with a hutch dominates one
long wall. A sofa covered with a kilim and a small table with a very large
TV set occupy the opposite wall. A kilim-type rug extends wall to wall
and a similar, smaller rug hangs behind the sofa on the flowery wallpaper.
The sofa is the fold-down type. I look around and surmise that this room
serves several functions. It is the parlor where guests are received. It is
also the family room because of the TV set, and it also is Lyuda's bedroom. The third room is a smaller version of Lyuda's room. It has a sofa/
futon, a wall unit, and a desk instead of the side table. From the books
and the posters on the wall, I know this is Timofey's room. He has just
turned eighteen and works as a night watchman on weekends at the same
factory where his mother works as a secretary in the director's office.
During the week Timofey, quiet and shy, is enrolled in an engineering
institute. I will stay in Timofey's room since he will be away working.

Each room has a double window on its short wall. The windows are
covered with white organdy curtains. One evening, I try to open a window because my room has grown unbearably hot and discover that the
windows have been taped shut. I ask Lyuda about the taping and she
says that all windows in Moscow—in all of Russia—are taped shut in
November and the tape is not removed until the following April.

Lyuda lives well. Hers is not one of the infamous "Khrushchevkas," a
type of apartment built in the 1960s during Nikita Khrushchev's reforms.
Russians remember Khrushchev for two things: He released political

prisoners from the concentration camps where Stalin had sent them by the tens of thousands; and he also launched a huge building campaign to ease housing conditions and overcrowding. Unfortunately, the new flats were tiny and ill designed, where one room opened into the next one, affording no privacy. When Khrushchev fell from grace, so did the Khrushchevka. It became universally hated. People wait for years to "move up" into an apartment like Lyuda's.

We spend most of the time in the kitchen at a birch table that also serves as the dining room. A sink, a stove, and a refrigerator, and birch cabinets line the far wall. A bulky cabinet without drawers occupies a sizable space near the door. An elaborate birdcage made from wrought iron and painted white sits on top of the cabinet. Inside the cage, an energetic parrot provides constant entertainment. The bird goes into ecstasies of chirping and cooing whenever addressed. It has mastered a number of Russian words, among them *pozhaluista* (please), and loves to show off and preen. Lyuda bought the parrot in Cuba. Eventually, I will see what's beneath the birdcage. Lyuda will place the birdcage on the table, unhinge the door on the front of the bulky cabinet, and step aside to show me a washing machine. She will do this with a gravity that borders on ritual and I will know that this is a rare and prized possession.

On this first morning in Moscow, Lyuda wants me to rest but I want to go to Red Square. We compromise by eating an early obeyd of chicken-fried steak and noodles, although it is barely eleven o'clock in the morning, before setting out.

Downtown Moscow reminds me of Washington, D.C.—another one of my former homes—since every important building is a government office of some kind. But Moscow's crowds are New York City crowds, energetic, always in a hurry, street smart. I am told that ten million people live in Moscow and another ten million visit it daily. These huge crowds mind their own business and hide behind a mask of stony indifference. They see you, but you are not noticed, which is quite an accomplishment. People shift only their eyes while taking an inventory of you. No one ever exchanges smiles.

Once we reach Red Square, I stop and stare. There is a Russian proverb, and now I understand it: "There is nothing above Moscow except the Kremlin, and nothing greater than the Kremlin except heaven." For nearly 850 years, this part of the world has revolved around Moscow, and Moscow around the Kremlin. Westerners think that Red Square was renamed after the Revolution, as many streets, squares, and cities were.

That is not the case. It's been called Krasnaya Ploschad since the seventeenth century, probably because of the deep, blood-red color of its brick walls. Smack in the center of the square is Lenin's tomb, red also, but of stone, not brick. Here behind the parapet the members of the Politburo used to stand to review the military might of the Soviet Union on the anniversary of the Bolshevik Revolution and on May Day. I suggest we join the queue in front of the tomb and see Lenin's mummy, but Lyuda vetoes the idea. She says Lenin's coffin is solid except for a small piece of glass through which the visitor can glimpse a portion of the face. "It could be anyone in there," she scoffs.

Lenin is déclassé, even in Moscow.

Red Square is a vast rectangle with a hump in the middle. The cobbled expanse slopes down to the right and left. I have read somewhere that the square is the length of five football fields. Because of its size, Red Square became the favored place for military parades and remained so until the dissolution of the Soviet Union. Here's how Zara Witkin, a California civil engineer who worked in Russia in the early 1930s, remembers one of the great shows of Soviet military strength:

> The military bands stationed in the Square blared forth a stirring march. The battalions sprang into motion. Rank by rank in brisk precision they marched past the Lenin Mausoleum saluting their leaders in the reviewing stand. After the infantry had passed, there ensued a lull, the air full of expectancy. Then, in a terrific charge over the stony pavement, galloped the cavalry. So headlong was their rush that several horsemen were thrown from their mounts and ridden down in the press. Stretcher-bearers quickly carried them off. Next came the light artillery, followed by the heavy motorized field pieces. Then, sinister, formidable, the ponderous tanks rumbled. For almost two hours the military divisions passed with heavy tread in review through Red Square.

To the left of Lenin's tomb rise the speckled domes of St. Basil's Cathedral, a church that even Stalin was too scared to dynamite in the ferocious 1930s, although he did blow up Christ the Savior Cathedral so that his tanks could have easier access into Red Square. Since the collapse of the Soviet Union, St. Basil's has been returned to the Orthodox Church, as has the Assumption Cathedral inside the Kremlin walls. The Kazan Cathedral, whose name derives from the icon of the Virgin of Kazan, has been rebuilt on its original site in the northeast corner of Red

Square, near GUM, the department store. The Cathedral of Christ the Savior was rebuilt to coincide with the 1997 celebration of Moscow's 850th birthday. However, the interior embellishment of the golden-domed, marble-clad church is still under way.

As we wait in line, Timofey tells me a grisly legend I have not heard before. Ivan the Terrible ordered St. Basil's built to commemorate his victory over the Mongols in 1552. When the church was completed, Ivan toured it with the architect. At the end of the tour, the czar turned to the architect and asked if he could duplicate a building as beautiful as St. Basil's. The foolish architect said yes, and Ivan had him blinded. There is a lesson to be learned from this legend: don't tell the truth if it might get you in trouble. Russians learned this lesson well, both under the czars and under Communism. Westerners, who don't understand this, accuse Russians of lying, which they will say they are not. This national aversion to being the bearer of bad news contributed, I think, to making Chernobyl the enormous disaster it became. When the reactor blew up, the leaders in Moscow were told, at least in the beginning, what they wanted to hear: "Everything is under control." Everything was not under control and would not be for months, years.

On this cold, blustery November afternoon, Red Square is teeming with activity. No one seems to notice the biting rain. We watch three soldiers goose-step from the Kremlin for the changing of the guard at Lenin's mausoleum. The ceremony interrupts newly made brides who are being photographed in front of the tomb in their wedding dresses, while relatives hold black umbrellas above the heads of the newlyweds. When I ask her about the picture taking, Lyuda says visiting Red Square following the marriage ceremony is a tradition dating back to the society marriage markets in centuries past, held annually in Moscow in the vicinity of the Kremlin. Today's brides leave their bouquets at the eternal flame burning nearby.

As we walk along the Kremlin walls, Lyuda points out the graves of Josef Stalin; Lenin's lover, the French revolutionary Inessa Armand; writer Maxim Gorky; and cosmonaut Yuri Gagarin. Lyuda says that nearly six hundred people are buried in the shadow of the walls. She has a surprise in store for me—she has obtained tickets to the Diamond Fund. These tickets are hard to get and Lyuda must have great connections, just as her friend Tania does in Kyiv.

The Diamond Fund is the depository of the crown jewels of the Romanov czars. Set in brilliantly lit, velvet-lined, bulletproof-glass cases, the jewels of Russia are extraordinary. Looking at them, I realize the difference between jewelry and jewels. In the cases lie pearls the size of almonds, sapphires the size of eggs, rubies as large as golf balls. The colored gems are surrounded by diamonds and embellished with gold and fanciful enamel. Each piece is more magnificent than the last one. Catherine the Great, especially, loved large ostentatious jewels.

A visitor can wander through most of the Kremlin's museums and churches at will, but in the Diamond Fund, where guards stand at the door and visitors must pass through a metal detector, movement is restricted by the tour guide. The electronic device has detected the camera in my purse and it has been confiscated, but I do get it back later.

When we leave the Diamond Fund and visit the three Kremlin churches that are open, I suggest that we stop at the Metropole Hotel for coffee since the day has grown cold and an early dusk has fallen. Lyuda says the bouncer will not let us in. I say, "Watch." At the hotel entrance, a burly man steps in front of us and barks, "For hotel guests only." Lyuda backs away. I hold my ground. "What did you say?" I ask in English, smiling brightly at him. "I don't speak Russian."

He jumps back as if I had hit him. "Pardon. Pardon," he cries, and bows us in.

The restaurant takes Western currency only. We order coffee and pastry and it costs fifteen dollars. But it was worth coming in just to see the expression on the bouncer's face, I say to myself as we sip and nibble at the pastries. This is when I am suddenly struck by the fact that I am beginning to understand the October Revolution—the great transforming event of the twentieth century in Eastern Europe. I am different from Lyuda and the people around me because I escaped being transformed by Communism. I am not afraid, while Lyuda is, as are the shuffling and distrustful crowds on Moscow's streets. Although it may exasperate me at times, I really don't mind being noticed because I wear a red parka. The West nurtures individuality, while Communism pulverizes it. Bolshevism expelled the kulaks, the merchants, the middle class, the thinkers, and the entrepreneurs and installed clerks and drones, docile and mute. The Revolution triumphed—but also made its own eventual downfall inevitable. Fear and drones cannot govern a nation forever.

If I had grown up in the Soviet Union, I doubt I would have dared to challenge the authority of the bouncer at the Metropole Hotel or, earlier, the guard at the headquarters of the Ukrainian Communist Party.

Lyuda noticed my interest in icons during our tour of the Kremlin's churches and suggests that I hire a car to Zagorsk, where I will see the finest icons of the Virgin Mary in all of Russia. She adds that she has seen enough Virgin Marys to last a lifetime, but Timofey and his girlfriend, Lana, about whom Lyuda has mixed feelings, will go with me.

The drive takes two hours, instead of the promised one. Sleet and rain obscure the countryside. We finally pull up in front of a monstrous stone wall. It is forty-five feet thick, two miles long, and is dominated by spires and onion domes of six incredible churches. A local priest was murdered in the shadows of this wall a year earlier, the act creating a national scandal and triggering rumors of ecclesiastical political shenanigans.

The Troitse-Sergeiyevsky Lavra, or Trinity Monastery of St. Sergius, is located behind the monstrous wall. The monastery's founder was St. Sergius, who is the patron saint of Russia. He is credited with single-handedly deflecting the Mongols from sacking Moscow back in the fourteenth century. In the seventeenth century, the monastery sheltered the boy-czars Peter and Ivan against mutinous palace guards. A hundred years later, Catherine the Great, who did not get along with the church, secularized most of the monastery's holdings.

The interior of the Troitse basilica is cavernous and dim, except for the glittering tomb of St. Sergius. I wonder if the sootiness is the result of the 1986 fire in which five monks died, or of five hundred years of smoke from votive candles. The cathedral's iconostasis once held the most famous icon of the Holy Trinity, which was painted specifically for the cathedral by Andrei Rublyev, who was one of Russia's greatest icon painters. I know from my reading that the icon on display is not the original but a realistically sooty copy. The original has been taken to Moscow.

Timofey and Lana leave me as soon as I say I am going to the cathedral. They go to the Historical Museum to examine contemporary glass and furnishings. I begin to understand why they did not mind accompanying me. I have surmised from their whispers in the car that they are thinking of getting married, although Timofey has not, as yet, shared his plans with Lyuda.

An enchanting soprano is singing inside the cathedral. The smoky air carries an overlay of sweetness imparted by the incense burner a priest is swinging energetically over the bent heads of the congregation. To honor St. Sergius, the monks celebrate a liturgy called the *akathist* from dawn until late in the evening. This service is conducted at a small altar adjacent to the tomb of St. Sergius. Some twenty kerchiefed, mostly older women have gathered and are singing the responses. They are led by the wonderful soprano. The voice belongs to a woman with a coarse, careworn face. She holds a large book with large Old Church Slavonic script, and as the priest finishes his chant, she echoes him in the melody of the response. As she sings, the priest swings the *kadylo* up and down and wisps of burning incense curl upward into the shadows of the enormous nave. The kadylo in which incense burns during services is usually made of silver and consists of a round container suspended from three short chains. During the longer responses, the priest turns toward the congregation and wafts the incense into the nave so that the congregation is enveloped in the sweet smell of the smoke. At such moments, as if the incense is transporting the singers to visions of otherworldly vistas, the singing seems to change into an ancestral Russian plaint and the deep lines on the soprano's face soften.

During the service, a steady stream of people, for the most part women, approach the main altar. They fall to their knees before the golden gate of the iconostasis, then creep, sometimes on all fours, to the dull silver sarcophagus of St. Sergius. Here they again prostrate themselves. There is a rag to wipe off the spot where they kiss the tomb and a platter for donations. But quite often, one of the petitioners will pass something to the priest, or drop something onto another platter in front of him on the altar. I am curious and decide to find out what these pilgrims are doing.

Timing my approach when no one is kneeling at the crypt, I creep forward and mimic the ritual I have observed. I wipe the crypt before kissing it fleetingly, drop some ruble notes on the collection plate, then dawdle, keeping my eyes on the pile of papers on the altar. The priest picks up a slip, scans it, then chants a petition. The mystery of the slips of paper is solved: these are written supplications to St. Sergius. I make my way back into the congregation and my red parka attracts several disapproving glances.

In the Historical Museum, the icons fill a large gallery and an adjacent room. Most are of the Virgin Mary, as Lyuda had promised. I spend a long time in that gallery and leave to find Timofey and Lana when the guard says it is closing time.

I leave Zagorsk with my appetite for icons whetted. The next day is Sunday and I ask Lyuda to take me to Izmailovo, Moscow's largest flea market, to buy an icon. Lyuda rolls her eyes and tries to talk me out of going. She tells me we will be robbed, especially since I am obviously an American. I do wear a red parka. An acquaintance of an acquaintance of Lyuda's went shopping at Izmailovo a few weeks back. She saw a winter jacket and bought it. As she was walking away with her purchase, two men approached her and said: "When you leave the market, you'll give the jacket to us."

The woman realized they meant business and spent the rest of the day looking for someone she knew with whom she could leave. But the day passed and she had to go home alone. The two thugs were waiting for her and relieved her of her purchase.

"Why didn't she get the militia to help her?" I ask Lyuda.

Lyuda just rolls her eyes at my naïveté.

We compromise. I will wear one of Lyuda's coats to Izmailovo.

At the park, I head for tables covered with *shkatulkas,* the wonderful lacquered boxes that replaced icon painting and church embellishment during the Soviet regime. The subject matter of the exquisite miniature paintings on the lids, and occasionally the sides of the boxes, was usually drawn from Russian mythology or folklore, reliable subject matter as far as the Communist government was concerned. Despite Lyuda's objections, I ask questions. One of the sellers says he is an artist, as are the other sellers around him. He and the others no longer want to work for the government-sanctioned collectives that produce the lacquered boxes. He is selling his work himself because he can earn more money doing so. I have read up on shkatulkas before coming to Moscow and know what to look for—the artist's signature and the name of the collective under the painting. Once I ascertain that these dissident artists come from some of the most famous collectives, I purchase several shkatulkas. I then let Lyuda lead me away to look at icons. As promised, I restrict myself to "How much?" and a few "das" and "nyets," and a lot of nodding and sympathetic listening.

I have perhaps two hundred icons to choose from, from large pieces obviously cut from an iconostasis, to small silver-clad ones, to old, dark icons where the features of the saint are barely visible. I buy an icon of St. Nicholas and one of the Virgin of Smolensk.

Lyuda stays at my elbow the entire time, in sharp contrast to her trying to disassociate herself from me when I was talking to the artists. She even offers her opinion on the icons and barters with the sellers. When we are ready to leave, the national cunning of self-preservation reveals itself in a simple act. She takes me by the elbow and waits until several people are departing, then pulls me in after her and we mingle with the group. Lyuda steps in front of me and engages a man in a conversation as we pass through the gate. All the way to the metro, the man flirts with her.

In the apartment, we examine my purchases minutely. Neither Lyuda nor Timofey can comprehend why I have spent money on old, chipped, bad-smelling icons.

Lyuda tells me that when she was growing up it was fashionable for Pioneers—children who belonged to a scoutlike organization that trained future Communists—to destroy the icons their parents had.

"We were taught to be atheists," Lyuda says. "Our leaders urged us to tear icons from the place of honor in our homes and throw them into the stove. This was a heroic act, since, usually, the Pioneer had his behind paddled by his parents."

"Did you?"

She smiles a toothy smile. "But I was held up as a shining example in school."

Chapter 19

THE CAT BURGLAR

I do not sleep well on trains. I like a steady, not a rolling bed, and the excitement generated by the trip keeps me awake. Dnipropetrovsk. Kharkiv. Poltava. I try the names on my tongue and they fill me with the same wonder I experienced when I first arrived in Kyiv. I learned about these cities in the Saturday afternoon lessons my mother gave me. Dnipropetrovsk was the city the German Army leveled during its retreat from Russia in World War II. This is where the rockets aimed at the West used to be manufactured. Kharkiv was once the capital of Ukraine, the stronghold of the Dnipro Cossacks. Poltava is famous for its beautiful embroidery and the soft and melodious speech of its inhabitants. This is the city where Peter the Great defeated Charles XII of Sweden and Hetman Ivan Mazepa, then leveled the town and killed all its inhabitants. What are these cities like to live in today? Will I ever have the opportunity to get off the train to stroll their streets?

I had wanted to take a daytime express train to Moscow and back, but Tania, as well as Volodia and Andriy, said such trains did not exist. Express trains between far-flung cities run at night. It is eminently sensible, Andriy explained with a straight, solemn face. "It's really a good idea to take an overnight train for a long journey. You get a good night's rest and you can go about your business the next day refreshed."

"What about a tourist who wants to travel sitting up during the day so that she can see the countryside?" I asked. I didn't add what I was really thinking: that the system of overnight trains is just another example of the lingering psychosis about spies that the Soviet regime has left behind.

Everyone I consulted considered my idea of touring strange. The point is to get to one's destination in the shortest possible time. Wanting to dawdle, wanting to make frequent stops and detours, is decidedly one of my American oddities.

So I went to Moscow and back at night. After all, I could not complain since Tania obtained the very best accommodations. First class is called the SV (CB in Cyrillic lettering) and consists of one or two cars in a train that may have thirty coaches. The special SV cars accommodate eighteen passengers in nine two-berth compartments, called coupes. I have a coupe all to myself to Moscow and back.

On the way to Moscow, I woke up several times, but when I looked out of the window, all I saw was dense fog and pale yellow lights shimmering in the distance. I got up with the first gray light so that I could glimpse at least a bit of the countryside. The day was unpromising, as was the landscape. I saw a gray sky, rain and occasional snow, a dreary expanse of fields interspersed with villages, their streets choked with mud and lined with shanties. Beyond the villages and the fields, forlorn groves of bare-branched trees dotted the horizon, while white-trunked birches along the edges loomed like ghosts. As we swept past one dilapidated train siding after another, the waste I saw was astonishing. Construction materials were piled into untidy heaps—lumber, window jambs, bricks, and even what looked like concrete mix—with no tarp to shield them from getting wet. Some of the lumber stuck out of the mud, but much of it had already sunk into the mire and the puddles. I remembered reading how central planning generated waste and defied logic: Each day a train from Moscow chugged to St. Petersburg with a load of concrete roof beams and passed on its way a train from St. Petersburg carrying concrete roof beams to a construction site in Moscow.

On the way back from Moscow, I decide to get up early again to compare the Russian countryside with the Ukrainian and be at the window when the train crosses the Dnipro River.

Before I left Kyiv, Volodia warned me to be careful. "Make sure you put all your luggage under your bunk," he advised. "Don't leave anything out."

But I am alone in the coupe, and I ignore his advice. I place my luggage across from me on the unoccupied bunk. The attendant brings hot tea and clean sheets and I reach into my purse, which is sitting on the bunk next to me, to pay her. When I go to bed, I leave my belongings on the bunk instead of stowing them away in the hatch below the seat.

The coach quiets down slowly. Doors bang open and shut as passengers make their way to the toilets, one on each end of the coach. A draft of cold air creeps into my coupe whenever someone goes out on the tiny platform between traincars to smoke.

I fall asleep. Sometime during the night I wake up because a sliver of light passes over my face. This surprises me because I realize in my half-awake state that my coupe door must be open a crack. I sit up, extend my hand and close it. A voice keeps whispering that this is strange because I know I had locked the door, but another voice points out that the train is rolling heavily and the lock must have sprung open.

I doze fitfully. Suddenly something tinkles. I sit up, thinking the empty tea glass, which the attendant had failed to collect, has rolled off the tiny table by the window and shattered. As I sit up, I reach for the light switch. My fingers connect with something warm, a body. It recoils. Instinctively, I grab. Somehow I manage to grab a wrist.

Just then, the door rolls open, the hall light streams in, and I see the cat burglar. He is crouching on the other berth, my wallet frozen in the hand I am holding.

I am shocked, but not terribly afraid. The first thought is: "Good grief, cat burglars do wear body suits and blacken their faces. It's not just a Hollywood invention."

The man is tiny and slippery. He tries to yank his hand out of my grasp, but I hold on. "Sit still," I say, "or I'll scream."

He stops squirming.

I take my wallet from his hand and place it next to me.

Suddenly he says, "What time is it?"

"What?" I demand.

"What time is it?" he insists.

Like a dummy, I glance down on my watch.

In that instant, the cat burglar slips out of my grasp and disappears through the half-open door.

I turn on the light. I get up and test the lock. It works fine. It has not been forced. I lock the door but don't feel much better. The cat burglar has a key to my coupe. What would have happened if he had been more aggressive or had had a knife?

I go through the motions of examining my wallet. It has a change purse that gapes empty. The clasp must have sprung open as the cat burglar fumbled in my purse. The change spilled out and, as it fell to the floor, tinkled. The noise of falling coins had awakened me. I look down. The kopecks lie scattered all over the floor of the coupe.

I do not asleep again. The paranoia I thought I had escaped by blending into the background and becoming "one of them" is running rampant. Who knew that an American, a foreigner, was in this coupe? Tania, who had bought the tickets. Lyuda knew also. She accompanied me to the train. The attendant, who had brought tea, saw me; yet I hardly said anything to her. Had this been a random burglary, or did someone always know where I could be found?

Chapter 20

BIRTH OF AN INDEPENDENT NATION

Not long after my return from Moscow, a monumental event in the life of Ukraine—and in my life—takes place. I am in Kyiv when "Little Russia" secedes from the Soviet Union. Like any child of political émigrés, I grew up with a dream. The dream was to see a Ukraine free of Russia. On December 1, 1991, and again on December 6, I witness the snapping of the 350-year-old chain.

Volodia asks me to write for *News from Ukraine* about the referendum on independence and the election of Ukraine's first independently elected president. I join a group of journalists from every part of the globe as Leonid Kravchuk, who is expected to win the presidency, casts his ballot, and I stay behind to talk to the voters after he and the press leave.

On this overcast election day, voters are casting their ballots with solemn and grave demeanor. People look thoughtful. They mark the paper ballots with a religious zeal that evokes the pilgrims in Zagorsk who prostrated themselves before St. Sergius in the hope that their petitions would be granted. Like pilgrims embarking on pilgrimages to fulfill their dreams or visions, Ukrainian voters believe that their future lies in the small rectangular pieces of paper they are depositing into tall, wooden ballot boxes aligned in a neat row in the middle of the hall. They approach the ballot boxes with a discernible air of ceremony. After pressing their ballots through the narrow slit on top of the box, these pilgrims turn away with shining, dreamy eyes, eyes brimming with tears. Or is the sheen fearful expectation? These pilgrims know that the occasion is momentous and their vote—their supplication—will alter their and their children's future.

"How did I vote? For independence, of course," says Natalia Bazhanova, who came with her husband and daughter. "We are deciding our destiny today."

An elderly woman leaning on a cane pauses to consider my question. "I voted in so many elections that I lost track of them long ago," she says. "But this one's special. Of course I voted for independence. Everyone I know did."

A few hours later, I accompany an election official, who is carrying a small version of the rectangular ballot box, on his rounds to housebound voters so that they, too, can vote. And as I watch these frail men and women mark the ballot with a pencil that trembles in their fingers, I am struck again by the gravity of the event. In this election, 84 percent of the nearly thirty-eight million eligible voters would vote. Of these, 91 percent would vote for national independence. Leonid Kravchuk wins the presidency with a 60 percent majority.

Ukraine's movement away from Russia—and here I am drawing a distinction between the Soviet Union and Russia—began when Ukrainians lost their awe and fear of the Muscovite Big Brother as glasnost unfolded. There was little to admire in the televised convocations of the Soviet Communist Party in Moscow or in the delegates when they spoke. Even on meeting the Russian secretary general, Mikhail Gorbachev, face to face, Ukrainians were not impressed. The man could be rattled. The icon flubbed his lines.

Here is a transcript of Gorbachev's remarks caught by a Kyiv microphone, as he addressed a crowd in a square off Khreshchatyk. "Listen, we coped after the imperialist war, after the civil war, when the country was in ruins. Nothing was left after that. But we coped. We coped. They predicted Russia would never rise again after the war, but we rose again." Then he adds, "For all the people who are striving for a good Russia . . . er, the Soviet Union, I mean . . . that is what we call it now, and what it is in fact, for them it is a bulwark."

The Kyiv crowd jeered, and the insidious microphone captured that jeering. Ukrainians were tired of having their republic lumped with Russia, tired of being considered Russians. Their city, Kyiv—their civilization—was five hundred years older than that of the Moscow upstart. And slowly Ukraine began to rebel.

There were other reasons that led to the break with Moscow, one of them being language. If the language is the soul of a nation, then Ukraine was on the verge of losing its soul and it foresaw that tragedy. After World War II, Russian increasingly became the language of commerce, of politics, and of the cities, which had burgeoned in the second half of the twentieth century. In the meantime, the rural population shrank. This demographic change was significant because ever since the time of the

Dnipro Cossacks, the conservative, religious peasantry had kept the Ukrainian language and the national traditions alive. In 1939, 58 percent of the population lived in villages, 29 percent were workers, and 13 percent were white-collar city dwellers. By the 1990s, the percentage of people living in the villages had fallen to 30 percent. In the cities, the new residents were increasingly Russified, not only through the insistent government policy but also by their neighbors, the immigrant Russians who settled by the millions in Ukrainian cities. Ukrainian became the language of the poor, the ignorant, and the backward. In the meantime, Soviet Ukrainian leaders, mimicking Gorbachev, were saying that their *babusias* (the diminutive form of babushkas, or grandmothers) spoke a quaint tongue, but that *Homo sovieticus* was a man above quaintness and folklore.

The language was dying not only in the anonymous high-rise apartments and on the sidewalks; it was also dying on the page. With few exceptions, Ukrainian writers were writing in Russian to get their work published. Those few who wrote in Ukrainian, such as the poet Vasyl Stus, had died in the Siberian gulag. Authorities destroyed Stus's manuscripts. The demise of Ukrainian in Ukraine at the end of the twentieth century was not yet an accomplished fact, not yet the inevitable future, but it was a possibility. With the exception of the Western Ukrainian minority, the cities of Eastern Ukraine had forgotten it. Russification was finally taking hold, and Ukraine, as a distinct nation, was dying.

Then the pivotal 1991 dawned. In January, Pope John Paul II legitimized, and thus resurrected, the clandestine Ukrainian Catholic Church by dispatching a cardinal to take up residence in Lviv. In March, local elections catapulted candidates of Rukh to power. In June, the Parliament, swept up in the fervor of the reformers, declared the primacy of Ukrainian laws over those of the USSR. Ukraine waited and watched as the coup unfolded in Moscow in August. A friend told me that on August 20, on the second day of the coup, tanks blocked the highway to the airport, as if someone was about to seize it, but nothing happened. As the coup collapsed, the Verkhovna Rada (which would become the Parliament) met and declared "the creation of the independent Ukrainian state—Ukraine." Not *the* Ukraine, not a colony of Russia, but Ukraine. And in this moment, the name, born eight hundred years before, finally achieved its meaning. *Ukraina* appeared first in the twelfth-century chronicles of the exploits of the Kyivan princes. It derived from the Indo-European root *krei,* which meant both "to separate" and "to cut." At the end of the momentous year of 1991, Ukraine does both. In

*Poet and parliamentarian
Ivan Drach speaking at a
rally of Rukh in 1991.
Photograph by Valentyn
Bondarenko.*

the fifteenth century, the word evolved to mean "borderland" and later
into the Ukrainian word for country. At the end of the momentous year
of 1991, Ukraine carries out the original meaning of its Indo-European
root. In the December 1 plebiscite and the formal act of secession by the
Verkhovna Rada on December 6, Ukraine cuts itself from the Soviet
Union and hastens the collapse of the empire three weeks later.

As I witness these events, I think often of my mother. If only she could
be here to see her dream of Ukraine's nationhood come true. If only she
could rejoice with the throngs crowding the Square of Independence,

once called the Square of the October Revolution, once a square dominated by a monstrous Lenin. The only physical evidence that he ever stood here is a plywood-shrouded, empty pedestal, the uneven wood covered with graffiti.

Of course, the road to independence was not that simple, and there were a number of other important reasons why the Soviet Empire disappeared. Yet, when someone asks me what brought about the downfall, I say, "Television." Television, satellite communications, and, yes, CNN and Ted Turner. My reasoning may be simplistic and perhaps too narrow. One could argue that President Ronald Reagan—my mother's favorite president and a man who suffered with the same illness that she did—and his lavish funding of America's "Star Wars" defense systems drove the Soviet Union to near bankruptcy as it tried to keep up. Yet I think that Cold War defense spending was not as important as the technological revolution that put satellites in the sky, which carried twenty-four hours of news from Turner's superstation. CNN created a global network of television images, which could not be blocked with the huge jamming towers that I saw everywhere in Ukraine.

But it wasn't only access, even if sporadic, to images from the West that opened the Iron Curtain; Soviet television itself demystified the Kremlin rulers. During Brezhnev's regime, a television set became a standard in practically every Soviet home. The saturation of apartments with television sets coincided with the advent of glasnost and access to incredible images. For the first time ever, television showed Politburo members not as giants on giant posters but as normal people, visitors in your depressing little flat. These people perspired like you did, picked their noses, and flubbed their lines. Television gave the "czars" of Communism a dimension that the masses had never experienced before. Brezhnev looked catatonic. Gorbachev was outshouted at the plenary session of the Communist Party.

Along with television and glasnost came the first communications satellites and CNN. If you tried hard enough, you could not only see Gorbachev being insulted by a stolid deputy from some forsaken kolkhoz, but you could also tune in to a CNN broadcast and glimpse that far-off magic land—the West. At a party in an apartment in the Darnitsa suburb of Kyiv one evening, one of the men was surfing channels. (I think there were four at that time.) Suddenly he tuned in to CNN. A satellite was passing in the heavens above Kyiv, someone explained to me. Around us conversation stopped as everyone turned to watch. No one in the room except me knew English. Yet, every one of the guests watched in fascination. They were waiting for the ads. When an ad came on, showing a store and a woman with a shopping cart going down the aisles in search of something like Hamburger Helper, everyone's eyes were glued to the screen. When the newscast resumed, I was inundated with questions. Are your stores really so big and so full of merchandise, or is this propaganda? Our leaders told us that we lived well, but when we see . . .

Not only in Ukraine but throughout the Soviet Union, people were receiving proof through their television sets that Moscow had been lying for years, both when it rewrote history and lied about the past and when it talked about present-day life in the West. Rumors of a consumer utopia were not a CIA-planted lie but the truth. "Is it really like this in America? You don't have to stand in line to buy goods?" I was asked again and again by wide-eyed people ready to be disenchanted with their lot. And I did everything to disenchant them. "Yes, yes, yes!! It is true," I said.

The return of the diaspora augmented the increasingly unstoppable flow of information, and, once again, crafty Josef Stalin was being proven right. At the end of World War II, he had declared that those who had been to the West would "contaminate" those at home with the information they brought back and, therefore, had to be shot or sent to Siberia. Stalin had been correct to fear news from the West. News spreads. The power of instant news was well demonstrated in the failed coup d'état in Moscow, when Boris Yeltsin listened to CNN reports in the barricaded Russian "White House." If news is not controlled, if it is not packaged—as Evgeniy, the Afghanistan war veteran and student, insisted it had to be—then people will make up their own minds about the truth of events. They did so when they heard the news of the putsch, saw the drunken and frightened coup leaders, and turned to Boris Yeltsin, who dared to challenge the tanks.

On election day, the deliberate act of voting is in sharp contrast to the disarray of counting ballots. These are tabulated one at a time by hand. Andriy had arranged with the election commissioners in the Lenin precinct in central Kyiv for me to observe the count. The election commissioners and the representatives of the two principal candidates, Kravchuk and Vyacheslav Chornovil, the candidate of Rukh, sit on three sides of a rectangular table. The fourth side is reserved for the ballot boxes, which are brought up to the table one at a time. Each box is unsealed and its contents are unceremoniously dumped on the table. Blue ballots mingle with white ballots and pink ballots. One color signifies the presidential vote, the second one, the independence vote, while the third one is a vote on a local issue. The fluttering scraps of paper first are separated into three piles by color, and only then are the ballots counted. I sit about ten paces from the table. An armed soldier stands next to me. The two representatives of the candidates monitor each scrap of paper. I can imagine how, with no observers present, piles of votes could simply dispear.

Ballot counting takes most of the night, but few sleep that night, and I certainly have no intention of going to bed. As the morning after the election dawns clear and brisk, I stand with thousands of other people in the Square of Independence and cheer. In front of us, a huge trident painted in blue is emblazoned on the plywood surrounding the pedestal from which Lenin once ruled.

The swearing in of Leonid Kravchuk as Ukraine's first president and the accompanying vote by Ukraine's Parliament to ratify the plebiscite on secession are not anticlimactic. I am fortunate to obtain an invitation to the swearing-in ceremony in the Parliament building, decorated with blue and gold bunting, festooned with golden tridents. The crowds wear their Sunday best. Friends hug. Sentimentalists weep. Acquaintances congratulate each other on a job well done. Champagne flows. Tables sag under the numerous platters of zakuski. Conversations rise in crescendos of hope, of joy, of faith in the rosy future. When the choir, assembled in the gallery above the floor of the Parliament, breaks into the once forbidden Ukrainian anthem, a tremor I remember to this day courses through my body, and I too let the tears flow down my cheeks unchecked. The great hall of the Parliament as well as the streets and the squares reverberate with cheers as the hammer and sickle flag of the Soviet Union is lowered and the blue-and-gold flag of Ukraine is raised to replace it. The red star yields to the golden trident, and the rule by the penal colony recedes into history. Or, as the *International Herald Tribune* will trumpet, the Soviet era is cast on the trash heap. In between the two events, I sit down to write about the election:

> Independence fever turned into a solemn rite December 1 as voters in Ukraine streamed to the polls in record numbers to approve the nation's separation from the Soviet Union and to elect the nation's first president.

I am packing, since I am going home in time for Christmas. People come to my room with many requests. Several students from the university have completed applications to journalism schools and colleges in the

Leonard Kravchuck, first Ukrainian president, campaigning in 1991. Photograph by Valentyn Bondarenko.

United States and ask me to mail their packets once I reach America. Several professors have prepared résumés, which they want me to circulate in American academia. Others come with letters and packages they ask me to post in the West since they do not trust their own postal service.

One day, there is a knock on the door. I open it to Andriy Ivanovich, a fair-haired and bespectacled doctoral candidate at the university, who has mentioned to me that he wants to study in the United States. He carries a huge bag and I groan inwardly at the thought of taking all those things on the plane.

He marches into my room, places the bag on the chair by my desk, and begins to set the desktop for a meal. A white tablecloth appears, then two plates and the necessary utensils. Next come the food packets: sausages, cheese, sauerkraut, pickled vegetables. Last to emerge from the quickly deflating bag are a bottle of vodka and two tumblers, the medium kind we use for on-the-rocks drinks.

Andriy Ivanovich steps back and surveys the impromptu meal with satisfaction. He invites me to sit down, heaps my plate, then his, with zakuski, and begins eating. I follow his example. We speak about many things, among them his unfulfilled wish to invite me to his home to dinner, not carried out because of the prolonged absence of his wife from Kyiv. He fills both tumblers to the brim with vodka and hands me one. He takes the other, raises it, says, "To your health," puts his head back and pours the contents of the tumbler into his mouth. I take an experimental sip and choke on the fire exploding in my mouth. My nose begins to run.

"What is it?" I croak.

Andriy Ivanovich has not flinched. Only his eyes are watering. "Strong, isn't it?" he says. "My grandmother made it. She has a first-class still."

After toasting the success of my return journey, Andriy Ivanovich pulls an envelope from his pocket and gives it to me. It contains a résumé and a letter of application, which he asks me to circulate in America.

The following day, another man comes. He is old and bent over. He has carefully written in block letters his request. He is a Jew who miraculously survived the Nazis. His sister, however, was separated from him. Over the years he has heard rumors that she is alive. He asks me to forward his request to the American Red Cross. His message reads:

> Brother Searches for his Sister: Ungerfeld, Simon, is searching for his sister Rose, 60 years old, who was born in the city of Ustryky Dolni in the former Drohobych oblast. She was hidden during the war from the Germans by good people. She may have immigrated. She may be a Catholic. She may have two children. If someone knows her whereabouts, or those of her children, please call me at 8 Levit St., flat 143, Lviv, or by telephone 72-34-10.

I meet Lisa at the Lenin metro stop because she, too, has heard I am leaving and has a package for me to take to the West. She is pretty and blond. She wants to send keepsakes to her family in America. She gives me two tightly wrapped packages. I wince since I know that I will be asked in Frankfurt whether I am carrying unopened packages and if I am, I will have to unwrap them before my luggage is accepted on the plane. I tell Lisa this, but she assures me that the packages contain nothing either dangerous or of value, just a few keepsakes. She does not offer to open them, as I have hoped. The night before departure, I slit open the wrapping. Inside I find gold bracelets. It is too late to contact Lisa. I was given a notice by customs on my arrival that I cannot take gold out of the country. I put the bracelets on my wrist, and luckily, they pass customs. I later repackage them and send the gifts to Lisa's family.

I pack and repack. I give away almost all the clothing I brought with me. Yet, I have trouble fitting in the icons, the lacquered boxes, the newspapers, the canisters of film, and all the other things I have collected or bought as presents. Andriy is amused. "How did you manage to amass all of these things in a land famous for the absence of consumer goods?" he asks. Eventually, everything somehow fits, even the jars of caviar.

At the airport, I see again that life does not move in a straight line away from a starting dot, but rather in great circles, and that, in time, we return to our starting point. Although I have tried to be a Ukrainian for several months, I am once again an American in a hurry. The assumed identity comes off like the skin of a molting snake. I find the two-hour wait for the plane unacceptable. I find the thorough search of my baggage equally unacceptable, and the failure of my jars of caviar to pass customs—I have slid them into a pair of boots for safekeeping, an action the custom clerk regards as a clumsy attempt at smuggling—outrageous discrimination. I do not conceal my opinions. I complain, and Volodia and Andriy, who have accompanied me, shrug and laugh. Haven't I learned anything about patience and waiting, they ask?

The time to leave is here. I shake hands with my two friends, then decide that's much too formal and hug each one in turn. As Katia and my mother were my guides to the past, Volodia and Andriy became my guides to present-day Ukraine. I hug them and thank them again, then say, because I am suddenly sure, "I'll be back."

I follow the other passengers out onto the tarmac to board the plane. The day is cold and painfully clear. On the runway, the snow glints like the shards of shattered mirror. The Malev Airlines jet takes me to Budapest and from there I fly to Frankfurt, where I catch a big DC10 home.

Chapter 21

RETURN OF THE CRIMEAN TATARS

Only five months have passed, but Kyiv looks a little poorer and the queues are a little longer. What is most worrisome is that the euphoria of the independence vote has vanished. Volodia meets me at the airport. He is pleased with the gift I have brought him, two pounds of coffee beans flavored with almond extract. He had written that these beans make the best Turkish coffee.

We exchange the latest information in our lives. He tells me that *News from Ukraine* is on the ropes because the governmental subsidy through the Ukraina Society is ending, while the paper shortage has grown worse. I tell him that I am back under the auspices of the Ukrainian National Association, a fraternal organization founded in North America at the turn of the century, and Prosvita, the literacy society in Ukraine. The UNA has agreed to find bilingual teachers willing to go to Ukraine to teach English to students from the primary grades to college level, while Prosvita will ensure transportation and lodging for those who come. When I saw the announcement of this project, I called for an application, on which I stated that I would like to be posted somewhere in the south, Crimea being my first choice. I was delighted to learn that I would teach near Yalta and that my students would be at the high school and college levels.

However, minor difficulties arise immediately. I discover that the train ticket to Crimea is for *platzkart*. This time, however, laden with a heavy suitcases filled with textbooks, I am unwilling to risk third class. A five-dollar bill secures a second-class overnight coupe with three other passengers. During the night, the weather turns cold and rainy, the large drops spurting as if from a spigot. The morning is foggy and gloomy, the countryside flat and lushly emerald. Since daybreak I've been standing at the window in the corridor opposite my compartment, thinking about the changed, sadder Ukraine. Being on one's own is not as easy as it seemed five months ago.

The train is paralleling the Dnipro, the maker and soul of Ukraine, a river closely bound since the dawn of history with the people who became Ukrainians. Herodotus called the river Borysthenes; the Romans called it Danapris. A vial of Dnipro's water and a lump of the black soil of the steppe are what Ukrainians take with them into exile. I remember that when I stood on the banks of the Dnipro for the first time, I took off my shoes and waded in, unmindful of the frigid water or the stares.

The Dnipro is the third largest river in Europe, after the Volga and the Danube. At its headwaters in Belarus, the Dnipro is a small river. Before it reaches Ukraine, it takes on several tributaries and becomes a river to be reckoned with. In Ukraine, more tributaries feed it. The largest of these is the Prypiat. Prypiat waters cool the Chernobyl nuclear plants; into the Prypiat, then into the Dnipro, the exploding Number 4 reactor spilled its radioactive isotopes. Dnipro water is what Kyiv and the villages, towns, and cities of central Ukraine drink and use to irrigate crops. It is said that the Dnipro has carried the radiation from Chernobyl to the Black Sea. I boiled Dnipro's water for tea in Kyiv, and I will do likewise in the Crimea, because the Dnipro has been diverted to that peninsula.

I try to fathom the gray, unhurried river as it spills wide into marshes crisscrossed with canals. The train is slow, the river is slow moving and solemn. From the train window I contemplate the passing steppe. The morning dew shines, quivers on the blades of emerald marsh grass and, beyond the grass, on the planted fields that touch the sullen horizon. As the morning ripens, we swing away from the river toward the Perekop Isthmus to the east. Despite the irrigation canals, the lush greenness is replaced by a barren and brown landscape. It remains so all the way to Semfirepol.

Another difficulty arises upon my arrival. The people responsible for picking me up at the station miss the train's arrival and I spend several hours sitting on my suitcases amid the clamoring crowds, not unlike other middle-aged women, who are also waiting to be picked up. By late afternoon, I have had enough. I hire a taxi to Frunzenskoe, on the other side of the Crimean Mountains.

As the four-cylinder Lada struggles up to the spine of the peninsula, we pass miles of fences that were painted bottle green in honor of Richard Nixon. The paint on the fences is peeling and some sections of the fence have collapsed in disrepair, but the driver assures me that when

Overnight train to Crimea. Photograph by Ania Savage.

Nixon visited Leonid Brezhnev in 1974, the sixty-four-mile route to the Black Sea dacha where the two Cold War warriors met was in spanking good order. The driver relishes telling the story. He keeps glancing at me in the rearview mirror and I know he is also relishing the fare in dollars we have agreed upon. Before we reach the coast, he will confide that the fare is equivalent to the monthly pension he receives as a retired officer in the Red Army. He says the hyperinflation that followed independence has wiped out his savings.

At the pass over the Crimean spine, the taxi driver points out the Kutuzov Fountain. He says it honors the famous Russian field marshal who, as a twenty-six-year-old colonel, stemmed a charge by Turks and lost an eye in the process. The fountain is not working and has not been for some time. The pool surrounding it is caked with dried mud and littered with garbage. Thus far, Crimea has been a hot, dusty, and noisy disappointment.

I once heard that drama is created in the approach. What that means comes home to me at the moment the taxi crests the pass, and Crimea suddenly opens before us. The view is one of the most spectacular I have ever seen. Craggy purple peaks, some still dusted with snow, rise to meet a limitless expanse of clear blue sky. Beyond them and at the point where the land should merge with the sky, a sparkling ribbon of azure stretches from east to west. This is the Black Sea, cyan in color, not black.

Saved from being an island by the five-mile-wide Perekop Isthmus, which, like a wrist, links it to Ukraine and the body of the European mainland, Crimea sticks out into the Black Sea in a clenched fist. The 105-mile-long spine of mountains rises along the southern edge of the peninsula, not unlike the row of knuckles on a clenched fist. The Crimean Mountains, in places mere palisades and in other places pinnacles soaring to four thousand feet or more, shield the coved, rocky southern coast from harsh arctic winds and create a balmy microclimate long renowned in Europe.

As we begin our descent, the weather changes. The heat and dust are carried away by the Black Sea trade wind made famous thousands of years ago by Greek sailors. The last of the clouds drifts off also. The sky and the air are so clear that my eyes hurt. The road crosses a heavily wooded ridge of Tchatyr Dag, the highest mountain at 5,125 feet, before descending into Alushta, an ancient town settled by explorers from Genoa. Here the road forks to follow the rocky coastline east and west. We take the westerly fork—to Yalta. On the left of the road is the startlingly blue sea; on the right, cliffs rise in abrupt walls crowned with spires, domes, and pinnacles, evoking images of ancient battlements. The road is edged with flowers, vines, and slender Italian cypresses that nod their narrow tops in the breeze from the sea. Sometimes the road hangs precariously on the flank of a palisade while the cliff plunges down into the sea with dizzying abruptness.

Frunzenskoe, twelve miles east of Yalta, is tucked away in a cove formed by shaggy Bear Mountain. I had not been able to find Frunzenskoe on a map and am relieved that it does exist and is not a mistake in the letter of confirmation I received. Frunzenskoe was named after Mikhail Frunze, an early Red Army commander who gave his name to the Frunze Military Academy in Moscow, which was for many years the Soviet Union's West Point. He is one of the people buried along the Kremlin's walls. Lyuda pointed out his gravesite when we went sightseeing in the Kremlin. Frunzenskoe was built in the 1960s as an exclusive enclave for the faculty of the Frunze academy, whose professors are retired generals.

Three sanitariums, which are Soviet-style resorts, hem in the town's main square. Between the square and the iron gates to the resorts, several dozen high-rise apartment buildings and a few shops serve the people who work in the resorts. Two of the resorts are for military personnel— rocketeers, I am told. The third, and largest, is for KGB employees, although, officially, the KGB no longer exists in Ukraine or in Russia.

I will live in Frunzenskoe for almost two months

I board with Tatiana Ivanovna Bedryk. Raised in central Ukraine, she worked as a schoolteacher in the 1950s in a poor village in Western Ukraine. During one of the periodic famines triggered by a crop failure, she moved to Crimea. "We survived by catching fish and gathering mushrooms in the mountains," she says.

In Crimea, Tatiana Ivanovna became a teacher of Ukrainian at a local Russian elementary school. To teach Ukrainian under Brezhnev was brave. To teach it in Crimea, where the population was drawn largely from retired Red Army personnel, was doubly brave, or foolhardy. She did it anyway. Tatiana married Volodia, a Russian, whose family also came to Crimea in search of a better life. Volodia is a merchant sailor and easy-going. It does not trouble him that Tatiana, now retired, is again focusing attention on herself by inviting an American to live with them. She has helped organize the class I will teach.

"I'll be off sailing soon," Volodia says, shrugging off questions about the inconvenience my presence will create, but the summons does not come while I am there.

Tatiana Ivanovna dresses in shirtwaist dresses, wears high-heeled sandals, and colors her hair henna. Volodia feels that if he puts on a clean shirt he is "dressed up." He loves to garden and leaves the affairs of the house in Tatiana Ivanovna's capable hands. Her astuteness has gained them an enviable four-room apartment. It not only has a separate living room and a balcony but also a view of the Black Sea. I am given the guest room, which is furnished with a convertible sofa, a table and chair, and a wardrobe. The view southeast toward the sea is unencumbered and most mornings I wake up with the dawn and watch the sun weave gold strands across the water.

The first morning after my arrival, I am awakened by a "Hup, one, two, three—hup, one, two, three," in Russian. I look out of the window to see a detail of army recruits. They are on their way to a construction site, and I will hear them march by every morning except Sundays. Two apartment buildings are under construction, and both are under the jurisdiction of the military.

The school where I will teach is not in Yalta but in an even smaller town than Frunzenskoe. The town is called Maliy Mayak, or the small lighthouse. The big lighthouse is in the harbor in Yalta. I had not been told I would commute, and I hasten to arrange transportation. I can either take the bus, which apparently gets so crowded in the mornings that a man from the bus line stands at some depots and pushes people

A queue for bread in Alushta. Photograph by Ania Savage.

in, or hire a taxi. As I make my inquiries, I meet Frunzenskoe's taxi drivers. Every one of them says he's a retired Red Army colonel. Two volunteer their services. They say they will charge me cut-rate fares to drive me to class, thus enabling me to avoid the morning crush, but will not pick me up, when the buses run erratically. They tell me they cannot waste precious petrol shuttling up the coastal road for a one-way fare. I resign myself to the midafternoon bus.

The class is held on the second floor of the local school, in a classroom that serves as a laboratory during the school year, judging from the many vials and rows of Bunsen burners in the cabinets against the back wall. Two large windows offer a distant view of the sea and the room is washed by morning sunlight. Nearly thirty students crowd in on the first day. After a few days the class settles at twenty-two, ranging in age from eight to thirty-three. A mother sends a note with her second grader begging me to take him on. "How else will he succeed unless he learns English?" she writes.

Although the class is for intermediate students, the knowledge of the intermediate students extends not much past the English alphabet. Two students know some English. One of them is Vitaly Leonidovich, who is the oldest at thirty-three. A Russian from Moscow, he is thin, intense, and as pale as if he had just come from Siberia. He takes copious notes and stares at me intently throughout the first class. The class lasts four hours, from eight to noon. I designate a five-minute break at ten, an unheard of slackness of academic discipline, Vitaly Leonidovich informs me. He stays in his seat during the break on the first day and continues to do so throughout the course. The second student who knows English is Lena, a beautiful sixteen-year-old girl, who spent a month in California the year before on a student exchange.

I immediately discover that the textbooks I have brought with me are not suitable for this class. The reading comprehension textbook is much too difficult even for Vitaly Leonidovich. The conversation manual is culturally inappropriate. In it, two cartoon characters meet on the street and begin a conversation about where they work, who their friends are, what they think of the latest books, and so on.

"The KGB asks questions like that," Lena blurts out.

Stalin's purges are long gone, and these young people were children during Brezhnev's crackdowns. Yet the lessons and habits of eschewing revelation of oneself live on. How many stories have these children heard about cousins or neighbors who were dispatched to the gulag because during a chance conversation they said this or that? How many people disappeared because they were not circumspect in answering questions? These lessons are fixed in the national consciousness and influence even a teenager's behavior and outlook. I put the book of questions away.

I have one politically and culturally neutral English primer, which I had purchased just in case, after examining the textbooks I had been given. I had thought I would probably get at least one student who knew very little English, but I had not expected to get an entire classroom of beginners. The primer is essentially a beginner reader. It contains drawings of young people. The action in a drawing is rendered in a simple sentence below the drawing. The primer is not much different from the "See Jane run" text I had read many years earlier to learn English.

I decide to get the primer copied and distribute it to the students. I soon discover that this task, simple to execute in America, is impossible to accomplish in Yalta. "Nyet," says the Intourist office, which has a copy machine at the Yalta Hotel. There are no business printers or copy centers in Yalta, although Kyiv has them. Vitaly Leonidovich offers to help. On the first Sunday after my arrival, we drive back over the spine of the Crimean Mountains to inland Semfirepol. To our disappointment, Vitaly Leonidovich's contact in the capital says he does not have enough paper to duplicate the primer twenty-two times. I think he panicked when we were introduced and wants nothing to do with a foreigner, let alone with copying a foreign book. Vitaly Leonidovich and I drive back to Yalta empty-handed, and I find out that his dream is to learn English well enough to translate English technical manuals into Russian.

Eventually, a solution surfaces. I buy a ream of paper from Intourist and Vitaly Leonidovich finds someone at one of Yalta's sanitariums willing to copy the primer after hours. I give Vitaly twenty-five dollars for the copy machine operator, and two days later, Vitaly Leonidovich staggers into class, his arms overflowing with primers neatly bound in gray cardboard.

By the middle of the second week, everyone in Frunzenskoe knows a foreigner is living in a private flat. In class, everyone has learned the alphabet and we are composing simple sentences. Still, no one will talk in class. The girls sit on one side of the room; the boys on the other. If I pair them to do conversations from the text, they giggle. Lena is the worst. She is acutely aware of boys. They notice her because she has matured into a woman early and has flashing eyes, a golden skin, and a seductive mouth. All the girls envy her and copy her behavior. Giggling and blushing become the class norm.

Then I hit upon a solution. I have brought several magazines with me, among them *Glamour* and *Mademoiselle*. Lena and the other girls are enchanted. The boys are interested also because the pictures show pretty girls. Part of the lesson is spent reading headlines and advertisements aloud from the magazines. Vitaly Leonidovich frowns upon such dalliance. I wish I had brought a copy of the *Economist* to give him and gain his approval.

Since the course is sponsored by two Ukrainian organizations, I have been told: "Teach in English. If need be, use Ukrainian, but no Russian." But no one in class speaks Ukrainian. The students may have Ukrainian surnames and perhaps there's a grandmother who has taught them a few folk songs, but their outlook and language are Russian. Only Vitaly Leonidovich is ethnic Russian. But is it any wonder that the students are not cognizant Ukrainians? The language and culture of Crimea are Russian. Thus, we evolve a dialect for the class. It consists of two parts English, one part Russian, and one part Ukrainian.

Crimea combines natural beauty with a rich history. The peninsula is filled with ruins of many nomadic people, among them Cimmerians who were known to Homer and Herodotus. Scythians, an Asiatic tribe, drove out the Cimmerians, who settled in Europe and became known as the Goths. Ptolemy, Strabo, Pliny, and the geographers and historians of the Greeks and Romans described Crimea and its people. St. Andrew came through Crimea on his way to the northern steppes, and catacombs similar to those built by the early Christians in Rome can be found in the limestone cliffs. Merchant seamen from Genoa and Venice traded with Crimeans and established colonies along the southern shores. Until they were deported en masse to central Asia by Stalin after World War II, the southern portion of Crimea was primarily inhabited by Moslem Tatars, descendants of the Golden Horde that swept across Europe in the thirteenth and fourteenth centuries. The Tatars were the last of the ancient migratory tribes. The Tatars became subjects of Constantinople and gnawed at Imperial Russia's flanks until Catherine the Great's conquest of the Turks.

Crimea did not change rulers again until this century. In 1954, Nikita Khrushchev gave the peninsula away on a whim to Ukraine. When the Soviet Union disintegrated, Crimea became part of Ukraine, much to Russia's chagrin and the perplexity of Crimea's 2.5 million inhabitants, mostly Russians, who replaced the deported Tatars.

The Crimean Mountains, but for the granite pinnacles, are covered with dense forests; wild geraniums, violets, irises, and many wildflowers I had not encountered before grow in the meadows. On the lower slopes, the forests recede to permit vineyards and the towns are surrounded by a greenbelt where local people till small plots on which they raise vegetables and fruit trees. Sour and sweet cherries grow in abundance, as do tiny, nectar-filled apricots. On my way home from class I stop to buy fruit or berries, such as gooseberries or currants, from truck farmers or from local residents who are enjoying a bumper crop in their small garden plots in the greenbelt. Viticulture was introduced in Crimea after the conquest by Catherine the Great, and the peninsula became famous for its wine, which is sweet and heavy, and for champagne, which is light and delightful.

A bushlike plant Tatiana Ivanovna called "Spanish stock" grows abundantly on the shoulders of the coastal road. It has a flower not unlike a sweet pea, aromatic and brilliantly yellow. It is impossible to miss this flower since it grows on huge, swaying bushes and seems to capture the dazzling sun and the sparkling water in its brilliant blossoms. Following the 1974 summit in Moscow, Richard Nixon traveled with Leonid Brezhnev to Crimea. In his memoirs, Nixon mentions the "gold wildflowers" along the road.

Anton Chekhov, who lived in Yalta, the peninsula's most famous resort, wrote that Crimea reminded him of the French Riviera. Mark

Twain, who docked at Yalta in 1867 to visit Czar Alexander II, said, "To me the place was a vision of California." Alexander Pushkin, who spent three weeks at Gurzuf, a hamlet two miles from Frunzenskoe, described Crimea thus: "A happy southern sky, an enchanting region, scenery which satisfies the imagination—mountains, orchards, the sea."

From my window I can see Bear Mountain rising in a giant hump from the sea to separate Frunzenskoe from Yalta. According to a Tatar legend, Bear Mountain was once a great bear in love with a golden-haired maiden, who unfortunately loved a human. When the maiden sailed away with her lover, the great bear rushed to the shore and tried to suck the water to bring the maiden and her boat back to shore. The maiden escaped, but a thousand years later, the bear can still be seen, his shaggy fur changed into the thick pine forest, his mighty head a great cliff lapping the sea.

One afternoon, I put on my boots and climb up the shaggy flank of Bear Mountain, called Auy Dag by the Tatars. In the valley below I see Artek, the famous All-Union Pioneer Camp for deserving Soviet children. With connections, Elena Bonner was able to spend a summer here once, although she was not a hero child who had picked a record number of bales of cotton, caught a spy, or raised pigs to feed the Soviet Army. Bonner remembered that the camp's air was scented by the sea and the oleanders and that the campers visited famous Bolsheviks vacationing nearby. She had climbed unchanging Bear Mountain as I was doing now, but the camp where Bonner spent the summer holiday has changed. The buildings are no longer filled with children. The grounds are forlorn and quiet except for a group of Tatars cooking a meal over a small fire. They look at me with dark frightened eyes, but I smile and say hello and walk on past them. Tatars are migrating back to Crimea and demanding the return of their ancestral lands. Confrontations between the Russian colonizers and the returning Tatars are a weekly and occasionally a daily occurrence reported cautiously in *Vechirnii Krym (Evening Crimea)*.

I later hear, "Give us another hundred years and Crimea will again be Moslem."

Chapter 22

THE CLOSED CITY OF SEVASTOPOL

Soon after my arrival, Tatiana Ivanovna takes me to the KGB sanitarium and down to its private beach. She times the excursion for when one of her friends is on guard duty at the iron gate that bars unwanted visitors. "You wouldn't want to swim off the public beach," Tatiana says. "It's filthy."

The grounds are immaculate, the vegetation a lush jungle, and the geraniums planted in pots lining the boardwalk have blood-red heads as big as cabbages. A Soviet-era sanitarium, despite a name that evokes images of a recuperative hospital, is a country club resort. There are some eighty such resorts in the vicinity of Yalta. Some sanitariums are large and luxurious, as is the KGB one. Others have smaller grounds and fewer buildings and are not on the seashore. Until the collapse of the Soviet Union, government departments or agencies, trade unions, or local workers' cooperatives underwrote the cost of sanitarium vacations. I look around to see if a guard will stop us from enjoying the KGB grounds. "Don't worry," Tatiana says. "No one cares now."

But someone does.

I had been wondering about my assignment to Frunzenskoe. A one-time occurrence can be ascribed to coincidence, but the same thing happening twice in a row may show a hand at work. In Kyiv, I was steered into obtaining living quarters at the former school for spies, where I knew I could be watched, and I was. When I applied to come back and teach, I was sent to live in a town controlled by the KGB. I am waiting for something to happen, and it does.

A few days after my arrival, someone bangs loudly and forcefully on the apartment door. I am preoccupied on the telephone and don't pay much attention. Telephoning usually is an exercise in sheer futility. Most often, the telephone refuses to connect. At other times, you are suddenly listening to someone else's conversation and they yell at you to get off the line. This time the phone connects and I inquire if one of the retired colonel taxi drivers is free for an excursion into the mountains. But then the insistence of the banging refocuses my attention. Suddenly I'm thinking that loud banging on the door is the first sign of an impending arrest or interrogation. I pause in mid-sentence as Tatiana Ivanovna opens the door a sliver and then slams it shut. She runs into the room and tells me not to get off the phone until the visitors are gone. I turn away from the door and do as I am told. The visitors are two militiamen. They say they have been told that Tatiana Ivanovna is renting a room to a tourist. If that is so, the tourist has to pay a tourist tax. The Frunzenskoe city hall has no record of a payment being made.

Tatiana Ivanovna says she is not boarding any tourists, which is technically correct, and the militiamen leave. Both of us are worried. Later, when Volodia comes home, Tatiana Ivanovna tells him about the militia's visit. He considers possible repercussions, then shakes his head and says, "Everyone knows about Anna Ivanovna. They just found a pretext to come and look at her."

After the militia's visit, other funny things happen. A young man appears in class. He says he wants to learn English desperately and asks for private lessons. I explain that I am planning a trip into the mountains and apologize that I cannot help him. He says he will take me sightseeing and we can speak English. He is so insistent that I agree, and we set the excursion for the following day after class. Kostia would have been handsome had it not been for a bad overbite, which is that much more noticeable because he has several gold crowns, which make him look like a chipmunk chewing a piece of gold foil. He speaks reasonable English but spends the entire time questioning me rather than describing the sights — Oleksander Antonovych all over again. Kostia and I enter a sanitarium between Maliy Mayak and Frunzenskoe to admire a pretty pre-Revolution villa. I follow the overgrown formal gardens down to the sea, where a huge outcropping offers a panoramic view of the coast.

I suggest that we climb the rock. Kostia says rock climbing is for the young. I say I am young at heart. We climb to the top and I snap several photographs.

"What are you doing that for?" he asks with some alarm.

"Because it's pretty."

A few days later, I am walking back from the beach through the KGB gardens when I realize that someone is following me. I stop and turn around — it is still light and many people are about; I am not frightened.

A man significantly younger than I am, a handsome man with curly brown hair, engaging brown eyes, and a golden suntan, says hello and invites me to visit him in his guestroom. I laugh and turn him down, but he is set on changing my mind. He follows me to the apartment house where I live and, despite my protests, gets into the elevator with me. We ride up to the eighth floor as he pleads his case. Only when Volodia opens the door does the handsome man leave. I wonder what would have happened if Tatiana Ivanovna had opened the door.

Then one of my colonel acquaintances, the one who always plays twenty questions with me about my plans, calls to say he would like to introduce me around at the KGB sanitarium. Boris Fedorovich first shows me the hotels and the tunnel that connects them to the dining hall. The walls of this passage are tiled. Occasionally, the tiles create murals of sea animals. We also stop in the greenhouse, but the plants are sad and wilted since the weather has been very hot and the fan in the greenhouse isn't working. When we come to the administration building, Boris Fedorovich stops, his face growing animated as if he has just had a brainstorm, and asks whether I would like to come in and meet the director.

"Sure," I say.

We go inside, where I am asked to sit outside an office. Boris Fedorovich tells me he has to run an errand and disappears. A little while later, a secretary appears and says the director is ready to see me.

Dmitri Kurnakov has a pasty complexion as if he never goes down to the sanitarium's pebbled beach. He is dark-haired and has wide hips like an overweight woman. He waddles when he walks. I underestimate him from the start. He asks to see my passport. I say I do not carry it with me. He asks for some identification. I pull out my American driver's license, which is the compromise identification I carry at all times. While examining the license, Kurnakov asks me when I was born. For some reason, I do not want to tell him I was born in Ukraine. That old fear: *What will happen if they decided I belong to them?* suddenly surfaces. I lie blandly about the year of my birth, moving it to the year my parents registered as refugees in the American Zone in Germany. Then I remember that my age is on the driver's license and blush.

Kurnakov pretends he has noticed nothing. He keeps on asking age-related questions, trying to make me trip myself. How old was I when I finished high school? How old was I when I got married? How old are my children? I find myself sweating. In the space of a few minutes he has recreated a legion of fears I thought I had put aside. His voice, his manner, the sinister glint in his dark eyes scare me. Kurnakov leans toward me across the gleaming mahogany table. His breath smells of garlic. "You can speak freely," he says. "My recorder is not on."

It is as if he has slapped sense into me. I almost laugh out loud. He is acting out a ridiculous charade, a B movie scene. "Why don't you turn yours off, too?" he is saying.

Tatiana Ivanovna had told me that she had heard trouble was brewing at the KGB sanitarium. She said her dezhurna friends were saying black marketeering of gasoline had been uncovered at the resort. Certainly, the colonel taxi drivers always have plenty of gas in their tanks. I stare at Kurnakov, but say nothing.

"Anna Ivanovna, let's be frank," he presses on.

"About what?" I ask indifferently.

"I know what you are doing here."

"What is that?"

"We need not go into details. Let's just leave it at this: You mind your own business and I'll mind mine."

And suddenly I'm annoyed. Doesn't he have better things to do than worry about a middle-aged woman teaching a few young people and one adult? I say, "You know, the government in Kyiv gave me a visa."

He shrugs. "Then let me extend a welcome. You can come into the grounds anytime you want to. Just tell the dezhurna I said it was all right." He could have added: "I know all about you sneaking in," but does not, although I am certain he knows.

I think both of us want to be rid of each other. We both get up at the same time. He shakes my hand and returns to his desk. I open the door of his office and go out into the Crimean sun.

The militia do not return, Kostia does not reappear in my class, and no one tries to pick me up again.

I want to go to Sevastopol, but it is closed to foreigners because it is the home port of the Black Sea Fleet. I also want to see Balaclava, the site of the famous charge of the Light Brigade during the Crimean War (1853–55). Balaclava, too, is off limits because that is where Russian nuclear submarines berth. The barricade lies across the coastal highway a little way past Foros.

I ask Tatiana Ivanovna what can be done. She consults her dezhurna friends. One Sunday morning, when I have no classes, we go into the KGB sanitarium where a school bus is idling. The KGB officers' wives have organized an outing to Sevastopol. I will pretend I am one of them.

"Just don't talk to everyone, as you usually do," Tatiana Ivanovna admonishes. "I don't want to get my friends in trouble."

I follow her orders and pick a seat away from the other passengers. Both the guide and the bus driver know who I am. A small smile plays on their lips. We have arranged earlier that both will get a tip in dollars. I chuckle.

The coastal road to Sevastopol is rugged and reminds me of driving California's Big Sur highway. The road cuts into cliffs, rising and falling with them, often sweeping upward hundreds of feet before swooping down to just above the sea. The raging water forces its way between the mountains and nourishes narrow fertile valleys, or creates long deep bays and fjords. These sheltered coves hide nuclear submarines.

At the roadblock, a uniformed guard pokes his head through the open door. "From where?" he asks.

"The sanitarium in Frunzenskoe," the guide replies.

The guard salutes and the bus rolls past the barricade.

We approach Balaclava, which lies east of Sevastopol in a shallow, green valley. On October 25, 1854, during the Crimean War in which Turkey, England, and France fought against Russia, Lord Cardigan misunderstood his orders to "advance rapidly" against the enemy. On a plateau west of Balaclava, Lord Raglan, the commander in chief of the British Army, and his staff watched in horror as the Light Brigade charged hidden Russian cannons and was decimated. Of the 673 men who galloped down the mile-long valley, fewer than 200 returned. Also from a vantage point on the plateau, William Howard Russell, considered to be the first English-speaking journalist to serve as a war correspondent, followed the battle. His dispatch to the *Times* of London became the basis of Alfred Lord Tennyson's poem, "The Charge of the Light Brigade." This was one of the poems my teachers had made me memorize when I was learning English, perhaps because it mentions Cossacks and Russians.

In the distance I see a white obelisk. I wait for the guide to point it out, but she says nothing. On the way back, she again ignores Balaclava. Had I not promised Tatiana Ivanovna not to draw attention to myself, I would have quoted and translated a few lines from Tennyson's poem, which surely the women on the bus would understand, having grown up under Soviet rule:

Theirs not to make reply
Theirs not to reason why,
Theirs but to do and die.

I have read that in the spring the Balaclava battlefield is carpeted with red poppies blooming so thickly that the valley looks like a field of blood. In late summer, the valley is green.

Florence Nightingale was the "Angel of Crimea." She was the first woman to become a professional nurse, the first to follow an army into war, and the first to nurse the injured at the battle site. Florence Nightingale was thirty-four and already well versed in nursing when she was invited by the British Army, which had suffered enormous losses in Crimea, to establish a hospital in Scutari, on the Bosporus. Within weeks of her arrival, the hospital was functioning. She then went to Crimea where she established a field hospital in Balaclava. She remained in Crimea until the British pulled out. Her last act in Crimea was to erect a cross, twenty feet high, on a hill overlooking Balaclava. She requested that "Lord have mercy upon us" be inscribed on the cross. Our guide does not mention either Florence Nightingale, or the cross, or even Balaclava, as we trundle by in the KGB wives' excursion bus.

Sevastopol relishes the fact it has been totally destroyed twice, and our guide relishes telling the story of the famous assaults on the city. Before descending to the port, we stop at a diorama that recreates the first disaster in a panoramic painting by Roubaud, a member of the St. Petersburg Academy of Fine Art, who went to Munich to create the panorama in a specially constructed circular building. The painting, completed in 1905, depicts the storming of the city by the French and British on June 6, 1855. The scenes are of carnage, fire, death, and heroism. Here, a soldier is dragging a wounded friend from the line of fire. There, a soldier convulses in the final throes of death, his chest crimson with blood. And over there, a young sailor tries to raise the Russian flag as he is mown down by musket fire. Every scene is littered with corpses, dead animals twisted into grotesque poses, overturned wagons, spent ammunition, and bloody clothing. Only fourteen buildings were left standing after the siege by the French and English armies.

Our second stop is a vast museum of artifacts, photographs, and personal narratives from the Nazi siege during World War II. The guide tells a story of a brave fourteen-year-old girl—the photograph shows a dark-haired, hollowed-eyed, sullen youngster—who volunteered to deliver important orders, only to be caught, tortured, and put to death by the Nazis. This time the citizens of Sevastopol held out for 250 days, and again the city was leveled.

These memorials—the diorama was rebuilt in 1954—as well as several others occupy a low promontory or hogback that rises to about 150 feet. Both sides of this elongated hill slope down to the harbor, dividing it into two distinct fingers, the northern and southern sides. The sea pushes inland for nearly four miles, creating a deep, compartmentalized harbor that not only offers excellent shelter but is also easy to defend. The southern fjord is the commercial port. Two forts protect the northern naval base. A large fort called the Constantine battery guards the narrow entrance to the entire harbor and looks from the docks like a white gleaming box. In 1774 Prince Potemkin recognized the outstanding shape and depth of Sevastopol. The Russian fortress was built on the site of the Tatar village of Akhtair and the stone used for the new fortifications was taken from the ruins of the ancient town of Hersones.

Even today, the best way for going from the northern shore to the southern docks is by ferry. I see several bridges in the distance, but the guide says using a land route is time-consuming and a long way around. Our tour of the port begins at the monumental seagate called the Grafskaya Pristan, or "landing place for nobility." The portico is supported by a double row of Ionic columns. A staircase fifty feet wide has a dozen or so marble steps that lead to the water. Here the Russian czar and other distinguished visitors arriving by yacht were received with ceremony. The commercial port is bounded by Primorsky Boulevard, which offers beautiful vistas of the harbor. We stop to admire the Eagle Column, which rises impressively into the sky from an artificial rock just off the shoreline. Our guide relates how Russian warships were sunk in the harbor in 1854 to prevent the British and the French from landing. But one ship would not sink despite a hole in its flank and cannon fire from other ships. Finally, a sailor was sent to board her. He returned with the ship's icon of the Virgin of Smolensk, which had been forgotten. Immediately, the ship slipped silently into its watery grave.

The harbor is lined with dry docks, yards for shipbuilding, long rows of mothballed ships. The waters bristle with naval war equipment. If you narrow your eyes slightly, the sonars, radars, communication towers, and assorted other fixtures needed for electronic listening and spying resemble a forest of metal rods.

We are on our own after the tour. I wander around the city alone. It looks not much different from other ports I have visited, except that almost every male on the street is in uniform and every square seems to have an obelisk commemorating a battle. Sevastopol was founded as a great fortress, not unlike Gibraltar, and remains a fortress even though ICBMs and military satellites and rocket launchers have made the harbor's defenses obsolete.

On my way back to the bus in the late afternoon, I hear loud laughter coming from a store and poke my head inside. Two German tourists are examining a souvenir. An Intourist guide whom I met in Yalta is their interpreter. So much for Sevastopol being a closed city, and so much for my exploit.

Chapter 28

YALTA

Palaces and VIPs

Yalta entered the American consciousness in 1945. It was the site of the famous—or infamous, in the view of most East Europeans, including my parents—Yalta Conference. For a week in February, Franklin D. Roosevelt, Winston Churchill, and Stalin mapped the Allies' final assault on Germany and drew plans for postwar partitioning of Europe. Roosevelt was ensconced in Livadia, the Crimean palace of the Romanov czars. The large and graceful reception halls of the white, Italianate palace were used as the conference meeting place. Churchill was assigned to the Tudoresque palace of Prince Mikhail Vorontsov, the man who "civilized" Crimea for Catherine the Great. This palace, beautifully preserved to this day, overlooks the sea a few miles west of Yalta. I visit both Livadia and Vorontsov's castle several times but cannot get permission to see the palace of Prince Yusupov, where Stalin stayed and where Khrushchev as well as Brezhnev spent their holidays. Prince Yusupov is famous as the man who killed Rasputin, the mad monk who held sway over Czarina Alexandra, the wife of Nicholas II, the last czar.

Crimea's famous mild climate did not cooperate during the Yalta Conference. It was unseasonably cold and cloudy, weather similar to the miserable 1854 winter of the Crimean War when snow fell. The photographs on display in Livadia show Churchill in a winter coat. An unlit cigar stub sticks belligerently out of his downturned mouth. Roosevelt, his face drawn and very pale, is bundled in a cape, seemingly wondering why he has come to such a miserable place. (Livadia does not have central heating.) Only Stalin looks unperturbed, and as I study his photograph, I think I see a glimmer of satisfaction in those heavy Georgian eyes. He will gain the most at Yalta.

The rooms where the conferees met are now open to the public, as is a wing filled with photographs and memorabilia of Nicholas II and his family. This wing opened during glasnost.

A more recent addition is an incongruous wax museum. The guide, a pert woman with a small flashlight in her hand, takes us inside the darkened room and in a somber voice talks about the "martyred family of Nicholas II." She strokes each of the life-sized, lifelike figures with a her penlight and gives detailed biographies as well as a detailed and rather grisly recounting of how each member of the czar's family died. The museum also has a wax figure of Rasputin. He seems to be about to pounce, his eyes wide and bulging. Next to Rasputin stands Prince Yusupov, erect and patrician, although a scowl distorts his waxen features. An old, kerchiefed woman in our group curtsies before the czar and czarina and bends to kiss the czarina's wax hand.

Yalta residents are confirmed celebrity watchers. The best gossip is about Mikhail Gorbachev, who set Yalta on its collective ear when he bypassed the "perfectly adequate" Yusupov palace and built an Italianate villa about twenty-five miles west of Yalta at Foros. This is the place where he spent three days under house arrest during the coup attempt.

Excursion boats run regularly from Yalta past the Foros villa, which is situated close to the shore and is easily visible. A Black Sea Fleet ship, its top deck buzzing with radar and sonar, is anchored in front of the red-roofed villa during my stay and is the topic of much speculation since, by all accounts, the villa remains empty.

The road leading down to the villa is closed to traffic. I convince one of the cab-driving retired colonels not only to drive me to Foros but also to pull off the main coastal road so that I can walk to the edge of the cliff and take a peek. He does this with a great deal of reluctance, and as soon as I take a photograph, he drags me back to the cab, the engine of which has been left running. Apparently, shortly after the coup, he drove out to look at the villa himself. Before he knew what was happening, soldiers surrounded him. He somehow talked himself out of trouble.

By sheer coincidence, Sasha from Donetske calls me at Tatiana Ivanovna's (I had sent him a postcard soon after my arrival) and tells me that since I'm in Yalta I should drive out and look at Gorbachev's Foros house. He says he and his wife and daughter were vacationing at a modest sanitarium in Foros during the coup. "We knew something was happening because suddenly the sky was filled with helicopters that hovered over the villa and the road was closed," Sasha says. "We were cooped up

Foros Villa, where Gorbachev was kept under house arrest for three days during the 1991 coup attempt. Photograph by Ania Savage.

for three days. Couldn't get out or go to the beach." He says he could see the red-tiled roof of the villa from the windows in his room at the sanitarium.

After Gorbachev's demise, the Foros dacha became the vacation villa of Ukrainian presidents, although superstitious Crimeans only shake their heads at the folly. The dacha is bad karma.

Then there's the matter of its fabled swimming pool. Apparently, Raisa Gorbachev was an exacting mistress when it came to the dacha's construction; marble floors had to be laid four times to meet her high standards. Although the villa is on the edge of the sea—on a little bluff that has a flight of steps leading down to the narrow pebbled beach—Raisa ordered a swimming pool. As I listen to this tale, the teller rolls his eyes to indicate the utter wastefulness of the Kremlin *nomenklatura*. In any event, a swimming pool was added to the construction. My tale bearer does not know whether the pool is an indoor or outdoor pool, or both, but he says he and everyone else in Yalta knows that Raisa ordered a tiled mural of a preening peacock to adorn the bottom of the pool. The mural was executed in Finland and a truckload of numbered tiles was dispatched to Foros. Soon the masons laying the pool bottom ran into trouble. There were too few tiles to complete the peacock's tail. Finland was called. The tile maker assured the callers that all the tiles for the pea-

Yalta beach. Photograph by Ania Savage.

cock had been shipped to Foros. My informer pauses, moves closer to me, and drops his voice. In this new life I am leading, I hardly notice that my informer takes me by the hand and draws me aside, away from the crowd of strangers and potential eavesdroppers around us on Yalta's Naberezhna Promenade. It is wise to act circumspectly when imparting a secret about the security organs. "Then they called the KGB," he whispers.

The KGB solved the mystery in short order. At some point during the unloading of the tiles, someone decided that no one would miss one box out of a truckload of boxes. The box found its way to the weekend flea market in Yalta near the harbor. The box of colorful tiles was snapped up. The KGB found it before the buyer had time to tile his bathroom with a piece of a peacock's tail. And the swimming pool in Foros was finished.

The cry "You speak English" carries from across the cavernous hall and echoes against its travertine-sheathed walls. A man who overheard my long-distance call home shouts the happy acknowledgment. The gangling, sunburned man with the rolling gait of a sailor bounds across the hall of the Yalta Telephone Exchange building and smiles down at me.

"You're American. Where from?"

"Denver."

"I'm from L.A."

Not only has he overhead some familiar sounds; his voice carries a note of entreaty. I know he will ask me to help him solve a problem. He thrusts his hand out in greeting. "My name's Jim."

Jim has abandoned the freighter that had brought him to Yalta but cannot communicate with anyone. He is trying to get a room for the night, the week, the month. He has fallen in love with Yalta.

"I'm trying to learn Russian," he says. "I love Russians. I've been to Murmansk, but that's very different. Brr. Not a place for a boy from L.A."

The information comes pouring out like water from a spigot while we wait for the clerk to take his telephone number and dial it. There is no direct transatlantic dialing available in Yalta at the time I am there. Once a connection is established, an operator switches the call to one of the telephone booths lining the wall. Jim wants to tell his family he isn't coming home.

He talks with the speed and pleasure of someone who has spent many hours without a language he can use with those he meets. And his manner radiates the openness of an American raised in California. I like him immediately, then realize that I have become homesick for the open and friendly behavior for which Americans are known.

No one is at home in Los Angeles, and Jim is disappointed. I tell him I know where he can get a bed for the night and we leave the telephone exchange. I am taking Jim to the Intourist office, where I know several clerks who speak a smattering of English. They, like the rest of the post-Soviet society, are engaged in a constant search for hard, convertible currency as a hedge against the collapse of their own in the raging inflation. Someone will take Jim in if he pays in dollars.

Just before we reach the Intourist office, a couple emerges from Yalta's town hall, where civil marriage ceremonies are performed. The bride is wearing a summer dress and a white veil, while the groom looks stiff in a borrowed dark suit.

"Hold on," Jim cries and he joins the other well-wishers with his camera.

The groom glowers; the bride blushes. Jim kneels before them and snaps away, a veritable *paparazzo*. He smiles, already dreaming of a new life in Yalta. He does not see the urban decay because there is no money for upkeep. He does not see the broken panes of glass in a nearby shop window, or the smeared walls, or the cigarette butts on the pavement that mix with the nodules of spit drying in the sun. There is no money to wash sidewalks.

"This sure beats Murmansk," he says. "The only thing I don't like are the pebbles on the beach. But the sea, that's great. It's like Baja. I could stay here forever."

Chapter 24

ANCIENT CITADELS

Crimea, perhaps because it has been the home of many peoples, is a land of legends. One of the most famous is the legend about the fabled Fountain of Tears in the ancient Tatar capital of Bakhchesarai:

Stern was Crimean Khan Krim Girey. He pardoned no one, pitied no one. He ordered all the boys in his family, who stood higher than his chariot wheel, executed so no one would challenge his power. Years passed. The young khan grew old and his heart softened. A young slave was brought to him one day. She was small and thin, a mere girl. Her name was Diliare.

Diliare did not warm the old khan with gentleness and love, but the elderly khan nonetheless fell in love with her. For the first time in his long life he realized that the heart can ache, that it can suffer, that it can rejoice, that the heart is alive. Diliare did not survive for long. She withered in imprisonment, like a flower without the sun. And when a beloved dies, the heart weeps with tears of blood. Only when Diliare died did the khan fathom the depths of his love.

The great khan called Omar, the master artisan, to him and said: "Build me a memorial of stone. I want the stone to bear my sorrow through the ages; I want the stone to show how a man's heart weeps."

For a long time Omar pondered the khan's words and wondered how to transform stone into the tears a man sheds. He carved a petal of a flower on a piece of white marble, then a second petal and a third. In the center of the flower he carved the eye of a man. From this eye, heavy tears would fall onto the stone. They would fall continuously, all day and all night, without stop for years and ages.

And thus to this day, in Bakhchesarai's palace, a fountain weeps. It weeps day and night.

Everyone I meet assures me the Fountain of Tears is worth a trip and, having hired a car, a driver, and a guide, I set out across the mountains to the northwestern slope. Bakhchesarai, once a crowded and proud city, is today a sleepy and dusty town, its glories destroyed and forgotten. It was built in the fifteenth century by the descendants of the Mongols at the far end of a narrow valley with steep, easily defended sides. It could be—and was—protected by horsemen and lancers. For nearly three hundred years Bakhchesarai's khans plundered Ukraine and Russia, taking many hostages, who were either ransomed or sold to Turkey as slaves. Bakhchesarai's dominance ended in 1783 when Russia conquered Crimea and the last khan abdicated. The khan's palace, partially burned during the war, was refurbished for Catherine the Great's triumphant tour of the conquered lands in 1787, with only a nod to its Oriental antecedents. In the subsequent two hundred years it was renovated twice more, in 1837 for Nicholas I's visit and again in 1900. The palace became a museum in 1920.

Bakhchesarai means "palace of gardens" in Turkic, and the palace gardens live up to that description. Beyond a masonry wall, the palace opens into a series of pavilions linked by gardens and sheltered patios. To the right is the oldest pavilion, probably erected in 1503 when the Crimean khan detained Alevisio Novi. The Italian architect had been summoned to Moscow by Czar Ivan to build one of the Kremlin cathedrals. The khan ordered Novi to design and build a palace and did not release the hapless architect and his craftsmen until the work was completed fifteen months later. The only vestige of Novi's decorative work is an imposing set of doors.

The guide at the palace leads a group of tourists, including me, through a garden, into a great hall. The walls are whitewashed and lack the ornate decorations that embellished the first pavilion we toured. The guide steps aside and gestures grandly to the right and left. In one corner, a large fountain gurgles. A smaller, more intricate fountain occupies the opposite end of the hall. The guide tells me this is the fabled Fountain of Tears, but I find that I am disappointed. The fountain is much smaller than it appeared to be on a postcard I bought in Yalta, and the iron deposits in the water trickling over its face have discolored the white marble. On closer inspection, however, the intricate carving is quite lovely. The guide describes the probable history of the fountain and its likely removal from its original site at the sequestered mausoleum where Diliare is buried.

In the Fountain of Tears, water trickles from an eye that is carved as the center of a five-petaled flower. Beneath the eye is a petal cup that, as it overflows, directs the stream of water into two smaller cups. These two cups, in turn, channel the water's flow into another large cup, and so on down the fountain's face. Blood-red roses are floated each day in the cup directly below the weeping eye. The presence of roses has its own soulfully Russian legend.

In 1820, Alexander Pushkin, sent into exile by the czar, visited Bakhchesarai. His companion on that trip—which Pushkin describes in a letter as scrambling across the mountains while holding onto the tails of Tatar ponies—was Sofia Potocki. She was a member of the same distinguished Polish family that founded Stanislaviv, now Ivano-Frankivske, in the Carpathians, which my mother, Katia, and I visited the summer before. Sofia was beautiful and blond, and Pushkin, who loved beautiful women on principle, fell madly in love. She married someone else. Sofia is said to have told Pushkin a legend that came down in her family about a seventeenth-century Princess Potocki (Diliare) who was captured by the Crimean Khan Girey and who died in captivity. The palace and the fountain inspired Pushkin's poem "Fountain of Bakhchesarai," in which he says:

Fountain of love,
Fountain that lives!
To you I bring two roses.
I delight in your silent discourse
In your poetic tears.

Whether Pushkin actually brought roses to the fountain is not known, although the guide assures us the story is true and is the reason why red roses are floated in the fountain's cup each day. What is known is Pushkin's disappointment with the palace. He found the renovations insensitive and the upkeep indifferent. I learn this later when I read Pushkin's letters. Pushkin wrote: "I went through the palace feeling a great dismay at the poor condition in which it is kept and at the pseudo-European renovations in some of the rooms."

Diliare's octagonal mausoleum is crowned by a graceful white dome. Below the dome is an inscription in Arabic characters, which the guide translates as: "This is the tomb of Diliare, beloved wife of Khan Krim-Girey, died in 1746. She was a Christian." The mausoleum is in the cemetery where khans of the Girey dynasty are buried.

Chafut-Kale, the ruins of the fortress of the Jews on a mesa in the Crimean Mountains. Photograph by Ania Savage.

Above Bakhchesarai, cliffs hide much more ancient settlements and offer panoramic views that stretch to the Sea of Azov far to the east and north to the beginning of the great steppes. My guide, though he has lived in Crimea all his life, has never been up these cliffs and doesn't want to go. After a light lunch under an almond tree, I put on my climbing boots and scramble to the summit of the cliffs.

High up under the sun, I find a town preserved in stone. The narrow passage into the town winds past cliffs and granite outcroppings, then suddenly opens onto a mesa. I find myself standing on an ancient street, still discernible by two deep ruts worn into the rock during the passage of centuries. The street is lined with tumbled dwellings. Walls of many houses crowd one another as the street ascends the rocky face. At intervals, narrow, shallow alleys of more walls and gaping foundations bisect the street. I am at Chafut-Kale, the fortress of the Jews, once inhabited by Karaites, a tribe of Jews who did not believe in the Talmud. The place is deserted, yet I feel the throb of life. I pause to listen to the secret movement and am reminded of the deserted cliffs in Colorado that suddenly come alive when a shy ptarmigan darts out in order to lead you away from her nest and her hatchlings. The ancient ruin intrigues me and I linger away the afternoon in the town of stones. As I explore the ruins, I come to the mesa's edge where I find an Islamic structure that is a graceful, domed mausoleum. Later I will learn that this is a memorial to the daughter of a khan from Bakhchesarai. The khan's daughter fell in love with a Jewish prince from Chafut-Kale and ran away to marry him. The infuriated khan attacked the Jews, and in the battle that ensued, the Jewish prince was killed. Having nothing left to live for, the prince's bride threw herself from the cliffs. I think of the Western tale of Romeo and Juliet and how similar cultures are, in their tales and their hatreds.

And then, as I begin my descent, a plump brown hen flies at me, clucking. I look around and see a pale wisp of smoke rising from one of the standing stone houses. I recall the throb of life I sensed when I entered.

Chapter 25

OF CAMISOLES AND SOAP OPERAS

One day when none of the retired colonels is available and I am taking the bus to class, I see a radiant young girl, self-consciously wearing a white camisole trimmed with lace. She is obviously aware of how the skimpy garment enhances her beauty and her golden skin. It is also obvious from the label sewn in the back that the garment has come from the West. Other girls on the bus, among them some of my students, look at the girl in the white camisole with round, envious eyes. I study the garment for a long time, trying to figure out why it looks familiar; then I know why. I have such a camisole among my undergarments back home. Suddenly, I am seeing my mother standing at the window in Lviv and with a sad smile, relating the story about Russian officers' wives who wore French negligees to the Lviv Opera House in 1940. Upon occasion I have wondered if anyone ever went up to the Russian officers' wives and told them they were wearing garments that belong in the boudoir. Would anyone ever tell the radiant girl she is wearing an undergarment in public? But does it really matter what the wives wore and what this girl is wearing, as long as their choices pleased them?

As I looked at the girl proudly wearing the camisole, I think that life repeats itself.

Three times a week, at 8:20 in the morning and at six o'clock in the evening, stores empty and queues disappear. Instead of shopping or standing in line, women gather in front of a TV set. On one such afternoon, two grandmothers, their three daughters, and their four granddaughters, plus a neighbor come together. I am the eleventh woman in the room. Because I am both a foreigner and a guest, I am given the best seat in the room: a comfortable chair right in front of the screen.

The men are told to go outside and smoke. As they leave, they snicker, and their sons and grandsons follow suit. One hoots, "Haven't you cried enough already?"

We are gathered to see an installment of "The Rich Also Cry," a Mexican soap opera, which is all the rage. The principal characters of the soap are members of a prominent family, not unlike those in the series "Dynasty" or "Dallas."

The action revolves around Luis Alberto, the dashing, spoiled errant son, and Marianna, his dark-haired, virtuous, kind and loving—and misunderstood—bride. I saw an installment of "The Rich Also Cry" in Kyiv when a dinner party was delayed so that the female guests could focus their undivided attention on the six o'clock installment, which was a repeat. I become hooked on the soap in Crimea. Tatiana Ivanovna and I watch every evening episode. She feels sorry for me because I must miss the morning telecasts to go teach at the school. Later in Odessa, I cannot obtain a room because the two clerks are watching the telecast. They suggest that I go to a canteen for a cup of coffee and come back. Instead, I stand at the counter and watch the flickering black-and-white monitor in the back office through the open door. Watching "The Rich Also Cry" improves my Russian by leaps and bounds. During my stay, Luis Alberto's and Marianna's marriage flounders.

The episode that attracts the ten women and me, and banishes the men, recounts how Marianna gives away her infant son to a street woman after Luis Alberto accuses her of having the child by someone else. This is heady stuff for the straight-laced society in which most Ukrainians and Russians live. The cities may be different and "Western" morality the vogue, but in the countryside and in staunchly conservative places like Crimea, adultery and illegitimacy remain taboo subjects. A man is honor-bound to acknowledge his child and marry the mother if she does not have a free abortion. During my stay in Ukraine, I would never hear gossip about a woman cheating on her husband, but stories about male infidelities were plentiful.

Throughout the episode, the two grandmothers cluck about Luis Alberto's "unmanliness."

Tatiana Ivanovna tells me there are some two hundred episodes of "The Rich Also Cry." A great deal of consternation occurred earlier in the year when new actors suddenly appeared in the roles of some of the secondary characters. But the female audience accepted the changes philosophically and the popularity of the soap did not diminish.

"She's like us," one of the women in the room explains. "She suffers and so do we."

In class, I ask for a show of hands from those who watch the Mexican soap regularly. Every one of the girls raises her hand and giggles.

"Everything is so beautiful, the clothes, the homes, the cars," says Olga, one of the older students. "We would like our lives to be like theirs."

A friend of Tatiana Ivanovna's comes to see me one evening, after making a formal appointment. I surmise that she wants me to post a letter for her in the West. Instead she asks me about "Dynasty." She has heard I am not only an American but also from Denver, the setting for "Dynasty." The soap is being shown in Poland and my guest has seen an end-of-the-season cliffhanger of a shoot-out at a wedding. I disappoint and distress her because I have no idea who survived the shoot-out and who did not.

"But Tatiana Ivanovna said you are from Denver," she complains bitterly. My mother was also a fan of "Dynasty" in the late 1980s, before Alzheimer's clouded her ability to turn on a TV set and follow the developing plot. She particularly admired Linda Evans, who became one of her favorite stars when she appeared with Barbara Stanwyck, my mother's favorite actress, in a series set on a ranch. "Big Country," I think, was the name of series. Once when I was visiting her and we were both watching "Dynasty," my mother turned to me and said: "Have you met any of these people since you live in Denver?" I laughed and said no, but in retrospect, I think that question marked the advent of her disease.

I did not encounter anti-Semitism in Kyiv, where I attended a service at a synagogue in Podil. Perhaps that city was sensitized by the calamity of Babi Yar. This is not the case in Crimea. I am at a party in Yalta when one of the younger men, perhaps thirtysomething, tells a joke, the butt of which is a Jew. The others laugh, not dutifully, as sometimes happens when someone says something that is not right, but with gusto. *Oh, dear.* That sinking feeling. If it had been only one joke, I probably would have said nothing. I am not especially brave, nor a crusader, nor particularly self-righteous, but someone is telling another Jew joke. I say, "The Jews have suffered a great deal in this country; leave them alone," and get up to leave. A half dozen voices protest.

"Anna Ivanovna, we are only having a good time," someone says.

"It means nothing," the hostess assures me.

I stay a little longer, then leave because I am sad.

On another occasion, I hire a guide to one of the ancient ruins and engage one of the retired colonels to drive us. The colonel is unusually

Left to right: Tatiana Ivanovna Bedryk, Ania Savage, Yaroslava Fedorivna Volococka, and an Intourist guide on the Naberezhna Promenade in Yalta, 1992.

quiet that afternoon and, at times, downright brusque. On our way back, having dropped off the guide at the Yalta bus depot, I ask the colonel what is bothering him.

"Why did you have to get a Jew as a guide?" he snaps.

Oh, dear.

"He came highly recommended, and besides, what does it matter?" I say.

In Crimea, the anti-Semitism is particularly aberrational since many of the ruins of which the people are so proud were left by Jews, including Chafut-Kale. I do not see any synagogues in any Crimean city, and the Catholic basilica in Yalta is a museum of Greek and Roman coins. But in Chafut-Kale there is a synagogue. Amid the dead streets and collapsed stone homes, I noticed a stone building that had been partially restored; the door was padlocked. I am told the building is a synagogue, maintained by Karaites who continue to live in Crimea. On that same mountain massif, perhaps a mile or so away as the crow flies but on an east-facing cliff face, there are ruins of a cave monastery built around the ninth century and used up to the sixteenth or seventeenth centuries. When I was in Bakhchesarai, I climbed to that monastery also, and I peered into the caves of the early hermits and wondered how they ever carried enough materials up the perpendicular faces to build a monastery. Half a millennium ago, Jews and Christians lived side by side in this narrow valley.

Tatiana Ivanovna is lying rather uncomfortably on the pebbly Crimean beach inside the KGB sanitarium. I am a few feet away enjoying the caress of the cool azure water, the imperceptibly moving tide, the panorama of the towering mountains that glint above us on the noonday horizon. The water lifts me, aware but not resisting, and soon I feel the pebbles under me. I have been washed ashore. When I sit down beside Tania, I ask: "How in the world did the Black Sea get its name?"

Tania explains. "Black is how we describe the mood of the sea in the winter. Volodia says it can turn violent in an instant. Look," she says, and I glance back over my shoulder. The calm sea has suddenly churned into white caps.

"A couple of years ago, I almost drowned," Tania says. "I came after a storm and the waves were high, but I went in anyway. The current caught me. Fortunately, a man, a strong swimmer, saw me and pulled me out."

She adds: "Talk to Volodia about the sea."

It turns out not to be an easy assignment. Volodia is reluctant to talk about the sea because it isn't an "academic enough subject" to interest someone like me. He does volunteer that he has sailed the Mediterranean and once or twice the Atlantic. He says the Black Sea changes faster than the other two. "One moment you are working peacefully on the deck and the next moment a wave is trying to sweep you into the sea."

As I nod enthusiastically, his eyes grow dreamy and he turns toward the window; the sea glistens like the silver scales of a gigantic fish. "And does it get cold," he says. "It's a special cold. It's thick and heavy, especially out in the middle where you can no longer see the shore."

After ascertaining that my interest is genuine, he speaks of the sea occasionally, notably if there is news concerning merchant shipping.

"You, of course, know about the ancient Greek mariners," he says one day. "They called the Black Sea treacherous because of the currents. The currents and the trade winds drove the Greeks to Crimea. Even now, with diesel engines, currents can make trouble."

The sea, the giver and the reaper, awed ancient Greeks. The awe exists among today's sailors, too. Early sailors feared sea dragons and mermaids, while today's mariners tremble at the sight of the jellyfish that grows in Black Sea waters into a modern monster. The ribbed jellyfish,

Volodia says, was brought from the Atlantic in bilge water. "They're getting bigger and bigger. I know a man who pulled up one weighing seventy kilos," he says. I do a quick calculation and come up with 150 pounds. A jellyfish weighing that much would be as big as a medium-sized animal, indeed a sea monster.

"We sometimes still spot dolphins," Volodia says, "but the seals—they're gone for good." He shrugs.

The Black Sea and its unusual biological composition have long fascinated scientists. Following the end of Communism, scientists, including those from Wood's Hole Oceanographic Institution in Massachusetts, accelerated their study of what one scientist called a "geological freak." It is believed that the sea consists of a surface layer of oxygenated water that is about 400 feet deep. This is where most of the life exists. Below this layer is a boundary zone that is a combination of oxygenated and stagnant water. This layer reaches to 650 feet below the surface. Below the boundary zone and extending to 7,250 feet is a layer of deep water that is devoid of oxygen and most life. This layer contains hydrogen sulfide. There is also a sediment layer at the very bottom, which is believed to contain radioactive fallout from Chernobyl. Scientists believe the Black Sea was created some 8,000 years ago. The sea level of the Mediterranean rose and spilled through the Bosporus into a fresh water lake that was the original sea. As salt water rushed in, the marine life adapted to fresh water died. This process produced the hydrogen sulfide, which remains trapped beneath the thin surface layer of oxygenated water.

"If you lower a piece of metal deep enough, it will come out black," Volodia says, offering empirical evidence of the hydrogen sulfide layer.

If you were to flip the Black Sea upside down, the escaping gases would kill everyone living on the coastline.

Chapter 26

CRUISE ACROSS THE BLACK SEA

When I first heard the name, I thought Feodor Chaliapin was a general, but I was mistaken. He was a world-class tenor who went to Italy, where the Italians wrote that it was crazy for Russians to export tenors to Italy, just as it was crazy for Russia to import wheat. Feodor Chaliapin might not have been pleased that once he was rehabilitated, a cruise ship was named for him. He wrote to Maxim Gorky, "I won't go back to those bastards dead or alive." But in 1972, Feodor Chaliapin's remains were returned to Moscow from Paris. The government treated this acquisition of bones as a great ideological victory. He lay in state at the Bolshoi Theater, then a procession took him to Novodevichy Cemetery for reburial. The ship naming came a short time later.

Two weeks before I am to leave Crimea, I take a cruise across the Black Sea on the aging *Feodor Shalyapin* (spelled with a different system of transliteration than the tenor used). Getting aboard is complicated since I have no visa for Russia, I am an American citizen, and I neither want, nor can I afford, to pay in dollars for a "foreigner's ticket." A friend from Kyiv lends me her internal passport, while a friend in Yalta buys the ticket for second-class accommodations. First class would focus attention on me, says everyone I consult. In second class I can disappear among the masses.

Vitaly Leonidovich comes to see me off and frowns the entire time. He is still frowning on the dock as *Feodor Shalyapin,* with an enormous heave and a deafening blast of horns, edges past the Yalta lighthouse into the sea.

I find myself in what I decide is cruise ship steerage, on absolutely the lowest passenger deck. The cabin is tiny. One bunk is against the left wall and a double bunk is on the right wall. Illumination is provided by a naked overhead lightbulb, since there is no porthole. I am relieved to discover that mine is the single bunk on the left. The double bunk is already strewn with an amazing quantity of women's clothing. Sitting on the floor is a small, thin, pale woman with an orange Afro. Henna orange. Her hair is standing out from her scalp for at least four or five inches in an orange halo. It looks as if that she has just experienced an electric shock that has made her hair stand on end.

She introduces herself as Sveta, no surname or patronymic. She points to the upper bunk, where an adolescent girl is sleeping under the pile of clothing, and says the child is her daughter, Ania. This introduction jolts my memory and I remember to introduce myself as Lyudmila, the name on my borrowed passport. After depositing my suitcase, I explore the cabin by opening a narrow door. I find myself in a cubicle. The bathroom is one of those strange, Soviet-era frugalities, a combination shower/toilet. The shower head is practically above the toilet. There is no shower curtain. I will discover that once you turn the water on, the entire cubicle is drenched.

Sveta turns out to be one third of an unusual trio of women. She and Zhenia and Tania, also with children in tow, decided to take the cruise together. Zhenia and Tania share a cabin on the deck above us. No husbands accompany these women and no husbands are ever mentioned. Sveta tells me that she and her friends took a similar cruise a couple of years earlier. Ania and the other three children, two boys and a girl, will spend most of the cruise running around and playing on the decks, although they will be pressed into service when one of the women wants to escape a tedious admirer. "Oh, it's way past my darling's bedtime," Sveta or Zhenia or Tania will cry, jumping up and sweeping the startled child into her arms and hurrying away.

For partying at night or when the company is congenial, the three women drop their inhibitions. They dress to the nines for the welcoming party the first evening and cannot believe that I have not brought evening clothes.

After much agonizing and changing, Sveta emerges dressed like a tart. She has on tight green sequined pants and a red silk top, which clashes awfully with her orange hair. The top, however, matches a pair of red stiletto heels. As Sveta is slim, Zhenia is fat. She wears a chiffon caftan over a long loose black skirt and a black floppy top. The caftan is trimmed with red and gold bands. The third woman, Tania, is the least flamboyant and wears a black shift and enormous gold hoop earrings.

Tania whispers to me that today is Zhenia's birthday. She and Sveta present Zhenia with a flower bouquet as we leave for the evening's entertainment in the lounge on the top deck. Sveta finds a table for us by prancing along the edge of the dance floor until a couple of single men invite her to sit down. She points to us hovering behind her, and the men reluctantly invite us, too. A bottle of Crimean champagne appears and we toast Zhenia. Sveta goes off to dance with one of the men. The rest of us drink more champagne. I am embarrassed and ill at ease. I feel as if I am back in my adolescence at a high school dance, where boys stood on one side of the room and the girls on the other, each group pretending the other group did not exist. But if a boy marshaled his courage, crossed the room, and asked one of the girls to dance, those left behind writhed inside with envy. I am jealous of Sveta and her ease in gaining a dance partner. I drink another glass of champagne in a spate of annoyance.

Some time later, Zhenia, who has tossed down several more glasses of champagne, presses the bouquet she has received to her heaving bosom and floats onto the dance floor by herself. The chiffon caftan billows around her and she looks like a slow-moving sailing ship. The orchestra picks up on her mood and offers up a tango. Near us, a group occupying several tables begins to clap. Zhenia bobs in their direction and begins tossing the flowers to the men. They give her a standing ovation. When Zhenia sits down, one of the men who caught a gladiolus comes to our table with an unopened bottle of champagne. He says he is a Pole and he and his friends were touched by Zhenia tossing them flowers. The man bows to kiss Zhenia's hand. He clicks his heels in the very best Old World, Austro-Hungarian Empire manner. Zhenia beams up at him and extends her plump right hand while her left flutters on her heaving breast.

The Pole beams and kisses her hand a second time. I recall a story I once heard describing how, in the early days of World War II, the Polish cavalry charged German tanks, only to be decimated within minutes. Why did the Polish cavalry rush into certain death? Because that was the honorable thing for gentlemen to do. This Pole is kissing the hand of a tipsy woman because she has honored him with a gladiolus.

Zhenia now turns her attention to opening the bottle of champagne. She unwinds the metal wire holding the cork in place and tosses it on the table. Instead of popping the cork, she twirls the bottle above her head in ever faster circles, agitating the carbon dioxide inside. In a minute or less, the cork flies out and the champagne spews in a geyser, splashing her and us. Soon other men appear at our table. The party is off to a great start. The buzz of voices rises to a crescendo that is interrupted now and again by roars of laughter. Either Zhenia or sea travel, or both, have flung the Poles into high good humor. The Poles will turn out to be the friendliest passengers on board, laughing, joking, and fooling around, but I have to avoid them since to explain my accent, I told Sveta that I'm part Polish.

The passengers offer up a Babel of languages. Aside from the fair-haired, friendly Poles, there are the hard-drinking, loud-mouthed Russians, and the olive-skinned, saturnine, and self-effacing Georgians, who dress in black and eschew speaking Russian. There are also men wearing black fezzes with red tassels, men who bypass the evening entertainment to play cards on the deck and speak in a language I have not heard before. These men carry enormous wads of dollars, which they take out with great ceremony to peel off twenty-dollar notes whenever they lose a hand. There is also a woman who must have spent most of her life going barefoot. Her feet aren't swollen, but they are enormous, wide and flat. Her soles look like thick slabs of leather. The crust of calluses is like the armor on a turtle's body. I cannot take my eyes off her feet and I never see her wear anything but flip-flops.

Dress is casual, and few men wear jackets, but the women dress up, although not well. The seediness of the mainland reappears aboard ship. There are no babies aboard. The four children of the three women I befriend are the youngest passengers. If there is a captain, as I assume there must be, I never see him.

The first morning aboard dawns gorgeous. At 7:15, a pale moon hovers above a horizon of silky smooth, black-blue water. The sky is a cloudless pale blue and the air is perfectly still. By 9:30, clouds are rolling in and the sea grows angry and choppy. I remember what Volodia from Frunzenskoe said about the treachery of the Black Sea and examine the *Feodor Shalyapin* critically. She is an old cruise ship, showing her age. Rust has turned the iron deck into crumbling lace at the railings, so I stay away from the edge. When I look up at the ship's superstructure, the huge bolts that hold it together bleed their own rivulets of rust. I know that satellites plot storm systems and pinpoint their location. I also know that almost no place on earth is out of reach of some sort of communication. But this is a Soviet-era ship and technology alone cannot save an aging ship. All right, I decide, there's nothing to be gained in worrying about the seaworthiness of the ship. I go in search of the library, which has no books but does have bridge and backgammon tables and is away from the wind, now blowing at gale force.

At eleven o'clock, the storm ends as suddenly as it began. The clouds scud away, the sun comes out, but the wind remains strong and cold. I find a comfortable lounge chair in a sheltered corner of the second deck. It offers a great view of the frothing sea. The water has changed to coal black, which surprises me. From my window at Tatiana Ivanovna's flat, the sea would appear either azure or blue-gray, depending on the weather. When I went swimming, the water looked gray, which I attributed to the gray color of the pebbles on the beach and in the water. But here, miles from anywhere and below an umbrella of blue sky, the water is black. It is shiny black like molten coal, like a piece of polished ebony, like the deceptive, slick mud in Slavske. The darkness of the water is accentuated by the white, wind-driven caps of the tumbling waves. The water must be very deep here, I muse. It holds light far down inside like the fiery black opal.

The storm creates a quandary. No one wants to stay in the cabins, which, I learn, are uniformly small and cramped, and no one wants to face the elements on the exposed top deck. With the exception of the library, the public rooms remain dark and shuttered, so passengers congregate in the open stairwell between floors. Eventually, the crew relents and opens the disco and the bar. The partying begins early.

I spend most of the day on the deck, wrapped in all my warm clothes, watching the sea and regretting that I have not brought my red parka. At sunset, the wind sinks into a whisper, as if in awe of what is happening on the western horizon. There, the sun is a pulsating orange-red ball rolling slowly into a black void in which water and sky merge.

The bad weather destroys Sveta's Afro. That night at dinner her hair is limp and clings to her skull. I decide she must have used some sort of styling mousse, but dare not ask. I have been looking forward to dinner all afternoon. The night before, the first night's dinner had been excellent, although the service had been as gruff as on the mainland. The only time our server spoke to us was to rebuke us for not eating fast enough or for not finishing what was on our plates. If you did not eat fast enough, she whisked the unfinished plate away as soon as her assistant brought the huge tray heaped with the next course.

The first evening we were served a herring appetizer, a golden bouillon garnished with fresh herbs, lamb kebob with a julienne of carrots and string beans, and a selection of light and crumbly pastries, among them French napoleons. A glass of red wine, dry and full bodied, was served with the lamb. The primary ingredient of a good meal is, of course, good food. The second ingredient needed for a meal to be remembered is affable tablemates. We were assigned to tables by cabin number. Sveta tried to change the seating so that she could be with Zhenia and Tania, but the waitress simply said, "Nyet." Since no one at our table knows anyone else and since the Russian custom is to be reserved, because who knows who might be sitting right next to you, no one speaks to anyone else except his or her traveling companions. It is like being back in Slavske's dining room and being surrounded by five Politburo couples. But in Slavske, I had, at least, Katia and my mother. In *Feodor Shalyapin's* dining room, the only people willing to talk to me are Sveta and Ania, but only if I address them first. I try to make friends, but do not succeed.

The second night's dinner has deteriorated to the indifferent food served in mainland hotels. Sauerkraut coleslaw and semi-stale bread accompany "mystery meat." The meal is an oppressively silent affair interrupted by slurps and an occasional gale of laughter from the Polish party nearby. Our table is the first one to be finished, and the waitress compliments us on our speed.

The post-dinner entertainment the second night is a three-man act. One of the actors is dressed as Elvis Presley. He wears tight white polyester pants and a white jacket trimmed with gold braid. Beneath the jacket is a bare, hairy chest. The actor tries to gyrate like Elvis and sings "Hound Dog" in badly accented English. The second actor shows off Arnold Schwarzenegger muscles. He wears checkered baggy pants, which are held up by suspenders that dangle over a cut-off-at-the-armpits undershirt. He is playing the role of a peasant. The third actor is a fat man in an elegant suit. He later appears in a pink dress and a wig. The show is slapstick vaudeville.

The fat man does a monologue in verse. The subject is bad food and shortages, not bad politics. Then the muscled peasant comes back on stage. "I'm thinking of selling my pride and joy, my washing machine," the fat man dressed as a fat woman confides to him, and I remember Lyuda's washing machine in Moscow. "Why?" the muscled peasant asks. "Before, I couldn't get any soap with which to wash my clothing. Now, I have no clothing to wash."

People shout, whistle, and clap their approval while downing prodigious amounts of alcohol. The drink of choice is champagne. Tabletops are crowded with empty bottles—not one or two, but four or five. The hand-kissing Pole of the night before comes by to say hello and says there are thirty people in the Polish party. They boarded *Feodor Shalyapin* in Odessa.

It takes *Feodor Shalyapin* a night, a day, and a second night to reach a land of fables, the Caucasus. The northern and eastern shores of the Black Sea were known to and were explored and settled by ancient Greeks. They peopled the craggy shores, the granite peaks, and the deep gorges with supernatural beings, fickle gods, and larger than life heroes. Jason and the Argonauts found the Golden Fleece here. Prometheus is chained to a Caucasus peak in punishment for giving fire to humans. A fearsome tribe of man-hating Amazons inhabited inland gorges and scandalized nearby tribes. Alexander the Great explored the northern shoreline in search of a passage to the unknown steppes, while Pompey fought a battle here. Later, St. Andrew stopped to preach Christianity here. Shakespeare was fascinated by these shores and talked about the "frosty Caucasus" in his plays. Yet, until the Middle Ages, the northeastern shore of the Black Sea and the Caucasus Mountains that tower behind it were considered the end of the world. The mountains, running northwest to southeast between the Black and Caspian seas, are the boundary between Europe and Asia. This boundary was considered impenetrable until Russia built the Caucasus Military Road in 1863.

The Caucasus Mountains greet us the following morning. The wind has subsided during the night and the waves of the recent gale have dwindled into long rolls. Before noon, *Feodor Shalyapin* steams into Batumi, a port that was already a thriving city when Pliny mentioned it in the first century A.D. Batumi was once the capital of Colchis, a land of legendary wealth. This was where Jason acquired the Golden Fleece. I learn that the fable has a basis in fact. Even today, when shepherds drive their sheep to high summer pastures, they anchor fleeces of wool from their sheep in streams to trap grains of gold that are carried by the wild waters.

Batumi's old town lies near the port, while the new town climbs the low hills and spills from the port along the coast. The old town is a warren of narrow streets radiating from a central promenade that is lined with bazaar stalls and cafés. The bazaar smells of anise and nutmeg, mutton and chile peppers, overripe persimmons and ripening goat cheese. It is a world of men with hawklike features and women with flashing black eyes, an exotic, colorful, noisy world, never quite subdued by the surly conquerors from the steppes. In these parts, people have always been famous as goldsmiths and silversmiths. I don't come across gold trinkets—perhaps I don't know where to look—but I do see fabulous craftsmanship in copper and brass and stone. I succumb and buy an ornate bracelet with a huge agate eye and cufflike sides fastened together with an intricate lock. Some weeks later at the Kyiv airport, the bracelet will set off the metal detector of a customs clerk examining my baggage. The bracelet will be taken away, examined at length, and eventually returned to me. I think the clerk mistakes the burnished brass for gold. The bracelet will not be worth the trouble it causes. It is too ornate and too ostentatious for wearing in America and languishes in a drawer. The Batumi bazaar yields up other treasurers, but I resist. As I leave the bazaar, I head toward a side street where a crowd has gathered. Through plate glass, I glimpse a pale blue Volvo sedan in front of rows and rows of brand-new Japanese electronic equipment—television sets, VCRs, tape decks, boom boxes. I push my way to the entrance, only to be stopped by a guard brandishing a Kalashnikov. I do my nationality change. "*Ya Amerikanka,*" I say in broken Russian.

He looks at me but does not believe. "*U menya valuita* (I have hard currency)," I add, tapping my purse.

He grins and lets me in, and I wander around looking at the Sonys, the VCRs, the boom boxes, bottles of Johnny Walker Red, and other items one sees in airport duty-free shops, but I buy nothing. I am not even tempted. As I leave and smile at the guard with the Kalashnikov assault gun, I wonder why on earth I have bothered with this charade. I guess it is the obstinacy I learned as a journalist, wanting to get into places from which I am barred.

We see the Caucasus for the next three days. The mountains strain into the sky along the edge of the sea, although on their distant northern slope, I know that they sink indifferently into a bare and featureless plateau. I count three ranges of mountains behind Batumi. Bare and uninviting, the peaks tower above a narrow strip of cultivated land that is dotted with towns, sheltered azure coves, and fingers of dark forest.

My shipmates are an indolent, hard-drinking lot. They don't stop partying when we berth in Batumi, nor when we sail again. They stay on board in Sochi, our second port of call. Sochi is the Miami Beach of the Russian resort coast on the Black Sea. This is where Boris Yeltsin vacationed several times. Less than half of the passengers go sightseeing in either Batumi or Sochi. Most bake in the sun all day and drink. By the time the ship sets sail in the evening, most are lobster red. The Poles are particularly susceptible to the sun. The beautifully mannered Pole who presented Zhenia with champagne has turned a startling fuchsia, but he maintains his good humor and still bows gallantly over women's extended hands.

Sochi boasts sanitariums that are even bigger and more elaborate than the largest in the Crimea and a pebbled beach longer and wider than the one in Yalta. Sochi's rest homes were erected as showplaces of the "proletarian paradise." In 1936, André Gide was invited to visit the Soviet Union, including Sochi, and came back completely disillusioned. Explaining his rejection of Communism, he wrote: "When I visited Sochi I marveled at the number of sanitariums and rest houses that are being erected for the workers. . . . It is praiseworthy that all this semi-luxury should be provided for the use of the workers; nevertheless those who enjoy this comfort are all too often the new privileged class"—that is, Communist Party members.

Exploring Sochi, I spot a gold-domed church on a hill. I learn that it used to be a potato warehouse, one of the most onerous uses for a church during the Soviet regime. The potato fungus found a hospitable host on the icons, often decorated with paint that contained egg yolk and red wine. The fungus would eat away such paint, obliterating icons. A worker who has just climbed down from the scaffold inside the church tells me this. He is restoring the basilica of the Archangel Michael. In the vestibule, kerchiefed old women are selling long, thin yellow tapers, which visitors place in front of several restored icons. Somehow, the woman who sells me a candle knows instinctively I am not Orthodox and hesitates to take my money. Perhaps I do not light my candle the right way.

Aboard ship I have finally made a friend: She is blond, amusing, good-looking in a cool Grace Kelly way, and the cruise director. She immediately knows I am not from Lviv or Poland because she comes from those parts. But she does accept my story that I am a Ukrainian who has grown up in Germany. We go sightseeing together in Sochi and she sees dollars in my wallet. She asks me to exchange rubles for dollars since she is saving money for the next excursion, which will take *Feodor Shalyapin* to Turkey. I, perpetually cautious, exchange twenty dollars for rubles at the official rate, instead of the black market rate, which surprises her. She tells me about an Old World hotel in Odessa where I will spend a lovely day two weeks later.

I cannot figure out why we are docking at Novorossiisk, an industrial port with enormous tankers and cranes crowding the harbor. Novorossiisk is about five hundred miles south of Moscow and is the largest outlet for Russia's oil exports. I've read that the depth of this harbor is exceeded only by the depth of the fjords in Sevastopol. If the Black Sea Fleet is ever divided between Ukraine and Russia, Novorossiisk will become the headquarters for the Russian segment. Novorossiisk is a port of contrasts, having been divided into three areas: industrial port, military port, and commercial port. One side of the harbor rises steeply in a series of barren hills, scarred by excavations and pollution. At the base of these hills lie huge piles of all kinds of ores. One of the piles is sulfur, which is leaching chartreuse rivulets into the sea; I have once before seen raw sulfur during a tour of a chemical plant in the New Jersey Meadowlands. Container ships, freighters, and tankers are busy loading the piles of ore. A gravel quarry gouges one of the hills. A huge, billowing and belching cement plant throws off plumes of leaden smoke that first sink into the pit before floating in ragged streaks into the pale blue sky. Several tankers are taking on crude oil, which flows into Novorossiisk from Azerbaijan through the Baku-Novorossiisk pipeline. Next to the industrial disaster is the military port with a forest of masts of mothballed ships. The commercial port is compressed and to one side, a casual afterthought. The *Feodor Shalyapin* anchors here at a narrow concrete concourse that protrudes into the water.

Everyone is going sightseeing, to my surprise. Eventually I find out why the vodka and champagne drinkers are willing to abandon ship: buses are waiting to take us to a vineyard in the hills above the city. Wine tasting adheres to a strict etiquette in both Crimea and southern Russia and in no way resembles the casual wine tasting in places such as the Napa Valley. In Crimea as well as Russia, wine tasting is a serious business, requiring a solemn demeanor and a seriousness of mind reserved for monumental occasions. At the Novorossiisk vineyard, we are divided into groups. One group goes to see the winery, the second to see the vineyards, while the third group is ushered into a large hall for wine tasting. I am in the wine-tasting group. Stewards escort us one by one, each to a place at a table already set with five wine goblets of uniform size. There is also a goblet filled with water and a plate with four crackers, one to be eaten in each interval between wine samples.

After we are seated, stewards appear to pour the first wine. They fill each taster's first wine goblet to about one third of its volume. As soon as the steward is finished at our table, a man across from me downs the glass of wine as if he were downing a tumbler of vodka. His wife gives him a look of such utter disgust that he turns crimson and behaves himself for the remainder of the tasting. The rest of us wait for the sommelier to appear. In Novorossiisk, the wine expert turns out to be a woman in a gray, wrinkled housedress, not the elegantly dressed men I have admired at wine tastings in the Crimea. The expert's role is to describe the vintage, the grape used, and whatever else is significant about the wine and to invite the guests to sample it. No one except the expert speaks. No one offers opinions or asks questions. Everyone sits stone-faced and enormously serious. This is the case at Novorossiisk. Yet, instead of describing the bouquet and grape, the woman launches into listing wine's medicinal uses. Is this because five years earlier Mikhail Gorbachev condemned Russians' proclivity for liquor and ordered many vineyards destroyed? After all, this winery is a kolkhoz with an enormous hammer and sickle insignia at the entrance. We follow the same procedure in tasting four more wines, which grow sweeter and heavier but do not possess much of a bouquet. I do not like the wines, but am amused by the atmosphere. It is as if we were in a church.

It's fun to wander in Novorossiisk, despite my initial misgivings about a stop in an industrial city. The city is a thriving commercial center with many stores, markets, and vendor stalls. The streets are filled with people buying and selling all kinds of goods, from caviar tins from Vladivostok to bottles of red wine from the winery in the hills. I buy three icons in an antiquarian shop and come away with the impression that Novorossiisk is a freewheeling town, accustomed to foreigners and trade, and not as uptight as the rest of the country—the gray-clad sommelier at the winery notwithstanding.

Chapter 27

UKRAINE AS A FLEDGLING DEMOCRACY

In this part of the world, people have very long memories, perhaps because for decades they were forbidden to remember.

As I get ready to leave, I encounter the horrors of Slavske again. In Yalta a woman I met at the opening of a new exhibit at the Lesia Ukrainka Museum a few weeks earlier seeks me out. She asks me for my telephone number, but I don't wonder about her request. I assume that before my departure she will give me a letter to mail in the West. Instead, she calls to ask if we can meet on the Naberezhna Promenade in Yalta, not at the apartment.

She is a middle-aged, thin woman with hair cut short in a modish bob. The youthful hairdo is in sharp contrast to the deep lines running from her nostrils to the corners of her well-defined mouth.

We choose an outdoor table at a café overlooking the crimson waters of the sea at sunset. The cool trade wind, sweetened by the scent of subtropical flowers, ruffles her hair, and she pushes it away from her forehead. In profile, her angular features look masculine—not unlike Irena Sen's—above the white collar of her demure blouse. We talk about this and that while I wait, cautious, as she shores up her courage. I assume she will ask me to do something, see someone, or buy something in the West. I am wrong. She asks me to tell her about Slavske and its environs. She says she has heard I have been there. She is interested in the town because she was raised in Slavske, but left as soon as she could.

She sits across the small table from me with her back to the sea. We are less than a foot apart, but the distance between us grows to a half century. She leaves the present to enter her past, to return to Slavske. She speaks of her father, the Communist organizer. She says her father was the kolkhoz leader. Her father . . . Did any one in Slavske mention her father, who was sent to Slavske shortly after the war ended? The war. The war and its bloody aftermath have determined her whole life. Can I imagine—of course, I cannot—what it was like for him to bring his family to a place where everyone hated him and them? At home, he never spoke of what he did. Her mother remained silent also. She and her sister found out when they went to school. They were reviled in the classroom and in the yard.

Has she ever gone back? I ask. She shudders. No, never. She can never go back to Slavske. In the darkness, she fumbles for my hand and clutches at it. She clutches at my hand as she utters a string of evasions. Slavske is too far away. She has neither time nor money for such a long trip. Where will she stay? Then she capitulates and tells the truth: "I would be spit on if I showed my face there. My sister was."

In moments of pain, human features become distorted. She is no longer the coolly handsome woman I admired moments earlier. Her mouth skewers into the grimace of a stroke victim as she whispers, "My father killed."

Behind her, the sea has disappeared. I can find the water only when the yellow beam from the lighthouse at the mouth of the harbor sweeps toward the shore, catching the foamy crest of the waves in its light but never quite reaching the jagged rocks of the coastline.

"Now you know everything about me," she says. "Do you hate me?"

I shake my head, but I do not comfort her. Her tragedy is linked to the tragedies of Irena Sen, her two companions, and the two grave-diggers. One land, two histories.

Ukraine is a place where enforced isolation has obscured a history and a people. I sometimes wondered if a Ukraine really existed outside my mother's stories. And I also wondered: "How do you go back to a place you neither remember nor know?"

What are the ties that bind us to our past, I wondered. Blood, loyalty, common experiences, shared history and values, and, of course, memories. Neither my American self nor my Ukrainian self could lay claim to all. Blood was certainly a Ukrainian tie, as was a shared history, together with memories that were as shapeless as dreams. My life experiences and my outlook were American, as were my values, particularly those concerning the freedom of the individual and the equality of women. How was I to make sense of this hodgepodge?

I thought my mother's memories would serve as reference points as I sorted out who I was. But this did not turn out as I expected, or wanted.

I came to realize that she had idealized her past, had made it sound more glorious than it actually had been, had forgotten hardships. Her memories were not truths, nor facts. They had not been reliable in Slavske, in Krushelnytsia, in Zariche, or in Lviv. I now know that memories—such as the memory of a mass grave in a roadside ditch—give pain, like a festering wound.

Yet, going back became one of the highlights of my life. Going back changed me. Not unlike my mother, I had, for years, been living in a world of doubles. I had a past life and a language that I seldom, if ever, permitted to intrude on my present, safe life. I did the exact opposite of what my mother did—I lived for today, not yesterday. By choosing a husband who was not Ukrainian, I embraced America, opted for fluidity, and fell into the melting pot. As Bharati Mukherjee, the novelist, has pointed out, in marrying an American she succumbed to cultural and psychological "mongrelization." I did also. There was a time when I was estranged from most things Ukrainian, when speaking Ukrainian to my parents seemed foreign. I lost my fluency. Then I traveled halfway around the world to discover that the language was there waiting to be resurrected, that a heritage would not let itself be pushed into a dim corner. But as I was learning these truths, they were being filtered through my American self, and instead of feeling a victim of war, history, and geography—as my mother did—I came to see myself as a bridge.

One of the reasons I returned to teach in Crimea was because of a quixotic belief that people like me could be conduits of modernity and of the Western celebration of individual freedom at a crucial time in Ukraine's history. Both times I came back to America with new insights, bursting with stories that I knew I had to relate. As soon as I heard that first question: "How was it?" I knew I wanted to enact the history of my private experience on a public stage. I wrote "Comment" pieces for *USA Today*. I participated in a radio talk show; I gave lectures before any group that asked for one, from a Korean church congregation to the Kiwanis. I wanted those who heard or read about my experiences to say, "This is how it was when the Soviet Union collapsed. This is how the immigrant felt coming home. This really happened."

I was lucky to be in Ukraine during a time history will remember. I saw centuries of history being relived, reexamined, and reordered. Men and women on the streets walked smiling and elated, rejoicing at the end of tyranny. In the euphoria of freedom, everything was possible, nothing was impossible, not even instant democracy and a free marketplace. Why? Because Ukraine was unique. The new country had more land area than Poland, Czechoslovakia, and Hungary combined; a population as large as that of France; the fabled *chornozem* or black, rich earth; and factories that had been producing a quarter of the Soviet gross national product. Ukraine was bound to succeed, and the people with it. It took me the subsequent years to understand that I had been weaving my own fairy tale, as my mother had hers.

When we make a pilgrimage, we go to bear witness and our voices unite with those of the other pilgrims. This chorus not only validates our effort but also invigorates those who could not make the trek, or feared the journey. Perhaps this is why I wrote this memoir—to urge others like me to go back, to see and to understand.

There are other ways of examining pilgrimages. A priest in Muriel Spark's *Mandelbaum Gate* describes a pilgrimage as an act of devotion, which, like a work of art, is meaning enough in itself. As I consider this, I wonder whether I went back to affirm my Ukrainian heritage, and not because I was curious, or because an opportunity had presented itself. I came away from this experience much less the Ukrainian partisan, much less in awe and fear of Russia, but also more comprehending of Russia's grand past and why Russia eclipsed Ukraine. The great expanses of the north, the land's unyielding stubbornness, the long winters where cold is not an uncomfortable chill but a life-threatening enemy have a created a formidable people who grasp and won't let go. I admire tenaciousness.

Although Ukrainians and Russians are neither soul brothers nor fraternal twins, as Soviet propaganda in this century would have wanted the West to believe, the two peoples are, nonetheless, related. The kinship lies in the similarities of outlook, of melancholy, of doggedness when confronting hardships—and many points of shared history. The difficult years since independence both in Ukraine and in Russia bear out that the Russian and the Ukrainian nations are survivors. I am a survivor too.

My mother, in her way, was also a survivor. Although her legacy was contradictory, she brought me up to be the dispossessed—"the other"—but her life also showed me that even the dispossessed survive. What I did not know and what I learned by going back was that the state of being "the other" as well as a survivor are not only related but carry hidden benefits. In America I had experimented with a number of identities and found this alterability helpful in Ukraine also. I could be the Polish traveler, the German ethnic, the brusque American, and whatever other ploy was called for by the circumstances in which I found myself. I was not rootless but many-rooted.

In the end, I learned that life offers a choice, and choosing an active life, even if it is harder, is better than choosing a passive life, the life of a victim. Otherwise, one becomes like those tragic figures, fleeting shadows cowering in corners, whom I met in Donetske.

I went on a journey both to and from memories. I expected to learn, but I did not expect to be moved to the extent I was. I anticipated, even looked forward to, a resurgence of latent memories; but with the exception of those triggered by the Katyusha rocket launcher in Warsaw, they did not come. Yet all of my experiences were in some way touched by memories, not only my mother's, Katia's, or mine but also by the memories of those I met. And as I mined these memories—Angelina Nikolaevna's about Babi Yar victims, Sonia Petrovna's and Josef's about exile to Kazakhstan, those of the woman in Yalta about her childhood in Slavske—I learned that memories are both about remembering and about forgetting.

To refer again to Muriel Spark, who writes about lives as if they were pilgrimages, a pilgrim's response may be a matter of good or bad fortune, good or bad weather, friendly or unfriendly people the pilgrim meets. I was incredibly lucky that after Slavske I met many people who were kind to me—Volodia, Andriy, Sasha, Lidia Mazur, Tatiana Ivanovna, and even Sveta. I also had the extraordinary good fortune not only to be there at a historic time but also to see a country energized by a vision of a bright new future. I saw hope before it was dashed by reality.

My mother's memory failed rapidly in the mid-1990s. She soon forgot that she had ever gone back to Ukraine. More tragically, she did not care about or follow the changes that were occurring there. Ukraine no longer touched her soul, and when in a cogent moment she sat down to write a short codicil to her will, she asked to be buried in Trenton, New Jersey, not in her homeland. The memory of the homeland had been lost. When she died in 1997, I buried her in Trenton, next to my father.

Katia returned to Ukraine a year later with her older daughter, Christine, for another month or so. Irene, her younger daughter, planned to make the journey, but died too soon.

Archbishop Sterniuk, the holy man I met in Lviv, died on September 29, 1997, and ten thousand people marched in his funeral procession in Lviv. Veterans of the UPA, rehabilitated since Ukrainian independence, formed an honor guard as the casket was carried through the streets of Lviv.

The personal landscape in which I lived changed also. The journalism department moved from Shevchenko Boulevard near Khreshchatyk to the white marble building on Melnikova less than a year after Leonid Kravchuk, Rector Moskalenko's in-law, was elected Ukraine's president. The Center for Market and Entrepreneurship evaporated into thin air. The Ukraina Society elected the dissident poet and legislator Ivan Drach as its president and the organization's former president apologized for the years of vituperation directed at the diaspora. Volodia has taken a job as an editor for a publishing house, while Andriy, after several years at BBC, returned to Kyiv and has attained a notable career as an investigative television journalist. Sasha Dinges, my Russian German friend in Donetske, suffered a heart attack but is recuperating and continuing to work on behalf of the Volga Germans. My return to Ukraine has touched my family also. My son Michael enrolled in a Ukrainian language course in Ukraine and I spent several days with him in Kyiv following my return from Crimea. He subsequently spent a summer working in Kyiv in the Ministry of Foreign Economic Relations.

Some things, like the paper shortage, did not change. When Michael was leaving for his job in Kyiv, I was asked to give him a ream of fine bond paper. Upon his return he told me the paper was used to print the ministry's documents.

Perhaps because I'm a journalist, I seldom hesitated to open a door or strike up a conversation in order to learn how people lived and what they thought. I hope this book reflects what I discovered about my homeland. I have tried to present a vision of Ukraine as it existed at the time of the Soviet Union's collapse and in the first months of independence. The years since independence have not been kind. At the close of the twentieth century, more than half of the population of Ukraine is living below the poverty level. Crime is commonplace. Politicians are getting rich from the toil of overworked and underpaid citizens by corrupting the fledgling democracy. The reviled "coupon" currency was replaced by the *hryvnia* — the name of the currency of Kyivan Rus — but subsequent governmental restrictions have abridged its convertibility and its value.

But there have been strides forward, too. Ukraine has been successful at nation building. It is the only country of the former Soviet Union that has changed presidents (and is getting ready to do so for the third time) in free and fair elections. Today's Ukraine is a union of culturally, religiously, and politically different western and eastern provinces that have found a way to coexist and respect each other. Two histories, which

I first glimpsed in Slavske and later saw embodied in the granite monuments and the birch-cross-topped counter-monuments, have been assimilated into one history through tolerance. Although Ukrainian has become the language of the government, Russian continues to be the *lingua franca* in Eastern Ukraine, while Western Ukraine uses Ukrainian. I don't find this problematic. In countries such as the Netherlands and Switzerland, the population speaks several languages. In the western United States, including Colorado where I live, information at the public library and at the state government level is rendered in both English and Spanish. Similarly, southern Florida, where my mother lived, is bilingual and that multiculturalism adds zest to, rather than detracting from, daily life.

Perhaps of greater significance for the culture and heritage of Ukraine is the fact that writers are again writing and publishing in Ukrainian. Both the Uniate Catholic and the Orthodox faiths are thriving and people are returning in droves to their faith. Despite the economic crisis, the twelfth-century St. Michael's Golden-Domed Sobor (cathedral), dynamited by Stalin in 1936, was rebuilt and consecrated at the end of 1998, and neither the Catholics nor the Orthodox have demanded sole occupancy. Restoration of the eleventh-century Uspenski (Dormition or Assumption) Sobor at the Cave Monastery, dynamited in 1941 by the Germans, has begun. Perhaps one day the capital of Ukraine can once again boast of being "golden-domed Kyiv."

Politically, the Ukrainian Parliament (Vernkhovna Rada) has shared rule with the president during nearly a decade of independence. For this reason I argue that Ukraine's politics are more stable than those of its ex-Soviet neighbors, Belarus and Russia. In 1996, Ukraine adopted a constitution, which, bolstered by progressive policies of the government, protects fundamental civil liberties. There have been no anti-Semitic outbursts in the Verkhovna Rada and there have been no attempts to enact laws abridging the rights of minorities, as there have been in the Russian Duma. I think the Ukrainian nation has learned a valuable lesson in the twentieth century. The national conscience remembers the wartime atrocities against the individual that were perpetrated during both the German and Soviet occupations, as well as the bitter and bloody UPA war and the repression that followed. These experiences and a desire for normalcy are tempering, if not forestalling, unwise outbursts. Ukrainians, I think, have learned tolerance and accommodation. An example of prudence was the decision by the government to surrender its arsenal of nuclear weapons, inherited when the Soviet Union collapsed.

Ukraine is addressing the specter of Chernobyl, which continues to threaten Eastern Europe. Work between Ukraine and the G-7 countries is proceeding to find a way to stabilize and eventually remove the nuclear fuel from the ruined reactor that exploded on April 26, 1986.

And the press is free to speak the national mind most of the time.

Yet, some lessons remain to be learned. Different political forces continue to pull in opposite directions in the Verkhovna Rada. Unfortunately, the balance of power does not favor the national domestic forces of the democrats. Rukh, the Popular Movement of Ukraine, the strongest democratic party, has not been able to create a lasting and effective coalition of liberal factions and splintered into two shortly before Vyacheslav Chornovil, its leader during the 1990s, died suddenly in a car accident in 1999. One of Rukh's earlier successes was its coalition with the Crimean Tatars, who are becoming an increasingly important element on the peninsula. Mustafa Jemilev, the dissident and Tatar leader, was one of Rukh's successful candidates in the 1998 elections to the Verkhovna Rada.

Nonetheless, there are those who still dream of restoring the former USSR and its totalitarian system. Resurgent Communists have successfully blocked reform, including land privatization. Economic reforms, the promise of a stable currency, and control of inflation that would enable the citizenry to prosper have not been fulfilled.

In sum, Ukraine is still in transition and flux. Perhaps independence and self-rule happened too quickly—Volodia Kanash did point out on many occasions that dissidents and poets did not have enough time to learn how to govern before having rule thrust into their hands. Ukraine and its Slavic neighbors need more time for their transformation into truly democratic nations. Perhaps Ukraine, as well as Russia and the other countries that were in the Soviet bloc, will evolve into a uniquely Eastern European interpretation of democracy, one that reconciles the capitalism of the West with the socialism of the East. I look to the day when Ukraine ceases to be the country "on the edge" and becomes a full-fledged partner of Europe. This was a dream that my mother and her exiled generation dreamed, and I subscribe to this dream also.

Bibliographic Essay

CHAPTER I

The best, most exhaustive information in English on Ukraine, its history and culture, a view of its place and role in Western civilization, and its notable citizens (historic and current, both in the diaspora and in Ukraine) is available in the five-volume *Encyclopedia of Ukraine* (Toronto: Canadian Institute of Ukrainian Studies, University of Toronto Press, 1984, 1988, 1993). The longer entries are contributed and signed by experts in the field and many entries are followed by a brief bibliography or source list. I found the encyclopedia an excellent reference book on points of history and culture of which I knew little.

During the years of the Cold War, a number of books appeared about covert operations conducted by the United States against the Soviet Union. Some of these mentioned U.S. attempts to enlist Ukrainian guerrillas in the late 1940s and early 1950s to spy on the Soviet government. During this time also, Ukrainian exiles who came to the United States and Canada after World War II began to publish materials from the guerrilla war led by the Ukrainian Insurgent Army (UPA) that they had brought with them or had obtained from behind the Iron Curtain by other means. I read many of these books and mention below those I found most significant.

Presidents' Secret Wars: CIA and Pentagon Covert Operations since World War II (New York: W. Morrow, 1986) offers a description of the arrival of a UPA band in West Germany in 1947, the puzzlement among the Allies on what to do with these men, and the Allies' subsequent exploitation of the UPA remnants. The book also presents an even-handed analysis of the OUN and Stepan Bandera, OUN's most famous leader.

Harry Rositzke's *CIA's Secret Operations: Espionage, Counterespionage and Covert Action* (Boulder, Co.: Westview Press, 1988) offers a detailed description of Operation Redsox, which was launched by American and English secret agencies to use the UPA remnants behind the Iron Curtain to monitor Soviet military activities.

UPA Warfare in Ukraine by Yurij Tys-Krokhmaliuk (New York: Society of Veterans of Ukrainian Insurgent Army, 1972) is an exhaustive study in English of UPA ambush and battle tactics and bunker construction as well as a brief history of the UPA, OUN, and Ukraine. Now out of print, this book gives details of partisan training, schematics of bunker building, and lists of weaponry, together with verbatim reports of ambushes and battles. This is a handbook on how to wage a guerilla war.

Chechnya Calamity in the Caucasus by Carlotta Gall and Thomas de Waal (New York: New York University Press, 1998), also published in Great Britain by Macmillan, is a concise and objective account of the civil war and calamities in Chechnya. The authors trace the tragic history of the people of the Caucasus from the eighteenth-century invasions by Imperial Russia through Stalin's deportations to the 1994–96 war.

Amnesty International published three reports in 1997 on torture and abuse of human rights in Russia. I consulted all three reports. They are *Torture in Russia* (London: Amnesty International, International Secretariat, 1997), *Russian Federation, Torture, Ill-treatment and Death in the Army* (London: Amnesty International, International Secretariat, 1997) and *Russian Federation, Failure to Protect Asylum Seekers* (London: Amnesty International, International Secretariat, 1997).

CHAPTER 2

In *Lost in Translation: A Life in a New Language* (New York: E.P. Dutton, 1989), Eva Hoffman, who came to the United States as a teenager, speaks eloquently about the desires and difficulties of immersing oneself in the melting pot. Both Hoffman and Helena Znaniecka Lopata are of Polish heritage, but I found in Lopata's *Polish Americans: Status Competition in an Ethnic Community* (Englewood Cliffs, N.J.: Prentice-Hall, 1976) — which is a study of Polonia, the name given to Polish communities in the United States — numerous parallels between the Ukrainian and Polish immigrant ghettos.

CHAPTER 4

Ukrainian Nationalism, 1939–45 by John A. Armstrong (New York: Columbia University Press, 1955) is the definitive work in English on the OUN. Armstrong was a professor of political science at University of Wisconsin (Madison) prior to retirement and wrote about Soviet partisans during World War II before turning to the resistance in Ukraine.

OUN and the UPA are exhaustively analyzed in the twenty-nine-volume *Litopys UPA,* published in Toronto by a publishing organization bearing the same name (more volumes are forthcoming). Current volumes are being published in Ukraine, although Litopys UPA continues to maintain an office in Toronto. Each volume focuses on a geographical area where UPA developed and fought or on a particular subject, such as German documents on the UPA during the German occupation from 1941 to 1944 (volume 6). The books are in Ukrainian with a synopsis in English. Documents are presented in the original language with summaries in Ukrainian and English. The first volume appeared in 1978 and dealt with resistance against the Nazis during Ukraine's occupation by Germany beginning in June, 1941. I am in the process of translating volume 28, which is a memoir by Maria Savchyn, who joined the OUN at the age of fourteen and the UPA at sixteen.

Modern Ukrainian Short Stories, edited by George S. N. Lyckyj (second edition, Englewood, Co.: Ukrainian Academic Press, 1998) has parallel Ukrainian and English texts and several of the stories involve the UPA. I translated one of the UPA stories and one about a fisherman in Crimea.

The Second Soviet Republic: Ukraine After World War II, by Yaroslav Bilinsky (New Brunswick, N.J.: Rutgers University Press, 1964), also contains a good history of Ukrainian nationalism and UPA. The most recent history of Ukraine as well as of the Ukrainian nationalist movement is Orest Subtelny's *Ukraine: A History* (Toronto: University of Toronto Press in association with the Canadian Institute of Ukrainian Studies, 1994). Otherwise, there are few additional sources in English on the OUN and the UPA since this segment of Eastern European history has not interested Western scholars overly.

The definitive text on the Great Famine in Ukraine and Russia is Robert Conquest's *The Harvest of Sorrow: Soviet Collectivization and the Terror-Famine* (New York: Oxford University Press, 1986). The book served as the basis for a documentary of the same name that was shown in the late 1980s on William F. Buckley Jr.'s television program "Firing Line."

Negley Farson wrote poignantly about his disenchantment with the Bolshevik Revolution in *A Mirror for Narcissus* (Garden City, N.Y.: Doubleday & Company, Inc., 1957).

CHAPTER 5

A well-documented book in English on the Division Galizien (Galicia) is *The Ukrainian Division 'Galicia,' 1943–45* (Toronto: Shevchenko Scientific Society, 1988), a memoir by Wolf-Dietrich Heike, who was the division's chief of staff from January, 1944, to May, 1945, when it surrendered to the British Army. The division was formed in 1943, following the Red Army victory at Stalingrad. The Waffen-SS recruited Ukrainian young men for the division, but Adolf Hitler and Heinrich Himmler insisted that the division be referred to as Galizien (the German name for the province Halychyna, the capital of which is Lviv), not as Ukrainian. All officers were German. According to George H. Stein in *The Waffen SS: Hitler's Elite Guard at War, 1939–1944* (Ithaca, N.Y.: Cornell University Press, 1966), the Waffen (Armed) SS consisted of thirty-eight divisions. Of these, nineteen were composed primarily of foreign recruits, numbering approximately 500,000 men. The foreigners were mostly Eastern Europeans with Albanians, Belorussians, Bosnians, Bulgarians, Croats, Estonians, Hungarians, Latvians, Romanians, Russians, Ukrainians, and ethnic Germans from Eastern Europe forming the largest ethnic groups. The English memoir is a translation from German. John A. Armstrong wrote the introduction. My father's youngest brother, Roman Bojcun, joined the division when he was barely twenty and survived (with grave injuries) the division's defeat at Brody in 1944. Roman died in the 1980s.

CHAPTER 7

Several Ukrainian cookbooks have been published in English over the years, mostly in Canada. One of the most recent is *Festive Ukrainian Cooking* by Marta Pisetska Farley (Toronto: University of Toronto Press, 1991).

CHAPTER 8

When we were in Krakow, I went to Auschwitz and was deeply moved by what is preserved there. Mother and Katia did not go with me, as they did not go to see the mass grave at Slavske. I was struck by the indifference with which what happened at Auschwitz was treated by the guide who took us through the camp and by the hotel clerk who booked me for the trip. I later wrote an essay wondering whether their attitude was the result of their youth—both were young women, probably born in the 1960s—or whether they saw Auschwitz as "ancient" history or if human beings grow callous when exposed to a horror for a long time. The essay never found a publisher. Perhaps my visit to Auschwitz made it imperative for me to go to honor the dead at the fiftieth anniversary commemorations of Babi Yar.

When I returned to the United States I read several books about the Holocaust, including Elie Wiesel's *Night* (New York: Bantam Books, 1986). *Night* was originally published in Yiddish in a more expanded version, under title *Un De Velt Hot Geshvign*. I also read Nora Levin's *The Jews in the Soviet Union since 1917: Paradox of Survival* (New York: New York University Press, 1988) and *The Holocaust: The Destruction of European Jewry, 1933–1945* (New York: T. Y. Crowell Co., 1968).

CHAPTER 10

As I observed the turmoil on the Square of Independence in the fall of 1991, when the future beckoned with promises of an undreamed-of utopia, when impromptu orators stood on makeshift soapboxes to deliver their version of the truth, I came to understand their motivations. Throughout my adult life I had experienced the compulsion to define myself vis-à-vis Russia, more so than vis-à-vis the Soviet Union. Russia lay at the root of Ukraine's troubled history for the last 350 years, not the Soviet Union, which only perpetrated what czarist Russia had begun. Thus, I feel as compelled to give my version of Ukraine's history as I felt impelled in this book to speak of my family's past and use it as a background against which I (and other Ukrainians) can be analyzed and understood.

Despite what was accepted as truth for years in the West, Russians and Ukrainians are neither fraternal twins nor soul brothers. Over the centuries, the relationship between the two has ranged from uneasy to hostile. Although both nations claim Kyivan Rus, the medieval trading and cultural center on the Dnipro River, as the cradle of their culture and religion, the two peoples developed separately and differently. As Europe sank into the Dark Ages, Kyivan Rus flourished. Prince Volodymyr accepted Christianity and linked himself politically to Byzantium by marrying the daughter of Emperor Basil II. He was succeeded by his son, Yaroslav the Wise, who codified laws and brought under his rule the various tribes that inhabited the great steppes on either side of the Dnipro. Yaroslav strengthened the position of Kyiv as a

European power by marrying three of his daughters to the kings of France, Norway, and Hungary. The most famous of these daughters was Anna Yaroslavna, who married Henry I of France and ruled as regent following Henry's death in 1060. Kyivan Rus began its decline in the twelfth century because of dissension among the various princes, and in the thirteenth century, "golden-domed" Kyiv was reduced to rubble by the Mongol Horde. After the fall of Kyiv, western Ukraine came under Polish domination and became part of Poland and Lithuania. The Polish-Lithuanian commonwealth established an oppressive feudal system in the vast agricultural lands west of the Dnipro. Over the next century, runaway serfs (among them perhaps my ancestor Chybaty) banded near the Dnipro and evolved a military society, the Dnipro Cossacks. The word *kozak* is derived from the Turkic *kazak,* which means "free man." In the mid-sixteenth century, the Cossacks built a fortress called Sich on one of the islands in the sprawling, multichanneled Dnipro and regularly fought the Turks, who controlled the Black Sea and who made raids up the vast river for slaves. In 1648, Bohdan Khmelnytsky, hetman of the Dnipro Cossacks, led the war of liberation against Poland. The war was bloody; Polish landlords and Jews, who ran the area's commerce, were slaughtered. By 1656, Cossacks controlled a good portion of the area that is today's central Ukraine.

Russia developed from the principality of Suzdal-Vladimir that emerged as part of Kyivan Rus in the late eleventh century. This fact accounts both for Russia's name and the Russian claim to the Kyivan legacy. The Golden Horde overwhelmed the city-states of Suzdal, Vladimir, Yaroslav, and Moscow in three bloody years, 1236–38. These principalities remained vassals of the Mongols until Dmitri Donskoi of Muscovy defeated the Golden Horde. By the early fifteenth century, Moscow had become the leading Russian principality and its prince, Ivan III, united the principalities under his domain. He married the daughter of the last emperor of Constantinople and declared Moscow, the "Third Rome," the seat of Christian Orthodoxy. He also assumed the name of "caesar," which became the word *czar.* His son, Ivan the Terrible, organized Russia into a powerful centralized state. In 1610, Polish-Lithuanian forces sacked Moscow, but the Catholics were driven out two years later. The Polish-Lithuanian kingdom went into a decline, which made possible the revolt of Khmelnytsky. Besieged by Poles in the west and the Crimean Tatars in the south, Khmelnytsky signed a treaty of mutual aid with Czar Alexis Mikhailovich in 1654. The Treaty of Periaslav marks the beginning of Russia's domination over Ukraine. The treaty also lies at the root of the ongoing dispute between Russia and Ukraine over the Crimean peninsula, which was conquered and annexed to Imperial Russia by Catherine the Great in 1783. To mark the three hundredth anniversary of the Treaty of Periaslav in 1954, Nikita Khrushchev, a man known for liking the grand gesture, whether it was banging with his shoe on a desk at the United Nations or shipping missiles to Cuba, gave Crimea to Ukraine. Of course, in those years, no one could imagine Ukraine declaring its independence.

After Khmelnytsky's death, the Russian czar solidified his control over the Cossacks. Cossack hetman Ivan Mazepa (immortalized in Byron's poem "Mazeppa") joined King Charles XII of Sweden in a war against Peter the Great of Russia, but the two allies were defeated at Poltava in 1709. Peter the Great used Cossack labor to drain the swamps on which St. Petersburg was built, and Ukrainian *dumas,* mournful folk narratives chanted to the accompaniment of a stringed instrument called the *bandura,* speak of a city that arose on "the bleached bones" of the men of the Dnipro steppes.

In the eighteenth century, western Ukraine, which had reverted to Polish domination, became part of the Austro-Hungarian Empire, while eastern Ukraine was incorporated into the burgeoning Russian Empire. By then, the authority of the czar over the "Little Russians," as Ukrainians came to be called, was total. In 1863, the czar declared that "the Ukrainian language did not exist, does not exist and cannot exist." In 1876, Ukrainian books and the teaching of Ukrainian were banned.

A serf by the name of Taras Shevchenko focused Ukraine's dormant nationalism in the middle of the nineteenth century. His poetry was a rallying cry; his warning that "he who denies his mother tongue will be punished by God" was taken to heart by the Ukrainian population.

Not until November 20, 1917, did Ukrainians successfully revolt. As the Imperial Russian Army collapsed and civil war raged, Ukrainians formed two independent republics, one in the west, the other in the east, but the two failed to unite. In the post–World War I partitioning, western Ukraine became part of Poland, while eastern Ukraine was forced to join the newly formed Soviet Union in 1923. Joseph Stalin decimated eastern Ukraine. Ukrainian peasants resisted collectivization of agriculture, and to teach them a lesson, Stalin ordered the army to strip the countryside of all food and grain after the harvest in 1932. What followed was the Great Famine in which seven million Ukrainian peasants died. The existence of the famine was officially denied until Mikhail Gorbachev's *glasnost.*

During the 1920s and 1930s, caught up in the winds of nationalism blowing from Western Europe, the Organization of Ukrainian Nationalists arose in western Ukraine. Paramilitary and clandestine, the OUN attracted young people, especially university students, demanded autonomy for Western Ukraine, and was responsible for a number of assassinations of Polish government officials. The Polish government outlawed the OUN; many of its leaders were caught, sentenced, and executed. In 1939, as Poland crumbled, the OUN formed an independent government in Lviv and welcomed the Germans. The honeymoon did not last long, but the OUN's overtures to Hitler have echoed through the years. Hitler, however, considered Ukrainians and other Slavic people *untermenschen* — subhumans — and instituted a reign of terror. Thousands of young men and women were deported to Germany for slave labor; intellectuals were arrested and died in concentration camps together with the Jews and the Gypsies. One of my uncles died in the Janowska concentration camp in Lviv. My father found his partially cremated remains during the German retreat.

Young men who fled into the forests of the Carpathian Mountains in southwestern Ukraine and into the swamps of northeastern Ukraine to escape the deportations to Germany became the nucleus of the Ukrainian Insurgent Army (UPA). OUN members who had also fled into the forests after Hitler nullified the fledgling Ukrainian state began organizing the bands into a military force and gave the fledgling army a nationalist, anti-Communist ideology. By 1944, OUN had created a partisan army (20,000 to 40,000 fighting men, according to estimates) that ambushed and waged battles against Germans and later the Red Army. The UPA was armed with weapons the German Army left behind in its retreat. Some OUN leaders escaped to the West and settled in Munich, in the American Zone. Up until the early 1950s, UPA commanders were in courier contact with the OUN leadership in exile. The OUN's most famous leader in exile, Stepan Bandera, was assassinated in 1959 in Munich, West Germany. His assassin, a Ukrainian by the name of Bohdan Stashynsky, was tried and convicted in a German court in 1962. Stashynsky admitted that he had been specifically trained by the KGB to kill Bandera and that the assassination had been personally directed by the head of the KGB, Aleksandr Shelepin. John Barron described the plot and its aftermath in *KGB: The Secret Work of Soviet Secret Agents,* (New York: Reader's Digest Press, 1974). Robert Conquest wrote the introduction.

Because OUN had sided with Germany early in the war and because such information muddied the real reasons for the Ukrainian civil war, Moscow spread the propaganda inside the empire and in the West that Ukrainian nationalists were fascists. The intensive propaganda campaign against the OUN, former UPA soldiers, and members of the Division Galizien was waged until the dissolution of the Soviet Union. Even as late as 1999, a Ukrainian television producer was hard pressed to find funding for a documentary on Stepan Bandera. The name, which in Russian is coincidentally very close to the word *bandyora,* which means "bandit," makes people shy away. Stepan Bandera (1909–59) was born in the village of Stary Uhryniv, near the city of Kalush in the Ivano-Frankivsk *oblast.* His memorial, a life-size, bronze figure of a man in a flapping coat, is the third one. Vandals dynamited the previous two.

Although Stalin defeated the UPA, he failed to exterminate Ukraine's streak of independence. The UPA guerilla war in the Carpathian Mountains led to wholesale deportations and repressions throughout the western provinces of Ukraine. Villages were emptied and destroyed. Entire families were killed. Siberia was peopled with Ukrainian dissidents. Three out of every five prisoners in the gulag camps were Ukrainians. Historians believe that half a million Ukrainians were deported to Siberia after World War II. "There's just damned too many of them," Khrushchev reported Stalin complaining about Ukrainians. Ukraine's quiescence was short-lived. The Ukrainian democratic dissident movement emerged in the 1960s and, after a brief flowering, was crushed by a fearful Khrushchev.

A Russian will tell you that Ukrainians are obstinate, tenacious, and tough. Perhaps that is why eastern Ukraine, under the czars for 269 years and under the Soviets for another sixty-eight, never fully succumbed to Russification. Ethnicity and nationalism are very closely intertwined in Ukraine, and one is sometimes taken to be the other. Many Ukrainians resisted Russification by saying they were being ethnic. Often they got away with it. When they didn't, the authorities labeled their actions, such as having a library of Ukrainian books, as "bourgeois nationalism" and dispatched them to jail or Siberia. The unrelenting pressure from the center also had a secondary effect: it created pockets of hard-core, sometimes fanatic, resistance, especially in Western Ukraine. This resistance, in part, would fuel the collapse of the empire and was responsible for the counter-monuments in the Carpathian Mountains and the digging in Slavske.

Glasnost led to a rebirth of national awareness in both Western and Eastern Ukraine. In October 1990, several student protests and a student hunger strike resulted in the resignation of Ukrainian Prime Minister Vitaly Masol, the first and only such incident in Soviet history until Mikhail Gorbachev's resignation at the end of 1991.

CHAPTER 14

Yevgeny Yevtushenko has been translated widely into English. His description of Stalin's funeral is in *Yevgeny Yevtushenko, A Precocious Autobiography* (New York: E. P. Dutton & Co, Inc., 1963). My translation of his description of Stalin's funeral, which I did from the original when I was still in Kyiv, differs slightly from that in the English-language autobiography. A translation of "Babi Yar" is rendered as "Babii Yar" in *Yevtushenko, The Collected Poems 1952-1990* (New York: Henry Holt and Company, 1991).

CHAPTER 16

Many books are available about the Russian Germans. An overview of some of the materials is available on the Internet by using the phrase "Russian Germans" in a search engine. The most recent, applauded, and exhaustive book on the subject is *Deutsche Geschichte im Osten Europas: Rußland* by Gerd Stricker (Berlin: Siedler Verlag, 1997), reviewed as the definitive study of Russian-German history. It is one of a ten-volume series on Germans in Eastern Europe.

I used Joseph S. Height's *Homesteaders on the Steppes: Cultural History of the Evangelical-Lutheran Colonies in the Region of Odessa, 1804–1945* (Bismarck, N.D.: North Dakota Historical Society of Germans from Russia, 1975) and his *Paradise on the Steppe: A Cultural History of the Kutschurgan, Beresan, and Liebental Colonists, 1804–1972* (Bismarck, N.D.: North Dakota Historical Society of Germans from Russia, 1973). These hard-working and God-fearing people so intrigued me that I also read Hattie Plum Williams's *The Czar's Germans: With Particular Reference to the Volga Germans* (Lincoln, Nebr.: American Historical Society of Germans from Russia, 1975) and Fred C. Koch's *The Volga Germans* (University Park: Pennsylvania State University Press, 1977).

CHAPTER 17

An exhaustive study of the Ukrainian women's movement and the role it played in preserving the Ukrainian language and promoting literacy among the peasantry is Martha Bohachevsky-Chomiak's *Feminists Despite Themselves* (Edmonton: Canadian Institute of Ukrainian Studies, University of Alberta, 1988). The book traces the role of women in Ukrainian community life from 1884 to 1939.

CHAPTER 18

Pitirim Sorokin (1889–1969) was a young academic in Russia when many of his friends in the intelligentsia were arrested on orders of Lenin and Trotsky. Subsequently, these intellectuals were banished (as Alexander Solzhenitsyn would be in 1974) and Sorokin left the Soviet Union also. He obtained a professorship at Harvard University and wrote several books examining how revolutions, famines, and other calamities affect human behavior. I consulted three of his books. They are *Contemporary Sociological Theories* (New York: Harper & Row, 1928), *Man and Society in Calamity* (New York: E. P. Dutton and Company, Inc., 1943), and *The Crisis of Our Age* (New York: E. P. Dutton & Co., inc., 1941).

Zara Witkin (1900-1940) was in Russia after the Bolshevik Revolution. His memoir is *An American Engineer in Stalin's Russia: The memoir of Zara Witkin, 1922-1934* (Berkeley: University of California Press, 1991). Michael Gleb, who also wrote the introduction, edited the memoir.

CHAPTER 21

Elena Bonner remembered her childhood stay at Artek in *Dochki—Materi*, translated by Antonina W. Bouis as *Mothers and Daughters* (New York: Knopf, 1991).

I used *Traveling with the Innocents Abroad* (Norman: University of Oklahoma Press, 1958), which contains Mark Twain's original reports from his travels in Europe and the Holy Land, to learn more about Alexander II and his meeting with Mark Twain on August 26, 1867, in Livadia.

Anton Chekhov (1860–1904) mentioned Yalta and its streams of tourists often in his letters that are translated in *The Selected Letters of Anton Chekhov* (New York: Farrar, Straus and Company, 1966), Lillian Hellman, editor.

CHAPTER 24

The Crimean legends that I relate are from two books in Russian that I purchased in the Crimea. The books are volumes one and three of *Legendy*

Kryma, published in Moscow in 1913 and in Odessa in 1917, respectively. The translations are mine. I read the legend of Diliare and Khan Krim-Girey in a brochure I purchased in Bakchesarai. It is titled "Fontan Slez" (The Fountain of Tears) and was published in 1991 by L. N. Malyno-vskaya. The translation is mine.

In *Pushkin* (New York: Grove Press, Inc., 1967), David Magarshack offers a vivid portrait of Alexander Pushkin (1799–1837), which includes new research on Pushkin's companions and activities in Crimea.

CHAPTER 25

I returned from the Crimea fascinated by the Black Sea and found a book composed of newspaper letters written during the summer and autumn of 1910 when author William E. Curtis (1850–1911) traveled in the area. The book is titled *Around the Black Sea* (New York: Hodder & Stoughton, George H. Doran Company, 1911).

CHAPTER 26

The more I read about Feodor Chaliapin, whose surname is also trans-literated as Shalyapin, the more fascinating I found him. Born in Kazan to illiterate peasants, he went to St. Petersburg and became a star dur-ing the reign of Nicholas II. In 1901, he met Maxim Gorky and they became fast friends. In the early 1920s, Chaliapin was on a first-name basis with Lenin and Trotsky. He, however, could not stomach the So-viet system and emigrated, settling in Paris, as did many Russian émigrés. I consulted *Chaliapin, An Autobiography as told to Maxim Gorky* (New York: Stein and Day, 1967), which contains correspondence between Chaliapin and Gorky, and *Chaliapin, A Critical Biography* (New York: Knopf, 1988), as well as Chaliapin's autobiography that he published in Paris in French. It was later translated in English as *Man and Mask* (Gar-den City, N.Y.: Garden City Publishing Co., Inc., 1932).

Andre Gidé's (1869–1951) disillusionment with the Soviet system can be found in *The God that Failed* (New York: Harper & Brothers, 1950), a collection of essays by six writers who examine and reject Commu-nism. Richard Crossman was the editor.

CHAPTER 27

In Muriel Spark's *The Mandelbaum Gate* (New York: Avon Books, 1965), Barbara Vaughan, who is a half-Jewish convert to Catholicism, goes on a pilgrimage to strife-torn Jerusalem to rediscover who she is.

American Mosaic by Joan Morrison and Charlotte Fox Zabusky (New York: E. P. Dutton, 1980) records "the immigrant experience in the words of those who lived it." The authors present interviews with some 150 immigrants, starting with those who came to the United States in the early part of the twentieth century and continuing through to the immigration from Southeast Asia in the 1970s. The memories range from a few paragraphs to several pages and are presented the way the immigrant spoke while being taped; they thus contain the flavor and idiosyncrasies of the speaker's use of English. I found my mother, my cousins, and myself in these stories, as I did in the experiences and feeling of isolation I found in Shirley Geok-lin Lim's *Among the White Moon Faces* (New York: Feminist Press, City University of New York, 1996).

EASTERN EUROPEAN STUDIES
Stjepan G. Meštrović, Series Editor

Cigar, Norman. *Genocide in Bosnia: The Policy of "Ethnic Cleansing."* 1995.

Cohen, Philip J. *Serbia's Secret War: Propaganda and the Deceit of History.* 1996.

Gachechiladze, Revaz. *The New Georgia: Space, Society, Politics.* 1996.

Gibbs, Joseph. *Gorbachev's Glasnost: The Soviet Media in the First Phase of Perestroika.* 1999.

Knezys, Stasys, and Romanas Sedlickas. *The War in Chechnya.* 1999.

Meštrović, Stjepan G., ed. *The Conceit of Innocence: Losing the Conscience of the West in the War against Bosnia.* 1997.

Polokhalo, Volodymyr, ed. *The Political Analysis of Postcommunism: Understanding Postcommunist Ukraine.* 1997.

Quinn, Frederick. *Democracy at Dawn: Notes from Poland and Points East.* 1997.

Shlapentokh, Vladimir, Christopher Vanderpool, and Boris Doktorov, eds. *The New Elite in Post-Communist Eastern Europe.* 1999.

Tasovac, Ivo. *American Foreign Policy and Yugoslavia, 1939–1941.* 1999.

Teglas, Csaba. *Budapest Exit: A Memoir of Fascism, Communism, and Freedom.* 1998.